ALSO BY

Trumped Up: How Criminalization of Political Differences Endangers Democracy

Electile Dysfunction: A Guide for Unaroused Voters

The Case Against the Iran Deal

Terror Tunnels: The Case for Israel's Just War Against Hamas

Taking the Stand: My Life in the Law

The Trials of Zion

The Case for Moral Clarity: Israel, Hamas and Gaza

The Case Against Israel's Enemies: Exposing Jimmy Carter and Others who Stand in the Way of Peace

Is There a Right to Remain Silent? Coercive Interrogation and the Fifth Amendment After 9/11

Finding Jefferson: A Lost Letter, a Remarkable Discovery and the First Amendment in the Age of Terrorism

Blasphemy: How the Religious Right is Hijacking Our Declaration of Independence

Pre-emption: A Knife That Cuts Both Ways

What Israel Meant to Me: By 80 Prominent Writers, Performers, Scholars, Politicians and Journalists

Rights From Wrongs: A Secular Theory of the Origins of Rights

America on Trial: Inside the Legal Battles That Transformed Our Nation

The Case For Peace: How the Arab-Israeli Conflict Can Be Resolved

The Case for Israel

America Declares Independence

Why Terrorism Works: Understanding the Threat, Responding to the Challenge

Shouting Fire: Civil Liberties in a Turbulent Age

Letters to a Young Lawyer

Supreme Injustice: How the High Court Hijacked Election 2000

Genesis of Justice: Ten Stories of Biblical Injustice That Led to the Ten Commandments and Modern Law

Just Revenge

Sexual McCarthyism: Clinton, Starr, and the Emerging Constitutional Crisis

The Vanishing American Jew: In Search of Jewish Identity for the Next Century

Reasonable Doubts: The Criminal Justice System and the O.J. Simpson Case

The Abuse Excuse: And Other Cop-Outs, Sob Stories and Evasions of Responsibility

The Advocate's Devil

Contrary to Popular Opinion

Chutzpah

Taking Liberties: A Decade of Hard Cases, Bad Laws, and Bum Raps

Reversal of Fortune: Inside the von Bulow Case

The Best Defense

Criminal Law: Theory and Process (with Joseph Goldstein and Richard Schwartz)

Psychoanalysis: Psychiatry and Law (with Joseph Goldstein and Jay Katz)

THE CASE AGAINST
BDS

WHY SINGLING OUT ISRAEL

FOR BOYCOTT IS

ANTI-SEMITIC AND

ANTI-PEACE

ALAN DERSHOWITZ

A BOMBARDIER BOOKS BOOK
An Imprint of Post Hill Press

The Case Against BDS:
Why Singling Out Israel for Boycott Is Anti-Semitic and Anti-Peace
© 2018 by Alan Dershowitz
All Rights Reserved

No part of this book may be reproduced, stored in a retrieval system, or transmitted by any means without the written permission of the author and publisher.

Post Hill Press
New York • Nashville
posthillpress.com
Published in the United States of America

BDS: AN INTRODUCTION AND HISTORY

The Illegitimate Birth of BDS

The plot to boycott, divest and sanction Israel, and Israel alone—called BDS—was birthed at an anti-Semitic hate fest in Durban, South Africa, in 1991. Its grandparents on one side were the Nazis who organized the boycott of Jewish businesses, academics and artists in the 1930s. Its grandparents on the other side were the Muslim leaders who organized the Arab boycott of all Israeli and Jewish commerce in the years following the establishment of Israel. Its parents are the contemporary bigots who single out only Israel for boycott and seek to use this tactic to end the existence of the world's only nation state for the Jewish people. The illegitimate birth of this tactic reflects the anti-Semitic goal of its founders and leaders: to isolate, de-legitimize and ultimately destroy the nation state of the Jewish people.

Anyone who supports this bigoted effort in the belief that it is solely a protest against Israel's policies—such as continued occupation and settlement building—is being misled. The true goal of BDS is revealed by its history and chronology: The modern version of BDS started in 2001, just as Israel was offering, and the Palestinian leadership was rejecting, a Palestinian state in Gaza and on more than 95 percent of the West Bank, with an end to the occupation and settlements; and BDS became formalized in 2005, just as Israel was ending its occupation and all of its settlements in Gaza.

This book will prove beyond any doubt that the real objective of BDS is the anti-Semitic goal of ending the existence of the only nation state of the Jewish people and replacing it with another

Muslim-Arab state. Anyone who supports BDS is thus complicit—knowingly or out of willful blindness—in the world's oldest bigotry.

At the 2001 UN-sponsored World Conference Against Racism, Racial Discrimination, Xenophobia and Related Intolerance (WCAR) held in Durban, the Arab nations present promoted the tactic of de-legitimizing Israel by boycotting and isolating the nation state of the Jewish people. This tactic became known as the "BDS Movement." It was at this "so-called" anti-racism conference that the "Durban strategy" of de-legitimization against Israel took root; turning Israel into a pariah state among the community of nations. Based on the inapt South African paradigm, it provided the blueprint for the ensuing boycott of Israel by falsifying parallels between the former's apartheid-regime and Israel's territorial dispute with the Palestinians. As a result, calls for "anti-apartheid boycotts" became the "battle cry"[1] of the broad Israel-boycott strategy.

The countries, entities and NGOs participating in the UN conference accused the nation state of the Jewish people of racism, apartheid, genocide, and of creating a holocaust. Led by Yasser Arafat and his nephew, Nasser al-Kidwa, the Palestinian UN delegation—in conjunction with Western NGOs and nations belonging to the Organization of Islamic Cooperation—oversaw the Conference's final declaration of principles.[2] It stated:

> *"[We] call upon the international community to impose a policy of complete and total isolation of Israel as an Apartheid state as in the case of South Africa which means the imposition of mandatory and comprehensive sanctions and embargoes, the full cessation of all links (diplomatic, economic, social, aid, military cooperation and training) between all states and Israel.*[3]*"*

It is important to recall that at the time this resolution was being debated, Israel's Labor government had just offered to end its presence in the Gaza Strip and in more than 95% of the West Bank, and to agree to the establishment of a Palestinian state, with its capital in Jerusalem. It was Yasser Arafat who rejected this offer of statehood and instead ordered an intifada in which

4,000 people were killed. Addressing this rejection by Arafat, President Clinton said "you are leading your people and the region to a catastrophe."[4] Prince Bandar of Saudi Arabia characterized Arafat's rejection of the Israeli offer as not only a tragedy, but a "crime."[5] This chronology proves beyond any doubt that Israel's occupation and settlement policies—which they offered to end just before the current BDS movement began—are merely excuses for a bigoted tactic whose real goal is the elimination of the nation state of the Jewish people, as acknowledged by its leaders.

In the highly anti-Semitic milieu of the Durban Conference, U.S. Secretary of State, Colin Powell, ordered the American delegation to stage a "walk-out." This was his reason:

> *"Today I have instructed our representatives at the World Conference Against Racism to return home...I know that you do not combat racism by conferences that produce declarations containing hateful language, some of which is a throwback to the days of 'Zionism equals racism;' or supports the idea that we have made too much of the Holocaust; or suggests that apartheid exists in Israel; or that singles out only one country in the world—Israel—for censure and abuse."*[6]

Congressman Tom Lantos, the only Holocaust survivor to have served in the United States Congress, was a U.S. delegate at the Durban Conference. Writing about the blatant anti-Semitism he witnessed there, Congressman Lantos said:

> *"Another ring in the Durban circus was the NGO forum...the forum quickly became stacked with Palestinian and fundamentalist Arab groups. Each day, these groups organized anti-Israeli and anti-Semitic rallies around the meetings, attracting thousands. One flyer, which was widely distributed, showed a photograph of Hitler and the question 'What if I had won?' The answer: 'There would be NO Israel...An accredited NGO, the Arab Lawyers Union, distributed a booklet filled with anti-Semitic caricatures frighteningly like those seen in the Nazi hate literature printed in the 1930s. Jewish leaders and I who were in Durban were shocked at this blatant display of anti-*

Semitism. For me, having experienced the horrors of the Holocaust first hand, this was the most sickening and unabashed display of hate for Jews I had seen since the Nazi period."[7]

This then was the illegitimate birthplace of the current BDS strategy—immediately following Israel's generous offer to end the occupation and establish a Palestinian state.

While the Durban Conference gave rise to the new "internationalization" of the old Arab boycott, the Palestinians used this opportunity to "Palestinianize" the campaign so as to lend it legitimacy as a bottom-up Palestinian "movement."[8]

In the wake of these "gains" made at the Durban conference, in April 2004, Qatari-born, Israeli-educated Omar Barghouti co-founded the Palestinian Campaign for the Academic and Cultural Boycott of Israel (PACBI), which was tasked with "overseeing the academic and cultural boycott aspects of BDS."[9] The Boycott, Divestment and Sanctions "movement" was formally launched in July 2005—just as Israel was ending its military occupation of Gaza and uprooting all of its settlements there—and was endorsed by over 170 Palestinian political parties, organizations, trade unions and movements.[10]

The PACBI original "call for an academic and cultural boycott of Israel" in 2004 was based on the following principles:[11]

1. Refrain from participation in any form of academic and cultural cooperation, collaboration or joint projects with Israeli institutions;
2. Advocate a comprehensive boycott of Israeli institutions at the national and international levels, including suspension of all forms of funding and subsidies to these institutions;
3. Promote divestment and disinvestment from Israel by international academic institutions;
4. Work toward the condemnation of Israeli policies by pressing for resolutions to be adopted by academic, professional and cultural associations and organizations;
5. Support Palestinian academic and cultural institutions directly without requiring them to partner with Israeli counterparts as an explicit or implicit condition for such support.

Since 2004, Barghouti—who himself received his advanced degree at Tel Aviv University (a fact that flies in the face of his claim of a state-sponsored system of apartheid in Israel)—has been the key driving force behind the global BDS campaign. It is ironic that the leading advocate of a worldwide boycott of Israel—who has said that "all Israeli academics" are members of the "occupation reserve army"[12]—was himself unwilling to disrupt his own education and boycott the "Zionist" institution from which he was receiving his higher education.

Central to Barghouti's tactic has been the engagement of European governments, NGOs and grassroots organizations, as well as university campuses across the United States, in order to push the BDS campaign and grow its support base. As part of his overarching tactic of equating the global BDS campaign with the anti-apartheid movement in South Africa, Barghouti also formed a very public strategic "alliance" with South African human rights and anti-apartheid activist, Archbishop Desmond Tutu. Like Barghouti, Archbishop Tutu has a sordid history of demonizing Jews and their nation state.[13]

I was invited to debate Barghouti at Oxford Union, but the founder of BDS refused to debate me because according to his criteria I—as an American Jewish supporter of Israel—am subject to his boycott. He also refused to join me in a discussion sponsored by the Young Presidents' Organization (YPO), insisting that he conclude his presentation first, so that it is not seen as a debate, discussion or encounter with me. His bigoted boycott is also directed against non-Israeli Jews such as the singer Matisyahu—but not (at least according to some leaders of BDS) against Israeli-Arabs.[14] In other words, this is a <u>religious</u>, not a <u>national</u> boycott. That is anti-Semitism, pure and simple. BDS has increasingly been a hotbed of anti-Semitic activity and regrouped bigots of all stripes who feel comfortable with the language used by its leaders, such as Mr. Barghouti.

It is abundantly clear that Omar Barghouti is against the existence of Israel as the nation state of the Jewish people in any form. He confirmed this in a 2008 column when he declared:

"Forgetting for the moment the fact that it was born out of ethnic cleansing and the destruction of the indigenous Palestinian society, Israel is the state that built and is fully responsible for maintaining the illegal Jewish colonies. Why should anyone punish the settlements and not Israel? This hardly makes any sense, politically speaking...why should European civil society that fought apartheid in South Africa accept apartheid in Israel as normal, tolerable or unquestionable? Holocaust guilt cannot morally justify European complicity in prolonging the suffering, bloodshed and decades-old injustice that Israel has visited upon Palestinians and Arabs in general, using the Nazi genocide as pretext."[15]

Omar Barghouti himself has called for the "end [of] Israel's existence as a Jewish state," because he "opposes a Jewish state in any part of Palestine," which he defines to include even the pre-1967 borders of Israel. He opposes both the two-state solution and "binationalism." His goal is the "one-state solution," with that one state being another Arab state with a Muslim majority. When addressing mainstream audiences he claims that the goal of BDS is to "end the occupation," but he doesn't tell them that he believes Tel Aviv, Haifa, Jerusalem, Rechovot, Eilat and all the rest of Israel is "occupied territory" that must be liberated.

Barghouti also neglects to mention the role of the Palestinian leadership during the 1930s and 1940s having formed an alliance with the Nazi regime in general and Adolf Hitler in particular. The Grand Mufti of Jerusalem, Amin Al-Husseini, collaborated with the Nazis to prevent Jewish refugees from seeking sanctuary in what became Israel. He was instrumental in having Jews, who were on their way out of Europe, sent to death camps. After the war, he was declared a war criminal for recruiting thousands of Muslim Yugoslavs to murder Jews in Croatia and Hungary. Despite his Nazi collaboration—or perhaps because of it—he became and remained a hero to most Palestinians many of whom hung his picture in their homes. Following the Holocaust, Al-Husseini received asylum in Egypt, where he organized other German Nazis to help in efforts to destroy Israel.[16] So "Holocaust guilt" among the Palestinian leadership was an entirely appropriate factor to consider—though certainly not the only one—in supporting the establishment of two states for two peoples in mandatory Palestine.

The Economic Impact

In contemporary times, economic, cultural and academic boycotts of Israel have resonated in Europe, which is not particularly surprising when considering the rising tide of anti-Semitism on that continent. A recent NGO Monitor report revealed that members of the European Union are among the foremost backers of BDS.[17] This is a noteworthy revelation in light of the assertion of EU High Representative for Foreign Affairs and Security Policy, Federica Mogherini, in late 2016 that: "The EU rejects the BDS campaign's attempts to isolate Israel and is opposed to any boycott of Israel."[18]

The NGO Monitor report found "that 29 out of 100 EU grants administered through the frameworks reviewed, funnel funds to BDS organizations (€16.7 million out of €67.1 million—roughly 25%)... 42 out of 180 EU grantees in total support BDS—either through participation in activities and events, signing of petitions and initiatives, and/or membership in explicit BDS platforms."[19]

NGOs that receive grants from the EU must subscribe to its stated objective of promoting "peace, cooperation and human rights."[20] However, according to the NGO watchdog's findings, many of the prejudicial and highly politicized "boycott" organizations that the EU has funded seek to discriminate against the nation state of the Jewish people and oppose the EU's stated objective of a two-state outcome.[21]

The economic repercussions of European attempts to boycott Israel have had little discernible effect on Israeli trade or the economy at large. By contrast, it has had a noticeable effect on the Palestinian economy, which has been severely impacted when companies have decided to close down ventures in the West Bank to avoid being targeted by BDS.

Perhaps one of the most publicized calls for BDS was against the SodaStream factory in Ma'ale Adumim—a suburb of Jerusalem that Palestinian Authority leaders acknowledge will remain part of Israel in any negotiated resolution of the conflict—which had both

Jewish Israeli and Palestinian Arab employees. SodaStream was pressured to move its factory to an area in Israel where few, if any, Palestinian workers can be employed.

In recent years, the economic boycott—though having little actual financial impact—has been increasingly successful in de-legitimizing Israel on the world stage: several major investment funds and banks in Europe have joined financial institutions across the Arab world in publicly divesting from some Israeli, and Israeli-affiliated companies. European governments, including Germany, Norway and the Netherlands have also increasingly refused to provide grants or subsidies for companies that do business in the West Bank or East Jerusalem.

For example, Hewlett-Packard has been targeted because it uses parts manufactured by the Israeli tech giant EDS, which supplies the computer systems for the IDF and the biometric permit systems that track the movement of Palestinian workers through checkpoints in Gaza and the West Bank.[22] After facing mounting pressure, the Netherland's largest pension fund, *PGGM Investment*, also withdrew investment from Israel's five leading banks.[23]

In Germany, Spain and the United Kingdom trade unions adopted the boycott and ended partnership with Israel's *Histadrut* labor federation.[24] The boycott tactic also claimed success with French telecommunications giant, Orange, which is set to end its branding agreement with one of Israel's largest mobile companies, Partner Communication.[25] Other companies targeted by the official BDS tactic include: Ahava cosmetics, which was forced to shut its London store after countless threats;[26] Marks & Spencer for providing development aid to Israel; and Max Brenner chocolatier. These "successes" have been mostly symbolic, since the Israeli economy continues to thrive, even in the face of some European boycotts.

In the U.S., thanks to bipartisan support for Israel in Congress, economic boycotts have largely failed. Most recently, in March 2017, the bipartisan Anti-Israel Boycott Act was introduced in the U.S. Senate. The bill—which had 42 co-sponsors from both parties—expands on existing legislation that makes compliance with boycotts of Israel sponsored by governments illegal.[27] Several governors have also issued executive orders directing state entities not to invest public funds in companies supporting the "BDS" campaign against Israel.

I support anti-BDS legislation that prohibits economic and other means of discrimination against Israel, Israelis, or Jews, so long as it does not impinge on First Amendment rights to protest Israeli policies. Boycotts based on national origin or religion are as bad as boycotts based on race, gender or sexual orientation. The left wing food co-op that refuses to sell Israeli or Jewish products is no better than the baker who refuses to sell a cake to a gay couple or a landlord who refuses to rent to a black person. The academic who refuses to work with a Jewish Israeli scholar is no better than the bigot who refuses to collaborate with a Muslim scholar.

In addition to exerting economic pressure on Israel via an economic boycott, the BDS tactic has sought to isolate Israel via a broader "cultural boycott," including a boycott of Israeli academic institutions. Much like the economic boycott, the parameters of the academic boycott have differed widely: some campaigners have called on governments, foundations, and other academic institutions to cease funding and cooperating with Israeli universities altogether; others have sought a targeted boycott, or a conditional boycott, stipulating that to continue receiving funds, Israeli academic institutions must not cooperate with the IDF, or operate in the West Bank or illegal settlements.[28]

In the marketplace of ideas on college campuses and within academic institutions, an embrace of anti-Israel boycotts has coincided with the increasingly anti-Zionist (and often anti-Semitic) rhetoric of the hard-left. The radical left, whose worldview is often informed by selective 'anti-colonialism' and anti-imperialism, has largely embraced BDS and its effort to de-legitimize the nation state of the Jewish people. As I will demonstrate throughout the book, this trend is part of the hard-left's embrace of 'intersectionality'— the radical academic theory, which holds that all forms of social oppression are inexorably linked. Increasingly, hard-left radicals insist on a package of unrelated left-wing causes that must be embraced by anyone claiming the label of progressive—including the demonization of Israel as a racist, apartheid state.

Most recently, this was seen at the Chicago Dyke March—a parade geared towards that city's lesbian community—where, under the 'pretext' of intersectionality, some Jewish lesbians were told to leave the parade because their flag, which had a Star of David printed on top of the LGBTQ rainbow flag, "made people feel unsafe." They were also told that the march was "anti-Zionist" and "pro-Palestinian."[29]

Moreover, in the academic sphere, groups such as the Native American Scholars Association and the Americans Studies Association (ASA) have passed resolutions in favor of BDS. In 2014, when ASA President Curtis Marez was asked what the Israeli-Palestinian conflict had to do with their academic portfolio, he replied, "one has to start somewhere."[30] He did not explain why his organization chose to "start" with the world's only Jewish democracy and not with the world's many repressive tyrannies. Meanwhile, in 2013, the political science department at Brooklyn College voted to co-sponsor a campaign event at which only pro-BDS speakers would advocate a policy that is so extreme that even the Palestinian Authority rejects it.[31]

There have also, however, been some positive cases of student groups standing up to pressure and intimidation from BDS activists. On August 4, 2017, the student parliament at Goethe University in Frankfurt adopted a resolution condemning BDS, stating that it was analogous to Nazi boycotts of Jews in the 1930s. Student representatives from that university said that they adopted this position in order to push back against the rising tide of anti-Zionist and even anti-Semitic, sentiments in Frankfurt. This was what they said:[32]

> *"The call by the BDS [Boycott, Divestment, Sanctions] campaign to boycott products from the parts designated 'occupied territories' of the West Bank, East Jerusalem and Golan Heights stands clearly in the tradition of the national socialist Jewish boycott and the slogan 'Don't buy from Jews!'"*

Interestingly, shortly after the Frankfurt-based student group issued this resolution, the Deputy Mayor of Frankfurt, Uwe Becker, submitted an anti-BDS bill that bans municipal funds and public spaces from being used for activities promoting boycotts of Israel.

In language similar to that invoked at the Goethe student parliament in Frankfurt just days before, Becker said: "The BDS movement with its messages uses the same language the National Socialists once used to express: 'Don't buy from Jews!'"

In addition to the formal boycotts, many Jewish pro-Israel speakers are subjected to de facto boycotts. Universities and some departments in particular, are quickly becoming more political than academic. This trend threatens the academic freedom of dissenting students and faculty.

Meanwhile, artists are increasingly being pressured to cancel performances in Israel or collaboration with Israeli artists as part of the "cultural boycott." Most recently a group called Artists for Palestine UK issued an open letter to the band Radiohead, calling on the group to cancel its upcoming concert in Israel over the summer. The letter said: "Please do what artists did in South Africa's era of oppression: stay away, until apartheid is over."[33] Radiohead refused to comply with the boycott demand, and on July 12, released a statement stating that, "music, art and academia is about crossing borders not building them, about open minds, not closed ones, about shared humanity, freedom and expression."[34]

Many other artists have faced similar pressure and intimidation from radical BDS supporters. In an open letter in 2013, BDS advocate Alice Walker—who has a long history of bigotry against the nation state of the Jewish people and who described Israel's actions towards the Palestinians as "genocide," "ethnic cleansing," "crimes against humanity," and "cruelty and diabolical torture"— urged singer Alicia Keyes to cancel her concert in Israel. Ms. Keyes refused and responded with this statement: "I look forward to my first visit to Israel. Music is a universal language that is meant to unify audiences in peace and love, and that is the spirit of our show."[35]

BDS is Not a Universal "Movement"

The bigots who want to boycott, divest from and sanction Israel, and only Israel, seek to characterize their anti-Semitic tactic as a "movement." Among the goals of the so-called movement are "equality," along with justice and freedom. But in reality there is no such thing as the "BDS movement." A "movement" suggests universality, such as the feminist movement, the gay rights movement and the environmental movement. If there were a BDS movement that sought to achieve equality, justice and freedom, it would rank every country in the world in accordance with its failure to achieve the movement's goals.

Specifically, it would rank every nation by reference to two overriding criteria: 1) The seriousness and pervasiveness of its violation of basic human rights to equality, justice and freedom; 2) The inaccessibility of the victims to judicial, media and political relief. A true movement would then prioritize its protest activities—its boycotts, divestments and sanctions—according to the universal mantra of all true human rights movements: namely "the worst first."

It would not pick only one country, point out its imperfections, and focus ALL of its protest activities on that one country, to the exclusion off all others. Ranked according to the universal criteria outlined above, the list of countries with horrible human rights records and little or no access to relief would be quite long. It would include North Korea, Iran, Cuba, China, Zimbabwe, Myanmar, Belarus, Russia, Turkey, Saudi Arabia, Pakistan, Philippines, Venezuela, and Kuwait, among many others. Israel would be near the very bottom of any objective list, ranking behind every Arab, Muslim, African, and Asian country, as well as several Eastern European countries.

No reasonable person, including many supporters of BDS, would dispute this assessment. Even Peter Tatchell, a supporter of BDS whom I debated at Oxford Union in 2015, acknowledged this when he wrote:

> *"While I oppose Israel's occupation, I find it strange that some people condemn Israel while remaining silent about these other equally or more oppressive occupations. Many of Israel's critics are also silent about neighboring Arab dictatorships. And where are the protests and calls for boycotts against the tyrannies of Saudi Arabia, Iran, Burma, Zimbabwe, North Korea, Uzbekistan, Bahrain, Syria and elsewhere? Why the double standards?"*[36]

Indeed, the only nation subjected to the BDS so called "movement" is the one nation state of the Jewish people. There is something very wrong with that picture.

When only Muslim states were subject to the Trump administration's travel ban, the left was outraged. Why is there not similar outrage at subjecting only the nation state of the Jewish people to BDS? Many of those who most fervently support boycotting Israel demand that we end boycotts of Cuba, Iran, North Korea, and other tyrannical regimes. How can they justify this double standard?

For those who argue that's it is morally permissible to focus a "movement" only on the nation-state of the Jewish people, a true story from the past is instructive. Harvard's former president, Abbott Lawrence Lowell, sought to restrict the number of Jewish students admitted to Harvard on the ground that "Jews cheat." When Judge Learned Hand pointed out that non-Jews cheat as well, Lowell responded, "you're changing the subject—we are talking only about Jews!"

Well, you can't talk only about Jews when discussing a universal problem such as cheating. To focus only on Jewish imperfections, while ignoring all others, has a name: it's called anti-Semitism. The same name is applicable to a so-called "movement" that focuses all of its protests on the imperfections of the nation state of the Jewish people, when these imperfections pale in comparison with those of the vast majority of nation states, including every single Muslim and Arab state.

My Role in Fighting the Bigoted Goals of BDS

For over a decade I have taken a lead in opposing BDS. I have written dozens of columns, delivered hundreds of speeches, debated numerous supporters of BDS, consulted with lawyers who have litigated against BDS, advised legislators who have proposed statutory bans against BDS, spoken to university administrators who oppose student and faculty BDS initiatives, supported political candidates who have campaigned against BDS, encouraged alumni donors who want to pressure their universities against accepting

BDS, purchased products that have been targets of BDS, invested in financial companies that have resisted demands to divest from Israeli companies, and counselled students who are confused about the issue.

In this book, I bring together in one short volume the case I have made against BDS over the years in these different forums.

It is important to note that although BDS advocates tell students and others that its primary focus is on the areas captured by Israel after the 1967 War—what it refers to as Israel's "occupation"—in reality this is not the boycott campaign's origin, goal, or purpose. In both deed and creed the anti-Israel boycott is diametrically opposed to the very existence of Israel and to a peacefully negotiated two-state outcome.

The official, publicly proclaimed, objectives and tactics of the Boycott, Divestment and Sanctions campaign, referred to as "the call," are based on three key positions:

1. Ending its [Israel's] occupation and colonization of all Arab lands and dismantling the Wall;
2. Recognizing the fundamental rights of the Arab-Palestinian citizens of Israel to full equality; and
3. Respecting, protecting and promoting the rights of Palestinian refugees to return to their homes and properties as stipulated in UN resolution 194

These three declared positions do not truly represent the actual goals of the tactic. BDS cofounder Omar Barghouti opposes Israel's right to exist as the nation state of the Jewish people even within the 1967 borders. He confirmed as much when he declared:

"I am completely and categorically against binationalism because it assumes there are two nations with equal moral claims to the land. I am completely opposed to that..."[37]

Moreover, the Israel boycott tactic threatens the peace process by promoting extortion rather than negotiation, and discourages Palestinians from agreeing to any reasonable peace offer. The modus operandi of the anti-Israel boycott tactic is to distort history and international law, and de-legitimize Israel alone among the community of nations.

There Is Nothing New in BDS

BDS is a new name, but it is not a new tactic. Boycotts have been used to stigmatize and de-legitimize Jews throughout history. In the Middle Ages, Jews throughout Europe were legally disenfranchised and subject to widespread restrictions and boycotts—some of which existed until the advent of the nineteenth century. Jews were often made to live in ghettos, forbidden from owning property, and were forced to pay discriminatory taxes. Medieval anti-Semitism and the widespread demonization of Jews were often accompanied by blood libel accusations; namely, that Jews kidnapped and killed Christian children, using their blood on Jewish holidays for religious practices. Specifically, the anti-Semitic canard that Christian blood is desired by Jews to bake matzos on Passover, persisted for hundreds of years throughout much of Europe and the Middle East, and is still touted by some rabid anti-Semites today, including at least one notorious Jewish anti-Semite, about whom I write in this book.[38]

Moreover, when Hitler rose to power in April 1933 he ordered an immediate national campaign of "BDS" against Jews.[39] The word "Jude," accompanied by the Star of David, was splashed across Jewish-owned stores in order to deter Germans from shopping there, while SS officers stood guard outside with placards that read: "Go Back to Palestine" and "Jews are our misfortune."[40]

The Nazis' boycott also extended to Jewish culture and academia. In May 1933, books and oeuvres of European Jews—and anyone else deemed racially inferior or "un-German"—were thrown by German students and professors into bonfires as part of the Nazi purge or "cleansing."[41] It didn't matter if they were works of Freud or Einstein, Marx or Heinrich Heine; they all went up in flames. This was a prelude to Heinrich Heine's prescient and tragic prediction in 1821: "where they burn books, they will also ultimately burn people."[42]

In an infamous speech attended by some 40,000 Germans, Nazi Propaganda Minister Joseph Goebbels said that the boycott was a legitimate response to "atrocity propaganda" being spread by "international Jewry."[43] This was part of the Nazi narrative that Germans were the victims of Jewish "occupation" of the "*Vaterland*" (Fatherland.)[44]

In the wake of the destruction of European Jewry, the Arab world took note of the anti-Jewish boycotts and adopted its own strategy of "anti-normalization" of relations with their Jewish neighbors. Boycotts of "Zionist" goods and businesses in British Mandatory Palestine were prevalent, and when Israel's independence was declared in 1948 the newly formed Arab League crystalized this boycott into official policy.[45] The parameters of the Arab boycott were extended in the 1950's to include companies with "Zionist sympathizers"[46]—businesses with Jews in high positions or who engaged in commerce with the Jewish state. In 1966, for example, Coca-Cola bowed to Arab pressure when the company denied a bid from an Israeli firm to open a branch in Israel.[47] Films made by or starring Jewish (not necessarily Zionist) artists were banned, as were Jewish books, Jewish professors, and other Jewish influences. This was all before the 1967 War and Israel's military occupation of the West Bank and Gaza.

Despite peace treaties signed with Egypt and Jordan, the Arab League boycott of Israel remained official policy. Since 2002, some have re-implemented secondary boycotts targeted at companies that do business in the West Bank. For example, in part due to BDS pressure, in 2011 Saudi Arabia ended contracts with a French transport corporation that had operations in East Jerusalem (specifically building the Jerusalem light-rail.)[48] Hypocritically, many of the governments that have cooperated with BDS are themselves among the worst violators of human rights globally, according to several watchdog organizations. Several have occupied, captured, or disputed territories far longer than has Israel (which has repeatedly offered to end its occupation in exchange for peace). Russia has occupied territories in Georgia, Moldova, and most recently in the Ukraine; it also continues to repress minorities in Chechnya and the Dagestan region. In 1945, the Soviet Union occupied and ethnically cleansed the German city of Konsgberg, which it captured from the Germans. Russia continues its occupation to this day, having annexed the entire region. China continues to occupy Tibet, and oppress its native inhabitants, after invading and occupying that country in 1950. Northern Cyprus has been under the de facto control of Turkey since 1974. There are numerous examples of repressive regimes committing countless violations of human rights, military occupation or otherwise. None of these have been subjected to a boycott regime in any way comparable to BDS.

Importantly, the 2005 BDS "call" did not refer only to areas captured by Israel in the 1967 War, but also to the establishment of Israel in 1948:

> *"Thirty eight years into Israel's occupation of the Palestinian West Bank (including East Jerusalem), Gaza Strip and the Syrian Golan Heights, Israel continues to expand Jewish colonies. It has unilaterally annexed occupied East Jerusalem and the Golan Heights and is now de facto annexing large parts of the West Bank by means of the Wall...<u>Fifty seven years after the state of Israel was built mainly on land ethnically cleansed of its Palestinian owners,</u> a majority of Palestinians are refugees, most of whom are stateless"*[49] *(emphasis added.)*

Specifically, BDS calls for the right of return based on UN resolution 194. Article 11 of Resolution 194 has been interpreted by Palestinian representatives, and by many Arab states, as authorizing the so-called "right of return" of those Palestinian refugees to their former places of dwelling before the 1948 war, which has long been a point of contention between Israel and the Palestinian Authority.[50] Most international commentators agree that Resolution 194 was superseded by UN Resolutions 242 and 338, which marked the end of the 1967 War, and which provided the basis for the establishment of a Palestinian state along the lines of the pre-1967 armistice lines: the two-state solution. By adopting Resolution 194 as a baseline for the settlement of the Israeli-Palestinian issue, BDS is explicitly endorsing the alleged right of Palestinian refugees and their descendants to return to their former places of dwelling, that are now well within the borders of modern Israel. This could eventually make Arabs the majority within Israel and Jews the ethnic minority, rendering the two-state solution obsolete by creating two majority Arab states in Palestine, in clear violation of the UN resolutions that call for two states for two peoples.

In addition to its economic boycott, the BDS tactic explicitly denounces "normalization projects" with Israel. These projects include summer camps for Israeli and Palestinian children, joint business ventures between Israelis and Palestinians, and even academic dialogue designed to narrow differences. These are exactly the types of initiatives widely supported and promoted by liberal peace advocates like myself who are critical of settlements, but remain supportive of Israel and of a two-state solution.

Ten Reasons to Oppose BDS

In 2014, I wrote an article for *Haaretz*, which has been widely republished and circulated, outlining the "ten reasons why BDS is immoral and hinders peace." This outline, which I fill in by the remainder of this volume, is an appropriate way to conclude this introduction.

As a strong supporter of the two state solution and a critic of Israel's settlement policies, I am particularly appalled at efforts to impose divestment, boycotts, and sanctions against Israel, and Israel alone, because BDS makes it more difficult to achieve a peaceful resolution of the Mideast conflict that requires compromise on all sides.

The BDS tactic is highly immoral, threatens the peace process, and discourages the Palestinians from agreeing to any reasonable peace offer. Here are ten compelling reasons why BDS is immoral and incompatible with current efforts to arrive at a compromise peace.

1. BDS immorally imposes the entire blame for the continuing Israeli occupation and settlement policy on the Israelis. It refuses to acknowledge the historical reality that on at least three occasions, Israel offered to end the occupation and on all three occasions, the Palestinian leadership, supported by its people, refused to accept these offers. In 1967, I played a small role in drafting UN Security

Council Resolution 242 that set out the formula for ending the occupation in exchange for recognition of Israel's right to exist in peace. Israel accepted that resolution, while the Palestinians, along with all the Arab nations, gathered in Khartoum and issued their three famous "nos": No peace, no negotiation, no recognition. There were no efforts to boycott, sanction, or divest from these Arab naysayers. In 2000-2001, Israel's liberal Prime Minister Ehud Barak, along with American President Bill Clinton, offered the Palestinians statehood and the end of the occupation. Yasser Arafat rejected this offer—a rejection that many Arab leaders considered a crime against the Palestinian people. In 2008, Israel's Prime Minister Ehud Olmert offered the Palestinians an even better deal, an offer to which they failed to respond. There were no BDS threats against those who rejected Israel's peace offers. Now there are ongoing peace negotiations in which both parties are making offers and imposing conditions. Under these circumstances, it is immoral to impose blame only on Israel and to direct a BDS movement only against the nation state of the Jewish people that has thrice offered to end the occupation in exchange for peace.

2. The current BDS tactic, especially in Europe and on some American university campuses, emboldens the Palestinians to reject compromise solutions to the conflict. Some within the Palestinian leadership have told me that the longer they hold out against making peace, the more powerful will be the BDS movement against Israel. Why not wait until BDS strengthens their bargaining position so that they won't have to compromise by giving up the right of return, by agreeing to a demilitarized state, and by making other concessions that are necessary to peace but difficult for some Palestinians to accept? BDS is making a peaceful resolution harder.

3. BDS is immoral because its leaders will never be satisfied with the kind of two-state solution that is acceptable to Israel. Many of its leaders do not believe in the concept of Israel as the nation state of the Jewish people. (The major leader of the BDS movement, Omar Barghouti, has repeatedly expressed his opposition to Israel's right to exist as the nation state of the Jewish people even within the 1967 borders.) At bottom, therefore, the leadership of BDS is opposed not only to Israel's occupation and settlement policy, but to its very existence.

4. BDS is immoral because it violates the core principle of human rights: namely, "the worst first." Israel is among the freest and most democratic nations in the world. It is certainly the freest and most democratic nation in the Middle East. Its Arab citizens enjoy more rights than Arabs anywhere else in the world. They serve in the Knesset, in the judiciary, in the foreign service, in the academy, and in business. They are free to criticize Israel and to support its enemies. Israeli universities are hotbeds of anti-Israel rhetoric, advocacy, and even teaching. Israel has a superb record on women's rights, gay rights, environmental rights, and other rights that barely exist in most parts of the world. Moreover, Israel's record of avoiding civilian casualties, while fighting enemies who hide their soldiers among civilians, is unparalleled in the world today. The situation on the West Bank is obviously different because of the occupation, but even the Arabs of Ramallah, Bethlehem, and Tulkarm have more human and political rights than the vast majority of Arabs in the world today. Moreover, anyone—Jew, Muslim, or Christian—dissatisfied with Israeli actions can express that dissatisfaction in the courts, and in the media, both at home and abroad. That freedom does not exist in any Arab country, nor in many non-Arab countries. Yet Israel is the only country in the world today being threatened with BDS. When a sanction is directed against only a state with one of the best records of human rights, and that nation happens to be the state of the Jewish people, the suspicion of bigotry must be considered.

5. BDS is immoral because it would hurt the wrong people. It would hurt Palestinian workers who will lose their jobs if economic sanctions are directed against firms that employ them. It would hurt artists and academics, many of whom are the strongest voices for peace and an end to the occupation. It would hurt those suffering from illnesses all around the world who would be helped by Israeli medicine and the collaboration between Israeli scientists and other scientists. It would hurt the high tech industry around the world because Israel contributes disproportionally to the development of such life-enhancing technology.

6. BDS is immoral because it would encourage Iran—the world's leading facilitator of international terrorism—to unleash its surrogates, such as Hezbollah and Hamas, against Israel, in the expectation that if Israel were to respond to rocket attacks, the pressure for BDS against Israel would increase, as it did when Israel responded to thousands of rockets from Gaza in 2008-2009.

7. BDS is immoral because it focuses the world's attention away from far greater injustices, including genocide. By focusing disproportionately on Israel, the human rights community pays disproportionately less attention to the other occupations, such as those by China, Russia, and Turkey, and to other humanitarian disasters such as that occurring in Syria.

8. BDS is immoral because it promotes false views regarding the nation state of the Jewish people, exaggerates its flaws and thereby promotes a new variation on the world's oldest prejudice, namely anti-Semitism. It is not surprising therefore that BDS is featured on neo-Nazi, Holocaust denial, and other overtly anti-Semitic websites and is promoted by some of the world's most notorious haters such as David Duke.

9. BDS is immoral because it reflects and encourages a double standard of judgment and response regarding human rights violations. By demanding more of Israel, the nation state of the Jewish people, it expects less of other states, people, cultures, and religions, thereby reifying a form of colonial racism and reverse bigotry that hurts the victims of human rights violations inflicted by others.

10. BDS will never achieve its goals. Neither the Israeli government nor the Israeli people will ever capitulate to the extortionate means implicit in BDS. They will not and should not make important decisions regarding national security and the safety of their citizens on the basis of immoral threats. Moreover, were Israel to compromise its security in the face of such threats, the result would be more wars, more death, and more suffering.

All decent people who seek peace in the Middle East should join together in opposing BDS. Use your moral voices to demand that both the Israeli government and the Palestinian Authority accept a compromise peace that assures the security of Israel and the viability of a peaceful and democratic Palestinian state. The way forward is not by immoral extortionate threats that do more harm than good, but rather by negotiations, compromise, and good will.

The remainder of this book will lay out the case against BDS, as well as the case for a negotiated peace.

Making The Case Against BDS: 2009 - 2018

March 2, 2009
Hampshire Administration Does the Right Thing

A substantial majority of students at Hampshire College, as well as a majority of the vocal faculty, apparently still believe that Israel is the only country in the world from which Hampshire and other universities should divest. They seem not to care about the great abuses of human rights that are occurring in Iran, which routinely hangs children and dissidents; in North Korea, which tolerates no dissent; in Zimbabwe, which imprisons opposition candidates; in China, which occupies Tibet; in Russia, which engages in brutality against Chechnya; in Venezuela and Cuba, which are ruled by dictators; in Belarus, which is a throwback to Stalin's time; in Saudi Arabia, which practices gender apartheid; in Egypt, Jordan, and the Philippines, which routinely practiced torture against dissidents, and in so many other countries around the world.

This is not surprising coming from the Hampshire student body, many of whom have long been characterized by political correctness and groupthink, as well as by the vocal faculty dominated by knee-jerk, hard left throwbacks to the 1960s.

Life is difficult on that often-intolerant campus for students who dare to express support for the Middle East's only democracy that is fighting for its life against Iran-inspired terrorism and the threat of nuclear annihilation. I have received numerous emails from students, parents, and alumni recounting horrible treatment of students who dare challenge the anti-Israel groupthink.

But to its credit, the Hampshire administration has done the right thing. Though it did it quite belatedly, and largely in response to threats of a counter-divestment campaign, the president and chairman of the board have finally made it crystal clear that they are not divesting from Israel and that they will not divest from Israel. Indeed, they have agreed to buy stocks in companies that do business with Israel, even those on the hit list prepared by the virulently anti-Israel group that calls itself by the misnomer Students For Justice in Palestine. The last thing this group is interested in is justice. Its express goal is to end "the occupation of Palestine," which its leaders define to include all of what is now Israel. If they were interested in justice for Palestine, they would be seeking divestments from Hamas, which is murdering Palestinians and denying them any possibility of statehood.

In negotiations with the Hampshire administration over my call for a counter-divestment campaign against the school, I insisted that the following three conditions be met:

1. Publicly buy back the two stocks that the SJP demanded you sell that do not violate the Hampshire policy but that do business with Israel, and announce why you are buying them back.
2. Announce clearly that Hampshire rejected and will continue to reject the SJP efforts to single out Israel for divestment.
3. Announce publicly what you have said in your letter to me that those students and faculty who are claiming that Hampshire has divested from Israel are not telling the truth, are misrepresenting their authority to speak for Hampshire, and that no other school should use Hampshire's actions as a precedent for divesting from Israel.

The Hampshire administration agreed to these conditions, and I have issued the following statement:

> *"Hampshire has now done the right thing. It has made it unequivocally clear that it did not and will not divest from Israel. Indeed, it will continue to hold stock in companies that do business with Israel as well as with Israeli companies, so long as these companies meet the general standards that Hampshire applies to all of its holdings. As I previously wrote to*

> *President Hexter, if Hampshire did the right thing and made its position crystal clear I would urge contributors to continue to contribute to this fine school. I now do so. Indeed, I plan myself to make a contribution to Hampshire and to urge that my contribution, and perhaps others, be used to start a fund to encourage the presentation of all reasonable views regarding the Middle East to the college community. Debate about the Middle East is essential and criticism of any of the parties, when warranted, is healthy. What I condemned and continue to condemn is the singling out of Israel for divestment, unwarranted condemnation or any other sanction. I look forward to working together with Hampshire to assure that the marketplace of ideas remains open to all reasonable views on this important issue, and that students feel comfortable expressing views that may not represent the majority view on the campus."*

The matter is now closed between me and the Hampshire administration, but it is still very much open between me and the majority of Hampshire students and faculty who still support the bigoted singling out of Israel for divestments. I recently offered to send a small contribution to Hampshire to encourage open and balanced dialogue on campus about the Middle East. I hope Hampshire will invite me to participate in that dialogue. The Hampshire campus can sure use some real debate about the Israeli-Arab conflict, instead of dumbed-down brainwashing that passes for education in so many colleges and universities today. I would love to confront students and faculty who have hijacked the human rights agenda in their efforts to discredit the Jewish state. Let the student body hear all sides of these divisive issues and let them think for themselves and decide based on facts, not on propaganda.

April 28, 2009
Confronting Evil at Durban II

Last week I came face to face with evil, as I stood just a few feet away from Mahmoud Ahmadinejad. We were both staying in the same hotel in Geneva. He was there to be the opening speaker at Durban II, a review and reprise of Durban I, the United Nations-sponsored conference on racism that had turned into a racist hate fest against the Jewish people and the Jewish state. I was there—along with Elie Wiesel, Irwin Cotler, and others who have devoted their lives to combating bigotry—to try to prevent a recurrence of Durban I.

I first set eyes on Ahmadinejad when he walked into the hotel and waved in the general direction of where my wife and I were standing. We looked back contemptuously as my wife let out an audible hiss. He was about to be welcomed to Geneva by the Swiss president who made a special visit to the hotel in order to greet a man who denies the Holocaust while threatening another one, this time with nuclear weapons.

When the Swiss president was widely criticized for his warm and uncritical embrace of one of the worlds most evil and dangerous tyrants, he offered two justifications. First, because Switzerland was the host nation for the conference, he was obliged, as the president of the host nation, to greet a fellow head of state. This is patent nonsense. American presidents do not greet heads of states invited by the United Nations, unless they have also been invited by the United States. No American president has greeted Ahmadinejad when he spoke at the UN. Nor would President Obama—certainly without publicly and privately expressing disdain for his bigoted and dangerous views.

This leads to the Swiss president's second purported justification, namely that Switzerland represents the United States' interests in dealing with Iran, with whom it has no formal diplomatic relations. In other words, when the president of Switzerland extended a hand to Ahmadinejad, it was not only the hand of Switzerland, but also the hand of the United States. This, too, is nonsense compounded by overreaching. The United States had no interest in extending a hand of legitimacy to Ahmadinejad. Indeed the Obama government—

along with many other democratic governments—refused to legitimate this conference by its attendance. Other democracies, which chose to attend, publicly walked out of Ahmadinejad's bigoted tirade.

The Swiss president had no authority or right to act on behalf of the United States in the way that he did. The U.S. should find another government—one that understands the difference between good and evil and knows how to confront the latter—to represent it in its dealings with Iran. By his craven actions, the Swiss president has disqualified himself from serving in this important role. Neutrality should not be confused with legitimating evil and being complicit with bigotry, as the Swiss have been guilty of since they served as Hitler's banker during World War II.

Not only did the Swiss president legitimate, the Swiss security services protected him from the media. It was certainly appropriate for security to protect Ahmadinejad from physical threats, but they also sought to protect him from being embarrassed by difficult questions from the press, as evidenced by the following incident.

A bank of television cameras and reporters were waiting to interview Ahmadinejad after his meeting with the Swiss president. He was still in the meeting, and so I approached the reporters and suggested that they put several specific questions to him. The press was anxious to hear from me, but the security services physically removed me from the hotel, even though Ahmadinejad was nowhere to be seen.

My second encounter with evil occurred on the day of Ahmadinejad's speech. We, who were there to respond to Ahmadinejad's bigotry, were told that we could listen to his speech in a special room set aside for those who could not enter the actual room in which he was speaking. Several hundred people watched on a television screen as he walked up to the podium to rousing applause by many of the delegates. But the UN purposely decided not to translate his speech into English. All other speeches were translated but we were required to listen to Ahmadinejad in Farsi. I complained that the right of free speech goes both ways: It not only includes Ahmadinejad's right to express his horrendous opinions, it also includes his critics' right to listen to his words so that we can rebut them in the marketplace of ideas. When the UN authorities refused to translate his speech, I led a walkout from the overflow room toward the room in which he was speaking. I entered the room and took a seat several rows away from where he expressed some of the most horrendous views I had ever heard. To their credit, many of the European delegates walked out in disgust. I joined them, urging other delegates to leave as well and telling them that "silence in the face of evil is complicity." But most of the delegates remained and applauded Ahmadinejad when he made his extreme statements calling not only for the end of Israel but the end of all liberal democracies around the world.

It was then that I understood better how Hitler had come to power. Hitler rose to a position where he could commit genocide not as the result of anti-Semites, but rather because otherwise decent people put their own self-interests before the need to condemn his bigotry. As Edmund Burke observed many years ago, "all that is required for evil to succeed is for good men [and women] to remain silent." In that room, on that day, I came face to face with Ahmadinejad's evil. I expected that, but I also came face to face with a different kind of evil: the evil of a president of a great nation extending a hand of friendship to Ahmadinejad; and the evil of delegates of many nations applauding some of the most bigoted statements ever uttered from a United Nations lectern.

In the end, the forces of hate and bigotry were confronted by students, professors, and political figures who stood against Ahmadinejad and everything he represents. Ahmadinejad and the conference that reflected his worldview lost this round, but the battle against bigotry never stays won.

August 25, 2009
Sweden's Refusal to Condemn Organ Libel Is Bogus

The [now former] Swedish foreign minister, Carl Bildt, has refused to condemn a "blood libel" published by one of Sweden's leading newspapers, *Aftonbladet*. The article outrageously claims that Jewish soldiers in Israel killed Palestinians in order to harvest their organs. The writer of the article, Donald Bostrom, has acknowledged, according to *The New York Times*, "he has no idea whether the accusations are true." Yet a widely read Swedish newspaper was prepared to publish this undocumented and highly volatile accusation, without requiring its author to present any credible evidence.

This false accusation is reminiscent of the medieval blood libels that falsely accused Jews of killing Christian children in order to use their blood for religious rituals.

Not only has foreign minister Bildt refused to issue a personal condemnation of the current "organ libel," his foreign ministry explicitly disavowed the denunciation that was issued by Sweden's Ambassador to Israel, who had called the article "shocking and appalling." In a self-righteous statement, Mr. Bildt claimed that condemnation of the article would be inappropriate because freedom of expression is a part of the Swedish Constitution.

This is a bogus and ignorant argument, as anyone who understands freedom of speech will attest. I have devoted much of my life to defending freedom of speech and consider myself something of an expert on the matter. Nobody is talking about censoring the Swedish press or imprisoning the writer of the absurd article. What we are talking about is expanding the marketplace of ideas to include a completely warranted condemnation of sloppy journalism and outrageous accusations that foment an already increasing anti-Semitism in Sweden. Freedom of speech is based on an open and vibrant marketplace of ideas. No journalist is immune from criticism for bigotry and defamation, even from high-ranking government officials.

Recall that virtually every government official in Europe went out of their way to condemn the depiction of perfectly innocent cartoons that offended some Muslims by portraying Mohammed. (More recently, the Yale Press withdrew these cartoons and other classic art depicting Mohammed out of fear of violent reaction.) Without getting into the business of comparative offensiveness, no reasonable person could argue that depicting a long-dead religious figure comes anywhere close to falsely accusing contemporary Jews of murdering innocent Palestinians to steal their organs.

The reality is that the Swedish government, long known for its cowardice, simply does not want to get into a fight with the Muslim world, much as it didn't want to get into a fight with the Nazis during the Second World War. Sweden is perfectly willing to sell out the Jews in the name of neutrality, or in this case, in the false name of freedom of expression. Its silence is beneath contempt.

I am offended by Sweden's craven complicity with evil not only as a Jew, but also as a strong defender of freedom of speech. Freedom of speech carries with it certain obligations as well. One of those is to condemn false speech. The best answer to false speech is not censorship; it is truthfulness. By remaining silent in the face of the bigoted falsities contained in the *Aftonbladet* article, the Swedish foreign minister inevitably creates the impression that he sympathizes with the writer, and perhaps even with his conclusions. Mr. Bildt, too, has freedom of speech, which he has exercised on many occasions. By choosing not to exercise it on this occasion—or even worse, by exercising it to criticize the Swedish Ambassador to Israel for her condemnation of the article—Bildt becomes a facilitator of bigotry. He should be ashamed of himself. His country should be ashamed of him. And if his country is not ashamed of him, then every decent person in the world should be ashamed of Sweden.

Silence in the face of evil is not an option. As Edmund Burke reminded us many years ago: "All that is necessary for the triumph of evil is that good men do nothing." To that I may add, "Or say nothing."

September 4, 2009
Filmmakers and Writers Seek to Censor Israeli Film

A group of hard left filmmakers and writers from around the world have been using their celebrity to try to coerce the Toronto International Film Festival into banning Israeli films. Their petition, which is filled with misstatement of facts and rewriting of history, describes Israel as "an Apartheid regime." It focuses not so much on Israel's occupation of the West Bank since 1967, but rather on Israel's very existence since 1948. It characterizes Tel Aviv, a city built by the sweat of Jews largely on barren coastland, as illegitimate. It never mentions the fact that the Palestinians were offered and rejected statehood in 1938, 1948, 1967, and 2000–2001.

It fails to mention that when Israel ended its occupation of Gaza, the result was rockets being fired at Israeli schoolchildren and other civilians.

They claim that the inspiration for their censorship effort includes "former President Jimmy Carter," who they say has characterized Israel as an "Apartheid regime." Jimmy Carter has said many nasty things about Israel but he has expressly disclaimed any allegation that the Israeli regime itself is apartheid. He acknowledges that Israel is a multicultural democracy in which Arabs vote, serve in the Knesset, serve on the Supreme Court, and teach in Israeli universities. Many even volunteer to serve in the Israeli Army. His use—misuse in my view—of the word "Apartheid" was limited to Israel's occupation of the West Bank.

As Rhoda Kadalie and Julia Bertelsmann, two black South African women whose families were active in the anti-Apartheid movement, wrote recently,

> *"Israel is not an apartheid state...Arab citizens of Israel can vote and serve in the Knesset; black South Africans could not vote until 1994. There are no laws in Israel that discriminate against Arab citizens or separate them from Jews...South Africa had a job reservation policy for white people; Israel has adopted pro-Arab affirmative action measures in some sectors. Israeli schools, universities and hospitals make no distinction between Jews and Arabs. An Arab citizen who brings a case before an Israeli court will have that case decided on the basis of merit, not ethnicity. This was never the case for blacks under apartheid."*

Kadalie and Bertelsmann are critical of Israel's policies in the occupied territories but add that "racism and discrimination do not form the rationale for Israel's policies and actions...in the West Bank, measures such as the ugly security barrier have been used to prevent suicide bombings and attacks on civilians, not to enforce any racist ideology. Without the ongoing conflict and the tendency of Palestinian leaders to resort to violence, these would not exist."

At a recent concert by Daniel Berenboim, and an orchestra composed of Israelis and Palestinians held at the Young Men's

Christian Association in Jerusalem, I sat next to an Israeli Arab who was Israel's Minister of Culture. This is a cabinet position. The audience, too, was a mixture of Israelis and Palestinians, many from the West Bank. Hardly a feature of apartheid!

The ill-informed signers of the censorship petition ignore these realities, and in wrongly exploiting the apartheid analogy, they have devalued the antiapartheid struggle itself. According to Congressman John Conyers, who helped found the Congressional Black Caucus, applying the word apartheid to Israel belittles real racism and apartheid; the word "does not serve the cause of peace, and the use of it against the Jewish people in particular, who have been victims of the worst kind of discrimination, discrimination resulting in death, is offensive and wrong."

Instead of submitting their own film or writings into the marketplace of ideas, the censors seek to close down this marketplace to Israel. What are they afraid of? Why won't they compete in the open marketplace of ideas and try to influence public opinion in a manner consistent with freedom of speech, rather than employing the age-old weapon of tyrants, namely censorship.

The reason is clear. They know they would lose in an open marketplace of ideas. That is why they seek to close it to views different than theirs. "Speech for me but not for thee!," is the age-old mantra of censors.

Who are these censors? They consist mostly of obscure "activists" who nobody has ever heard of, but they also include Jane Fonda, who famously supported the Viet Cong and refused to condemn the Cambodian genocide. Other signatories such as Danny Glover, Alice Walker, and David Byrne are way out of their league when it comes to knowledge of the Middle East. They should know better than to be demanding censorship relating to a country about which they know so little. Moreover, I do not recall their names on petitions condemning—or calling for censorship of—such truly repressive regimes as Iran, Cuba, China, Zimbabwe, Syria, Egypt, Saudi Arabia, and other nations that discriminate against women, gays, dissidents, religious minorities, and others.

Imagine how the hard left would react if anyone tried to censor or boycott these writers and actors! They would cry "McCarthyism."

Yet McCarthyism from the hard left is as dangerous to liberty as McCarthyism from the hard right.

March 4, 2010
Let's Have a Real Apartheid Education Week

Every year at about this time, radical Islamic students—aided by radical anti-Israel professors—hold an event they call "Israel Apartheid Week." During this week, they try to persuade students on campuses around the world to demonize Israel as an apartheid regime. Most students seem to ignore the rantings of these extremists, but some naive students seem to take them seriously. Some pro-Israel and Jewish students claim that they are intimidated when they try to respond to these untruths. As one who strongly opposes any censorship, my solution is to fight bad speech with good speech, lies with truth, and educational malpractice with real education.

Accordingly, I support a "Middle East Apartheid Education Week" to be held at universities throughout the world. It would be based on the universally accepted human rights principle of "the worst first." In other words, the worst forms of apartheid being practiced by Middle East nations and entities would be studied and exposed first. Then the apartheid practices of other countries would be studied in order of their seriousness and impact on vulnerable minorities.

Under this principle, the first country studied would be Saudi Arabia. That tyrannical kingdom practices gender apartheid to an extreme, relegating women to an extremely low status. Indeed, a prominent Saudi Imam recently issued a fatwa declaring that anyone who advocates women working alongside men or otherwise compromises with absolute gender apartheid is subject to execution. The Saudis also practice apartheid based on sexual orientation, executing and imprisoning gay and lesbian Saudis. Finally, Saudi Arabia openly practices religious apartheid. It has special roads for "Muslims only." It discriminates against Christians, refusing them the right to practice their religion openly. And needless to say, it doesn't allow Jews the right to live in Saudi Arabia, to own property, or even (with limited exceptions) to enter the country. Now that's apartheid with a vengeance.

The second entity on any apartheid list would be Hamas, which is the de facto government of the Gaza Strip. Hamas, too, discriminates openly against women, gays, Christians. It permits no dissent, no free speech, and no freedom of religion.

Every single Middle East Muslim country practices these forms of apartheid to one degree or another. Consider the most "liberal" and pro-American nation in the area, namely Jordan. The Kingdom of Jordan, which the King himself admits is not a democracy, has a law on its books forbidding Jews from becoming citizens or owning land. Despite the efforts of its progressive Queen, women are still de facto subordinate in virtually all aspects of Jordanian life.

Iran, of course, practices no discrimination against gays, because its President has assured us that there are no gays in Iran. In Pakistan, Sikhs have been executed for refusing to convert to Islam, and throughout the Middle East, honor killings of women are practiced, often with a wink and a nod from the religious and secular authorities.

Every Muslim country in the Middle East has a single, established religion, namely Islam, and makes no pretense of affording religious equality to members of other faiths. That is a brief review of some, but certainly not all, apartheid practices in the Middle East.

Now let's turn to Israel. The secular Jewish state of Israel recognizes fully the rights of Christians and Muslims and prohibits any discrimination based on religion (except against Conservative and Reform Jews, but that's another story!) Muslim and Christian citizens of Israel (of which there are more than a million) have the right to vote and have elected members of the Knesset, some of whom even oppose Israel's right to exist. There is an Arab member of the Supreme Court, an Arab member of the Cabinet, and numerous Israeli Arabs in important positions in businesses, universities, and the cultural life of the nation. A couple of years ago I attended a concert at the Jerusalem YMCA at which Daniel Barrenboim conducted a mixed orchestra of Israeli and Palestinian musicians. There was a mixed audience of Israelis and Palestinians, and the man sitting next to me was an Israeli Arab, who is the culture minister of the State of Israel. Can anyone imagine that kind of concert having taking place in apartheid South Africa, or in apartheid Saudi Arabia?

There is complete freedom of dissent in Israel and it is practiced vigorously by Muslims, Christians, and Jews alike. And Israel is a vibrant democracy.

What is true of Israel proper, including Israeli Arab areas, is not true of the occupied territories. Israel ended its occupation of the Gaza several years ago, only to be attacked by Hamas rockets. Israel maintains its occupation of the West Bank only because the Palestinians walked away from a generous offer of statehood on 97% of the West Bank, with its capital in Jerusalem and with a $35 billion compensation package for refugees. Had it accepted that offer by President Bill Clinton and Prime Minister Ehud Barak, there would be a Palestinian state in the West Bank. There would be no separation barrier. There would be no roads restricted to Israeli citizens (Jews, Arabs, and Christians.) And there would be no civilian settlements. I have long opposed civilian settlements in the West Bank, as many, perhaps most, Israelis do. But to call an occupation, which continues because of the refusal of the Palestinians to accept the two-state solution, "Apartheid" is to misuse that word. As those of us who fought in the actual struggle of apartheid well understand, there is no comparison between what happened in South Africa and what is now taking place on the West Bank. As Congressman John Conyors, who helped found the Congressional Black Caucus, well put it:

"[Applying the word "Apartheid" to Israel] does not serve the cause of peace, and the use of it against the Jewish people in particular, who have been victims of the worst kind of discrimination, discrimination resulting in death, is offensive and wrong."

The current "Israel Apartheid Week" on universities around the world, by focusing only on the imperfections of the Middle East's sole democracy, is carefully designed to cover up far more serious problems of real apartheid in Arab and Muslim nations. The question is why do so many students identify with regimes that denigrate women, gays, non-Muslims, dissenters, environmentalists, and human rights advocates, while demonizing a democratic regime that grants equal rights to women (the chief justice and speaker of the Parliament of Israel are women), gays (there are openly gay generals in the Israeli Army), non-Jews (Muslims and Christians serve in high positions in Israel), and dissenters, (virtually all Israelis dissent about something). Israel has the best environmental record in the Middle East, it exports more life-saving medical technology than any country in the region, and it has sacrificed more for peace than any country in the Middle East. Yet on many college campuses democratic, egalitarian Israel is a pariah, while sexist, homophobic, anti-Semitic, terrorist Hamas is a champion. There is something very wrong.

March 20, 2010
Alan Dershowitz Address at AIPAC Policy Conference

Transcript:

The world should today be standing in awe and appreciation of Israel's amazing accomplishments and contributions.

No country has ever contributed so much to the world in so short a time. Israel's medical technology exports have saved more lives per capita than exports from any other country.

Israel has saved more Muslim and Arab lives than all of the Arab and Muslim countries combined.

Israel's high technology accomplishments exceed those of all of Europe and most of Asia. Israel has accomplished more for the environment than virtually any country in the world. Israel has taught the world how to fight wars against terrorism ethically and with concern for avoiding civilian casualties. No country in the world faced with comparable threats has a better record of human rights than Israel does.

When Justice William Brennan, probably the most liberal justice to serve on the Supreme Court, went to Israel he said, "If terrorism ever comes to the United States there is only one country from which the United States can learn how to balance human rights against the need to fight terrorism, and that country was Israel." The world should be so proud and appreciative of Israel, but instead, Israel is the only country in the world today whose legitimacy continues to be questioned, constantly questioned, constantly challenged.

It's more than ironic since no country has ever been established on a firmer foundation of law. Israel was established, after all, through declarations accepted by the League of Nations, by the United Nations, by international law; yet its legitimacy remains challenged. Compare it to other countries that started with the revolutions or simply grabbing a land of other people, Israel paid for every inch of its land, paid for it by money and paid for it by the blood of its children.

This process of de-legitimization began in earnest in 1975 when the United Nations took so much time and so much energy debating whether Zionism was racism. And do you know what else was happening in 1975 at the time the United Nations was involved in this ridiculous, bigoted debate? Millions of people were being murdered by genocides in Cambodia and the United Nations paid no attention to that at all. They were too busy de-legitimizing and condemning Israel. And then it moved from 1975 to the Durban Conference in 2001 where the Durban strategy of de-legitimization took root. They turned everything around. They accused Israel of racism, Israel of apartheid, Israel of genocide, Israel of creating a holocaust.

What they did is they inverted the entire concept of human rights and turned it against Israel. As a result of Durban, there were efforts to boycott Israeli institutions, institutions of learning, institutions that are trying to cure cancer and heart disease and Parkinson's. And yet efforts are made, to this day, in Norway as we speak, in England as we speak to boycott Israeli academic institutions.

You know what happened last time when they tried to boycott Israel and England? A few of us got together and put together a petition saying, "You know, if you boycott Israel, your universities, we will not speak at your universities." And we circulated a petition. We thought we'd get 400 or 500 signatures—11,000 American academics, Nobel Prize winners, presidents of universities—signed that petition.

And the message was clear, "If you try to boycott Israel it is you who will be boycotted and it is your universities that will suffer." Israel's universities are among the greatest in the world today and nobody should try to boycott its great academics and its great places of science.

And then came the concept that we call "guerilla lawfare," efforts to try to de-legitimize Israel by using legal tactics, legal means, using international law, using humanitarian law to try to turn it against Israel: divestment campaigns, distortion of human rights. When it came to Durban II, in 2009, we were ready and we went to Geneva and we fought back. And we won Durban II. They invited Ahmadinejad.

We invited Elie Wiesel.

We said, "Who is the person who speaks for human rights here today?" One of the proudest moments of my life was when I was arrested by the Swiss police for daring to try to confront Ahmadinejad and just ask him a simple question, "Do you deny the Holocaust? Have you ever been to Auschwitz? Which books have you read about the Holocaust?" Challenging him to debate his Holocaust denial. He denies the Holocaust while trying to bring another one upon the Jewish people of Israel and yet I was arrested for trying to confront him in a peaceful way. But at Durban the students stood up against Ahmadinejad. He was booed and people walked out on him and we won the second Durban encounter. And the important message is, "We fight back. We don't take these kinds of abuses sitting down."

And when Richard Goldstone—through his everlasting disgrace—agreed to serve on a commission that was so one-sided, we fought back. "One-sided?" Do you know who the three people serving on the commission were? One of them, a colonel from Ireland, who before he ever served on the commission believed that Israeli soldiers had taken out Irish soldiers and killed them in cold blood and he was going to get revenge. He believed Israel had no right of self-defense. He was serving on the commission. A British woman, who before she heard a piece of evidence said Israel was guilty of war crime. She was serving on the commission.

And a Muslim woman from Pakistan said, "You have to believe Palestinians, they always tell the truth." She was serving on the commission. And then, of course, to give the commission the certification of Kashrut, the Heksher, they put Richard Goldstone on the commission to sign on as the token court Jew so that when people argued with the contents of the Goldstone Report or tried to debate him, as I tried to debate him, his answer was, "No. I'm a Jew. My daughter lives in Israel. I must be correct. You can't question me, because I'm a Jew."

An argument ad hominem, which had nothing to do with the demerits of the Goldstone Report, that got everything backwards. And we now have videotaped evidence showing everything that Goldstone said was wrong. Israel tried desperately to avoid civilian casualties while Hamas fired from behind civilian shields. The point is that de-legitimation efforts, until now, have been limited primarily to the United Nations and European countries. It has never ever succeeded in the United States.

Why? Because in the United States—thanks to AIPAC and thanks to the fact that we have tremendous support among congresspeople and among the people of the United States—Israel is known to be America's great friend. Israel gets high ratings every time their public opinion polls and that's why every effort to de-legitimate in the United States up to now has failed. But I want to tell you about a new effort that's just beginning that has the potential to succeed if we don't fight back. The newest threat, the newest attempt, to import de-legitimation into the United States comes from people like Walt and Mearsheimer, who write a book that gets it all backwards.

Walt and Mearsheimer obviously says a lot of good things in some ways about AIPAC. He thinks you're the most powerful organization in the world; you control what the United States does. What he fails to understand is that the reason AIPAC is strong—and may you go from strength to strength and increase your strength—is because Americans support Israel and because Americans support Israel, congresspeople support Israel.

There is a lobby in Washington that has no public support, which is very powerful that Walt and Mearsheimer could've written about. It's called the Saudi lobby—no public support, great influence, and power. That's a paradox.

It's no paradox in a democracy that a lobby for a group that's completely popular and supported by the American public should have some influence in Washington. And then comes Jimmy Carter in an attempt to de-legitimate Israel by using that word apartheid.

Jimmy Carter, a man who wouldn't use the word genocide to describe what was going on in Darfur, because he says, "You have to be careful about how you use language," uses the word apartheid to describe Israel's only democracy. Carter limited this term to the West Bank.

But now the most recent argument and the most serious argument ever made against Israel in modern times is one that's recently been all over the Internet, namely that Israeli actions endanger American troops in Iraq and Afghanistan. It's all over the Internet and it's creeping into the mainstream media.

Headlines, "Israel: a danger to U.S. troops."—CNN, Rick Sanchez. "This is starting to get dangerous for us," Biden purportedly told Netanyahu. "What you're doing here undermines the security of our troops." (Reported by Yedioth Ahronoth.) United States tells Israel, "You are undermining America, endangering troops." "Israel is empowering al-Qaeda, Petraeus warns." "Petraeus: Israel's intransigence could cost American lives." Variations of this false and dangerous argument have now been picked up by Joe Klein in *TIME* magazine, Roger Cohen in *The New York Times*, Walt and Mearsheimer, Brzezinski, and others. Both Vice President Biden and General Petraeus have apparently disavowed this argument, though their statements continue to be cited in support of its conclusion.

Whatever the source, the argument has taken on, unfortunately, a life of its own and is being used in an effort to bring the de-legitimacy campaign to the United States of America. It is the most dangerous argument ever put forward in the ongoing campaign against Israel, because its goal is directly to reduce support for Israel among mainstream Americans, who like every one of us in this room support our American troops fighting abroad.

It is an ironic and insidious argument, primarily because the pillar of Israel's policy with regard to the United States troops is that Israel never wants to endanger our troops. That's why it never asks the United States' soldiers to fight for Israel as many allies, in fact, do. This argument seeks to scapegoat Israel for the deaths of American troops at the hands of Islamic terrorists. This argument has become a powerful weapon in the campaign to demonize and de-legitimate Israel in the minds of mainstream Americans. Most of all, it is an entirely false argument factually, entirely false.

There is absolutely no relationship between Israel's actions and the safety of American troops, none. Consider the year 2000–2001, what was Israel doing in 2000–2001 in—in November, December, January?

They were offering peace to the Palestinians at Camp David and Taba. They were offering the Palestinians a state on 100 percent of the Gaza Strip, 97 percent of the West Bank, a divided Jerusalem, $35 billion reparation package. What was going on during those months? Osama Bin Laden was planning the destruction of the World Trade Center.

There is no relationship between Israeli actions and hatred and actions by Islamic extremists against the United States. In 2005, Israel leaves Gaza—unilaterally leaves Gaza. That's exactly what everybody had been asking for and at the same time there was a slight increase against American troops in Iraq. During Operation Cast Lead and the recent Jerusalem building announcement there's been no significant escalation of violence against American troops in Iraq.

There is no relationship. It's made up out of whole cloth. I challenge those who are offering this argument, put up or shut up. Prove your point or stop making these bigoted arguments. They are wrong. And think—think of the implications—think of the implications of this argument. The implications of this argument are the de-legitimation of Israel in the minds of Americans. Why? Because for Muslim extremists it's not what America does. It's not what Israel does. It's what Israel is. It's what America is.

Islamic extremists cannot accept the concept of a secular democracy, a democracy that grants equal rights to women, equal rights to all. It's what they are that they hate, not what we do. That's why it's an important part of the de-legitimation campaign, Israel cannot do anything that would satisfy the Islamic extremists to threaten the United States troops. There's nothing Israel could do. If Israel made peace tomorrow unilaterally giving up all of its rights it would have no impact whatsoever. As long as Israel exists that is the grievance of Islamic extremists, and Israel is not going to stop existing to satisfy Islamic extremists.

Nor can the United States do anything to stop Islamic extremists from threatening Americans unless it were to pull out all of its troops in the Middle East, which it's not going to do. The point is there's nothing that Israel or the United States can do to stop these Islamic extremists. There is something, however, that the Palestinian Authority can do, by stopping the daily incitements against the United States from extremists. Just go on MEMRI.org. Just watch PA television. That's the incitement that puts American troops in danger, by stopping teaching its children to hate us, by stopping the naming of public squares in the West Bank after murderers of Americans and the murderers of Israeli children and civilians.

This square is being named after a murderer who killed an American woman and who killed many Israelis. When you do that and you say that you're naming the square in order to encourage your children to follow in the path of that murderer, you're inciting violence against American troops and against American citizens. So let us focus on those who hate America and those who incite terrorism against our troops rather than on a brave nation that loves America that helps it militarily and with intelligence and that never asks the United States for troops to protect it.

I want to mention just two propositions that I ask anybody who makes the case against Israel to dispute, two simple propositions.

Number one: if Israel's enemies were to lay down their arms, stop terrorism, and stop firing rockets, there would be peace. Does anybody dispute that? Number two: if Israel were to lay down its arms there would be genocide. That is the reality. That's the truth and those two statements must be kept in mind.

And then I want to talk just very briefly about three lessons of the Holocaust that I've learned in my friendship with Elie Wiesel. The first lesson is that morality without military power is not enough. We had morality on our side during the Second World War, but we didn't have the ability to defend the Jewish community. Thank God for Israel. Thank God for its military. Thank God for the ability that we now have to defend our morality. The second lesson—the second lesson is that military power without morality is dangerous. That's why the Israeli military learns lessons in ethics. That's why it has the concept of holiness of arms. That's why it has professors helping to shape ethical policies for the military. And the third one, and perhaps the most important one that Israel and all of us must keep in mind when dealing with Iran, is that you must always believe the threats of your enemies more than the promises of your friends.

And that's why Israel must be totally self-reliant. And so in closing, I want to thank you for showing support for this great, embattled nation. I want to tell you that the United States-Israel alliance is good for America. It's good for Israel, it's good for democracy, it's good for human rights, it's good for peace, it's good for the world.

And may the relationship between these two great democracies continue to go from strength to strength. Thank you very much.

May 12, 2010
Alan Dershowitz Speech at Tel Aviv University Upon Accepting Honorary Doctorate

In May 2010, I received an honorary doctorate from Tel Aviv University. My acceptance speech was denounced by several professors, who mischaracterized it as an "incitement" against professors who use the classroom to propagandize captive students. I then asked *Haaretz* to publish my entire speech, which follows:

I have the double honor and pleasure of accepting an honorary doctorate from one of the world's great universities, and also of delivering an acceptance speech on behalf of the other distinguished recipients of the honorary degrees. I know I speak for all of the degree recipients when I praise the incredible accomplishments both of Israel in general over the past 62 years and of Tel Aviv University in particular over the past 57 years.

No country in the history of the world has ever contributed more to humankind and accomplished more for its people in so brief a period of time as Israel has done since its relatively recent rebirth in 1948.

As one of the youngest nations in the world, and one of the smallest, Israel exports more lifesaving medical technology per capita than any nation in the world, and ranks among the top 2 or 3 in absolute terms. The same can be said for environmental technology, internet technology, and so many other areas of scientific innovation (Fortunately for the rest of the world, but unfortunately for Israel, it also exports some of its best scientists and other academics to American and European universities, because the Israeli government does not fund its universities sufficiently.) At the center of these contributions to the world are Israel's great research universities. And at the center of these universities is Tel Aviv. Barely half a century old, Tel Aviv University has surpassed most of Europe's ancient institutions of learning and is now the equal of virtually all. The publications, awards, and recognition of its faculty rival the best faculties in the world. I am tempted to say that Tel Aviv has become the Harvard of the Middle East, but then I would not be speaking for the rest of my fellow degree recipients who might not regard Harvard as the singular measure of excellence.

Instead, I will say that Harvard aspires to become the Tel Aviv University of America. Hyperbole aside, I can think of no university in the world that has achieved so much in so short a period of time as has the great university that has honored us tonight. Yasher Koach.

Looking at Israel's accomplishments over 62 years and Tel Aviv University's over 57 years, it would seem to suggest that Israel and its premier research universities have developed in tandem and with symbiosis. And to some degree they have. Israel's research universities have contributed immeasurably to the defense of Israel by the development of technological advances that support the mission of the IDF. And as Dan Senor and Saul Singer have brilliantly demonstrated in their remarkable book *Start Up Nation*, the IDF has paid back its debt to Israel's universities multifold.

The IDF has helped train and prepare many of Israel's most innovative young women and men for the university and then for their roles in research and technology. The Israeli military plays more than a critical role in defending the citizens of the Jewish state. It also plays an important social, scientific, and psychological role in preparing its young citizens for the challenging task of being Israelis in a difficult world.

All this is well and good. There is no reason why the state and its universities must have as high a wall of separation, as should the synagogue, the church, the mosque, and the state. But the university must play an important role in the informal system of checks and balances that is so essential to the health of the democracy. We all learn in school that the judicial, legislative, and executive branches of government must check and balance each other. But other non-state institutions must participate in this important system of checks and balances as well. These checking institutions include the academy, the media, religious institutions, and NGOs. The academy should not become too cozy with, or too reliant on the government. Great research universities must insist on independence from government and on the exercise of academic freedom.

Academic freedom requires that professors be free to challenge governmental policies, government officials, and the status quo. Israel boasts that the highest level of academic freedom in the world today—if not in theory, then certainly in practice. I emphasize practice, because few nations in the world—even those that in theory proclaim strict adherence to academic freedom—confront on a daily basis the kind of academic dissent experienced in Israel. Israeli academics regularly and falsely compare their nation to the tyrannical regime that murdered 6 million Jews.

Academic dissenters regularly and freely call on other academic institutions around the world to boycott the very Israeli universities which grant them academic freedom. Professors from this university are currently in Boston demanding the shutting down of an exhibit in the Boston Museum of Science featuring Israeli scientific and technological advances in medicine, clean energy and other contributors to humanity.

Israeli academics are free to challenge not only the legitimacy of the Jewish state but even, as one professor at this university has done, the authenticity of the Jewish people. Israeli academics are free to distort the truth, construct false analogies, and teach their students theories akin to the earth being flat—and they do so with relish and with the shield of academic freedom. So long as these professors do not violate the rules of the academy, they have the precious right to be wrong, because we have learned the lesson of history that no one institution has a monopoly on truth and that the never-ending search for truth requires, to quote the title of one of Israel's founder's autobiography, "trial and error." The answer to falsehood is not censorship; it is truth. The answer to bad ideas is not firing the teacher, but articulating better ideas that prevail in the marketplace. The academic freedom of the faculty is central to the mission of the university.

But academic freedom is not the province of the hard left alone. Academic freedom includes the right to agree with the government, to defend the government, and to work for the government. Some of the same hard leftists who demand academic freedom for themselves and their ideological colleagues were among the leaders of those seeking to deny academic freedom to a distinguished law professor who had worked for the military advocate general and whose views they disagreed with. To its credit, Tel Aviv University rejected this attempt to limit academic freedom to those who criticized the government. As Professor Shlomo Avineri, no right-winger, put it: "The attempt to 'protect' those who belong to the left while employing McCarthy-style methods against those associated with the right is nothing but hypocrisy, which has no place in academia."

Rules of academic freedom for professors must be neutral, applicable equally to right and left. Free speech for me but not for thee is the beginning of the road to tyranny.

Nor does academic freedom belong to the professor alone. As Amnon Rubenstein has brilliantly argued, academic freedom belongs to the student as well as the teacher. He has pointed out that Article 5 of the Student's Rights Law guarantees every student "the freedom to express his [or her] views and opinions as the contents of the syllabus and the values incorporated therein."

The right of the student's academic freedom, however, goes well beyond this law. It includes the right not to be propagandized in the classroom by teachers who seek to impose their ideology on students. It includes the right of the student to express opinions contrary to those presented by the teacher without fear of being graded down and without fear of being denied recommendations or job opportunities. Indeed, any professor who punishes a student for not agreeing with his controversial opinion is guilty of academic harassment, which is a variant on what we all would agree is an academic violation, namely sexual harassment. No teacher is permitted to threaten a student with lower grades or poorer recommendations if the student refuses to consent to sexual contact. Nor should any professor be permitted to threaten lower grades or recommendations if a student refuses to agree with a teacher's ideology. Students are the consumers of the university and consumers have rights that, if they don't trump those of the producer, are at least equal to them in the context of controversial ideas.

In their book *Start Up Nation*, Senor and Singer make a strong case that Israel's innovative excellence is in part of function of its non-hierarchical military structure: A young 19-year-old kid straight out of high school is encouraged to talk back to an officer if he or she thinks they have a better idea. Competition in the marketplace of ideas is encouraged in the IDF. It must also be encouraged in the academy where the right of a student to speak up and express controversial ideas is crucial. It is true that not all ideas are created equal and that those of the experienced professor may be better than those of the novice student, but the ultimate judge must be the open marketplace of ideas and not the raw power of the grader or recommender to impose his or her ideology.

But in most universities, not only in Israel, but throughout the Western world, the loudest and shrillest voices most often come from the extremes. Today it is the hard left. Yesterday it was the hard right. The burden should not only be on students to stand up to propagandizing professors who distort the truth in the name of extremist ideologies. The burden must be shared by professors as well, especially those who disagree with the extreme views. The other side of the coin of academic freedom is academic responsibility. It is the responsibility of reasonable and moderate professors to speak out against extremist views, whether of the hard right of hard left.

The silent center must not remain silent just because extremists are more opinionated and more willing to express their views. Moderates don't get a pass. They too have an obligation to speak out, not in the classroom but in appropriate forums outside of the classroom where different rules govern. Students deserve the public support of faculty members who quietly agree with them, especially when they feel vulnerable to the power of extremist faculty who believe that their unbalanced views represent the sole truth. Great universities have the right to expect their professors to contribute to the market place of ideas when irresponsible extremists try to hijack the university's hard-earned brand and misuse it to promote their own ideologies.

So let us join together in celebrating a great university that was born in conflict, came of age in conflict, and will continue in conflict. What else could be expected of an innovative house of learning in the Jewish state. Conflict, after all, is as old as Abraham's argument with God, Jacob's wrestling match with the angel, the Talmud's insistence on preserving dissenting opinions, and the tradition of Jewish jokes about two Jews, three opinions. A university without conflict may be suitable for China, Iran, or the former Soviet Union. But it could never find a home in Israel.

Conflict, while uncomfortable, is inevitable in a vibrant democracy. It is particularly inevitable in a vibrant Jewish democracy. To be Jewish is to be uncomfortable, to be unable to breathe a sigh of relief and declare that we can relax. Tension and conflict seems to be our destiny. It is also the road to learning, progress and innovation.

The alternatives to conflict are stagnation, certainty, and censorship, which have no place in a university. So let conflict continue, so long as no voices are silenced, all points of view valued, and the marketplace of ideas remains open. I am confident that moral clarity will trump hypocrisy, common sense will prevail over political correctness, and the process of searching for truth will be encouraged. Israel will survive its dissenters, as will this great university. While there will always be conflict, we all here today hope and expect that the state of Israel and the University of Tel Aviv will go from strength to strength.

June 3, 2010
Singling Out Israel For "International Investigation:" The Turkish Flotilla

In a world in which North Korea sinks a South Korean naval vessel killing dozens, Iran arms Islamic terrorists, who kill hundreds, Russia bombs Chechnya, killing thousands, and the United States and Great Britain, while targeting Al Qaeda and Taliban, kill an indeterminate number of civilians, only Israel is subjected to international "investigations" such as that conducted by Richard Goldstone and that being called for by the Security Council in the wake of the recent flotilla fiasco.

Why only Israel? Why is the United Nations silent about other situations that cry out for international investigations? Surely it's not because what Israel did was worse than what other member nations have done. Certainly it's not because Israel lacks self-criticism or mechanisms for internal investigation. Plainly it's not because the other "offenders" were provoked, while Israel was unprovoked.

There is only one answer—because Israel has long been singled out for public scrutiny and opprobrium by the United Nations in particular and the international community in general.

This is not to say that Israel has always been blameless. It foolishly took the bait and allowed itself to be provoked into overreacting to a well-planned provocation by so-called "humanitarians," who love only those who hate the Jewish state. The best proof that the flotilla had little to do with providing humanitarian aid to the people of Gaza and everything to do with breaking Israel's entirely lawful military blockade of a terrorist enclave, is Hamas' refusal to accept the food and medicine that Israel removed from the captured boats. The leaders of the flotilla admitted that their object was the same as Hamas'—not to provide humanitarian assistance to Gaza but rather to break the military blockade that is designed to keep rockets and other anti-personnel weapons from the hands of Hamas terrorists.

Israel should have been smarter in its efforts to enforce its blockade, but it did nothing illegal—and what it did do certainly doesn't warrant being singled out for the stigma of an international investigation.

If the United Nations is to get into the business of ordering and conducting international investigations, it must establish neutral and objective criteria for when such an investigation is warranted. These criteria must be equally applicable to <u>all</u> nations, and not merely to the Jewish nation.

Primary among the criteria must be "the worst first." Under that rule, investigations must be conducted in the order of the seriousness of the offense, not the unpopularity of the offender. Israel's actions in enforcing its blockade ranks fairly low on the pecking order of offenses, compared to those that have never been subjected to a mandated international investigation. Until and unless North Korea, Iran, Russia and other nations are required to undergo international scrutiny, the demand that Israel do so is illegitimate.

The second neutral criteria should be the capacity of the accused nation to investigate itself and to be subjected to domestic scrutiny and criticism. Here too Israel fares better than most. It has an active Supreme Court, a free and aggressive press and a responsive political system. It doesn't need dictatorial tyrannies telling it how to defend its citizens.

For international law to have any credibility, it must be applied neutrally, objectively, and fairly to all nations. Singling out Israel for special scrutiny and investigation, while far more serious offenders and offenses are ignored, is incompatible with the rule of law.

December 20, 2010
Bishop Tutu Is No Saint When it Comes To Jews

Among the world's most respected figures is South Africa's Bishop Desmond Tutu. His recognizable face—with its ever-present grin—has become a symbol of reconciliation and goodness. But it masks a long history of ugly hatred toward the Jewish people, the Jewish religion, and the Jewish state. Bishop Desmond Tutu is no mere anti-Zionist (though Martin Luther King long ago recognized that anti-Zionism often serves as a cover for deeper anti-Jewish bigotry.) He has minimized the suffering of those killed in the Holocaust. He has attacked the "Jewish"—not Israeli—"lobby" as too "powerful" and "scar[y]." He has invoked classic anti-Semitic stereotypes and tropes about Jewish "arrogance," "power," and money. He has characterized Jews a "peculiar people," and has accused "the Jews" of causing many of the world's problems. He once even accused the Jewish state of acting in an "un-Christian" way.

Were he not a Nobel Laureate, his long history of bigotry against the Jewish people would have landed him in the dustbin of history, along with a dishonor roll of otherwise successful people, whose reputations have been tainted by their anti-Semitism such as Henry Ford, Charles Lindbergh, Patrick Buchanan, and Mel Gibson. But his Nobel Prize should not shield him from accountability for his long history of anti-Jewish bigotry, any more than it should for Yasser Arafat, Jimmy Carter, and Jose Saramago.

Let the record speak for itself, so that history may judge Tutu on the basis of his own words—words that he has often repeated and that others repeat, because Tutu is a role model for so many people around the world. Here are some of Tutu's hateful words, most of them carefully documented in a recent petition by prominent South Africans to terminate him as a "patron" of the two South African Holocaust Centers, because he uses his status with these fine institutions as legitimization for his anti-Jewish rhetoric.

He has minimized the suffering of those murdered in the Holocaust by asserting that "the gas chambers" made for "a neater death" than did apartheid. In other words, the Palestinians, who in his view are the victims of "Israeli apartheid," have suffered more than the victims of the Nazi Holocaust. He has complained of "the Jewish Monopoly of the Holocaust," and has demanded that its victims must "forgive the Nazis for the Holocaust," while refusing to forgive the "Jewish people" for "persecute[ing] others."

Tutu has asserted that Zionism has "very many parallels with racism," thus echoing the notorious and discredited "Zionism equals racism" resolution passed by the General Assembly of the United Nations and subsequently rescinded. He has accused the Jews of Israel of doing "things that even apartheid South Africa had not done." He has said that "the Jews thought they had a monopoly of God: Jesus was angry that they could shut out other human beings." He has said that Jews have been "fighting against" and being "opposed to" his God. He has "compared the features of the ancient Holy Temple in Jerusalem to the features of the apartheid system in South Africa." He has complained that, "the Jewish people with their traditions, religion and long history of persecution sometimes appear to have caused a refugee problem among others." He has implied that Israel might someday consider as an option "to perpetrate genocide and exterminate all Palestinians."

He has complained that Americans "are scared...to say wrong is wrong because the Jewish lobby is powerful—very powerful." He has accused Jews—not Israelis—of exhibiting "an arrogance—the arrogance of power because Jews are a powerful lobby in this land and all kinds of people woo their support."

"You know as well as I do that, somehow, the Israeli government is placed on a pedestal [in the U.S.] and to criticize it is to be immediately dubbed anti-Semitic, as if Palestinians were not Semitic."

He has compared Israel to Hitler's Germany, Stalin's Soviet Union and apartheid South Africa, saying that they too were once "very powerful" but they "bit the dust," as will "unjust" Israel.

He has denied that Israel is a "civilized democracy" and has singled out Israel—one of the world's most open democracies—as a nation guilty of "censorship of their media." He has urged the Capetown Opera to refuse to perform Porgy and Bess in Tel Aviv and has called for a total cultural boycott of Jewish Israel, while encouraging performers to visit the most repressive regimes in the world.

He has claimed that his God sides with Palestinians, whom he compares to the Israelites under bondage in Egypt, and has sought to explain, if not justify, how Israeli actions lead directly to suicide bombings and other forms of terrorism.

He has been far more vocal about Israel's imperfections than about the genocides in Rwanda, Darfur, and Cambodia. He repeatedly condemns Israel's occupation of the West Bank without mentioning the many other occupations in the world today. While attacking Israel for its "collective punishment" of Palestinians—which he claims is worse than what apartheid South Africa did—

he himself has called for the collective punishment of Jewish academics and businesses in Israel by demanding boycotts of all Jewish (but not Muslim or Christian) Israelis. (This call for an anti-Jewish boycott finds its roots in the Nazi "Kauft Nicht beim Juden" campaign of the 1930s.) When confronted with his double standard against Jews, he has justified it on phony theological grounds: "Whether Jews like it or not, they are a peculiar people. They can't ever hope to be judged by the same standards which are used for other people." There is a name for non-Jews who hold Jews to a double standard: It is called anti-Semitism.

Tutu has acknowledged having been frequently accused of being anti-Semitic, to which he has offered two responses: "Tough luck;" and "my dentist's name is Dr. Cohen."

I am confident that President Obama was not aware of Tutu's sordid history of anti-Jewish rhetoric and actions when he awarded him the Medal of Freedom in the White House in 2009. The sad reality is that Bishop Tutu's beneficent look is the new face of the oldest of bigotries.

The decent people of South Africa have become aware of Tutu's bigotry, because they have seen and heard it up close. It is time for the rest of the world to recognize that the Bishop is no saint. When it comes to Jews, he is an unrepentant sinner.

Though he is now retired, he still has the opportunity to repent and to end the sordid history of applying an unacceptable double standard to the Jewish state, the Jewish people, and the Jewish religion.

February 2, 2011
How the Hard Left, By Focusing Only on Israel, Encouraged Arab Despotism

Now the hard left is finally talking about torture and other undemocratic abuses in Egypt and Jordan, as well as the despotism of virtually all Arab regimes. Do you recall any campus protests against Egypt or Mubarak? Do you recall any calls for divestment and boycotts against Arab dictators? No, because there weren't any. The hard left was too busy condemning the Middle East's only democracy, Israel. Radical leftists and campus demonstrators, by giving a pass to the worst forms of tyranny, encouraged their perpetuation. Now, finally, they are jumping on the bandwagon of condemnation, though still not with the fury that they reserve for the one nation in the Middle East that has complete free speech, gender equality, gay rights, an open and critical press, an independent judiciary and fair and open elections.

The double standard is alive and well on the hard left, and its victims include the citizens of Arab regimes who suffer under the heel of authoritarian dictators. Even more important, they include victims of genocides, such as those perpetrated in Rwanda, Darfur, and Cambodia—victims who did not prick the consciences of the hard left because the perpetrators were Arabs or Communists, rather than Americans or Israelis.

The same must be said for the United Nations, which rewarded Arab despots by according them places of honor on human rights bodies that devoted all of their energies to demonizing Israel. In a recent op-ed, Amnon Rubenstein, the conscience of Israel, has pointed out that the UN Human Rights Commission, to which both Egypt and Tunisia were elected, has gone out of its way to compliment both regimes. Egypt was praised for steps it has "taken in recent years as regard to human rights...." Tunisia was lauded for constructing "a legal and constitutional framework for the promotion and protection of human rights." Israel, on the other hand, was repeatedly condemned for violating the human rights not only of Palestinians, but of its own citizens as well.

Nor do I recall Bishop Tutu urging the Cape Town Opera to boycott Egypt, Tunisia, or Jordan as he urged them to boycott Israel. I do recall Jimmy Carter, who has falsely accused Israel of Apartheid, embracing some of the Arab's worlds worst tyrants and murderers. Many who claim the mantle of human rights ignore or even embrace the worst human rights violators and direct their wrath only against the Jewish nation.

The anti-American and anti-Israel hard left is a topsy-turvy world where the worst are declared the best and the best are condemned as the worst. This topsy-turvy view has become a staple of higher education, particularly among Middle East study programs in many colleges and universities. Among many on the hard left, where the only human rights issue of concern seems to be Israel's treatment of the Palestinians, the views of convicted terrorists Marwan Barghouti are preached as gospel. This is what Barghouti, who is serving a life sentence for planning terror attacks against civilians, but who remains among the most popular Palestinian leaders, recently said about Israel: "The worst and most abominable enemy known to humanity and modern history." It is this skewed view of modern history that runs rampant through the hard left and that gives exculpatory immunity to Arab and Muslim tyrants.

There is only one acceptable standard of international human rights: the worst must come first. Under that universal standard, any person or organization claiming the mantle of human rights must prioritize its resources. It must list human rights violators in order of the severity of the abuses and the ability of its citizens to complain about those abuses. It must then go after the worst offenders first and foremost, leaving right-left politics out of the mix. This standard must be applied by individuals, such as Bishop Tutu, by organizations, such as the United Nations, by the media, and by everyone who loves human rights. Until that standard is universally applied, despotism will continue, interrupted only occasionally by revolutions such as those taking place in Tunisia and Egypt.

The irony, of course, is that in the most repressive regimes, such as Iran, revolution is well-nigh impossible. Revolution is far more likely to occur is moderately despotic regimes, such as Tunisia and Egypt, where at least some basic liberties were preserved. It is the citizens of the most despotic regimes that need the most help from human rights activists. But don't count on it because too many so-called "human rights" leaders and organizations misuse the concept of "human rights" to serve narrow political, diplomatic or ideological agendas. Unless we restore human rights to its proper role as a neutral and universal standard of human conduct, the kind of tyranny and despotism that stimulated the current protests will continue.

March 31, 2011
Norway's "Boycott" of Pro-Israel Speakers

I recently completed a "speaking tour" of Norwegian universities on the topic of "international law as applied to the Israeli-Palestinian conflict." The sponsors of the tour—a Norwegian pro-Israel group—offered to have me lecture without any charge to the three major universities in Bergen, Oslo, and Trondheim. Norwegian universities, especially those outside of Oslo, tend to feel somewhat isolated from the more mainstream academic world, and they generally jump at any opportunity to invite lecturers from leading universities. Thus, when Professor Stephen Walt, co-author of *The Israel Lobby*—a much maligned critique of American support for Israel—came to Norway, he was immediately invited to present a lecture. Likewise, Ilan Pappe—a strident demonizer of Israel—from Oxford. Many professors from less well-known universities have also been invited to present their anti-Israel perspectives.

My hosts expected, therefore, that their offer to have me present a somewhat different academic perspective on the Israeli-Palestinian conflict would be eagerly accepted, since I have written half a dozen books on the subject presenting a centrist view in support of the two-state solution and against civilian settlements on the West Bank. Indeed, one of my books is titled *The Case For Peace*, and former President Bill Clinton praised my blueprint for peace as "among the best in recent years." But each of the three universities categorically refused to invite me to give a lecture on that subject. The dean of the law faculty at Bergen University said he would be "honored" to have me present a lecture "on the O.J. Simpson case," as long as I was willing to promise not to mention Israel. The head of the Trondheim school was more direct:

"Israel and international law is a controversial and inflamed theme, which cannot be regarded as isolated and purely professional. Too much politics is invited in this."

But is it less "controversial" and "inflamed" when rabidly anti-Israel professors are invited to express their "politics?"

Apparently, a pro-Israel perspective is more controversial, inflamed, and political than an anti-Israel perspective—at least at

Trondheim. The University of Oslo simply said no without offering an excuse, leading one journalist to wonder whether the Norwegian universities believed that I am "not entirely housetrained."

Only once before had I been prevented from lecturing at universities in a country. The other country was Apartheid South Africa where the government insisted on "approving" the text of my proposed talks on human rights. I declined.

But despite the refusal of the faculties of Norway's three major universities to invite me to deliver lectures on Israel and international law, I delivered three lectures to packed auditoriums at each university. It turns out that the students wanted to hear me, despite their professors' efforts to keep my views from them. Student groups invited me. I came. And I received sustained applause both before and after my talks. Faculty members boycotted my talks and declined even to meet with me. I was recently told that free copies of the Norwegian translation of my book, *The Case For Israel*, were offered to several university libraries in Norway and that they declined to accept them.

It was then that I realized why all this was happening. At all of the Norwegian universities, there have been efforts to enact an academic and cultural boycott of Jewish Israeli academics. This boycott is directed against Israel's "occupation" of Palestinian land, but the occupation that the hundreds of signers referred to is not of the West Bank but rather of every single inch of Israel. Here is the first line of the petition: "Since 1948 the state of Israel has occupied Palestinian land..." Not surprisingly, the administrations of the universities have refused to go along with this form of academic collective punishment of all Jewish Israeli academics. So the formal demand for an academic and cultural boycott has failed. But in practice, it exists. Jewish pro-Israel speakers are subjected to a de facto boycott. Moreover, all Jews are presumed to be pro-Israel unless they have a long track record of anti-Israel rhetoric.

Read the words of the first signer of the academic boycott petition—an assistant professor of Trondheim named Trond Andresen as he writes about the "Jews"—not the Israelis!

"There is something immensely self-satisfied and self-centered at the tribal mentality that is so prevalent among Jews. [Not]

> *only the religious but also a large proportion of the large secular group consider their own ethnic group as worth more than all other ethnic groups. [Jews] as a whole, are characterized by this mentality...it is no less legitimate to say such a thing about Jews in 2008-2009 than it was to make the same point about the Germans around 1938. [There is] a red carpet for the Jewish community...and a new round of squeezing and distorting the influence of the quite dry Holocaust lemon...."*

This line of talk—directed at Jews, not Israel or Israelis—is apparently acceptable among many in the elite of Norway. Consider former Prime Minister Kare Willock's reaction to President Obama's selection of Rahm Emanuel as his first Chief of Staff:

> *"It does not look too promising, he has chosen a chief of staff who is Jewish, and it is a matter of fact that many Americans look to the Bible rather than to the realities of today...."*

Willock, of course, did not know anything about Emanuel's views. He based his criticism on the sole fact that Emanuel is a Jew.

All Jews are apparently the same in this country that has done everything in its power to make life in Norway nearly impossible for Jews. Norway was apparently the first modern nation to prohibit the production of Kosher meat, while at the same time permitting Halal meat and encouraging the slaughter of seals, whales, and other animals that are protected by international treaties. No wonder fewer than 1,000 Jews live in Norway. No wonder the leader of the tiny and frightened Jewish community didn't get around to meeting me during my visit to his country. (The Chabad Rabbi did reach out to me and I had a wonderful visit with a group of Norwegian Jews at the Chabad house.) It reminded me of my visits to the Soviet Union in the bad old days.

The current foreign minister of Norway recently wrote an article in the New York Review of Books, justifying his contacts with Hamas, a terrorist group that demands the destruction of Israel. He said that the essential philosophy of Norway has always been to encourage "dialogue." But I'm afraid that that dialogue in Norway these days is entirely one-sided. Hamas and its supporters are invited into the dialogue, but supporters of Israel are excluded by an implicit, yet very real, boycott against pro-Israel views.

[Addendum: In 2013, Norway elected Erna Solberg as Prime Minister. While Prime Minister Solberg initially said she opposed boycotts of Israel, the boycott campaign remains strong and Norway is largely a bastion of anti-Semitism. And earlier this year, the city council of Trondheim, Norway's third-largest city, called on its residents to boycott all "Israeli goods." The national government has become more supportive of Israel since the election.]

April 5, 2011
South African Charge of Israeli Apartheid Rings Hollow

A recent speaking tour about Israel brought me to South Africa, following a visit to Norway. Both countries are hostile environments when it comes to the Jewish state. In Norway, the three faculties of the Norwegian universities refused to host me, but student groups broke the boycott against pro-Israel speakers by inviting me to speak. In South Africa, the boycott held and I was precluded from speaking at any university.

The South African boycott against me, as an advocate for Israel, was spearheaded by a sitting judge named Dennis Davis, who aspires to serve on South Africa's highest court and who authored an op-ed in the *Cape Times* headlined "Dershowitz is not welcome here!" It was co-signed by a dozen other mainstream lawyers and academics strongly opposed to Israel.

I was originally invited to speak to the faculty and students at the University of Cape Town but Judge Davis pressured the school to make it impossible for me to appear. The University's excuse was insufficient interest in my talk to warrant the heavy security my presence would have required. So instead I spoke off campus. More than 1,000 people, including hundreds of students, showed up for my talk. Another 1,000 people attended a second talk.

The justification offered by Davis for trying to censor me is that I have been critical of Bishop Desmond Tutu for calling Israel an apartheid state and for accusing the Jewish people of being "arrogant," "peculiar," "claiming a monopoly" on God, and on the Holocaust. He also accused me of being opposed to peace and of supporting Israel's occupation of the West Bank, despite my long-term support for the two-state solution and the end of the occupation. And he totally mischaracterized my views on torture, collective punishment, and academic freedom. (For a full rebuttal to Davis's pack of lies see my response in the *Cape Times* Edition 3.28.11 and 3.31.11)

I am critical of Bishop Tutu's call for boycotts against apartheid Israel, because it is a totally false charge. Israel is the only nation in the Middle East that does not practice any form of apartheid: Jordan prohibits Jews from becoming citizens or owning land; Saudi Arabia practices gender apartheid; all Muslim countries engage in sexual orientation apartheid; Hamas is notorious for its anti-Christian apartheid; and the Palestinian Authority has said that "no Jew" will ever be allowed to live in a Palestinian state. Israel, on the other hand, is a racially diverse country in which Arabs serve in the Knesset, on the Supreme Court, on university faculties, and even in the Cabinet. The court that recently convicted Israel's former president of rape included an Arab judge. Nothing like this ever happened in apartheid South Africa.

Indeed, Tutu's South Africa remains a far more segregated country today than Israel. Poor blacks live in segregated temporary settlements, and de facto apartheid can be seen throughout South Africa.

Moreover, the South African government, the African National Congress, and Bishop Tutu himself have far worse human rights records than does Israel. They have supported some of the most despotic regimes in the world, simply because the despots who head these regimes in Libya, Iran, Cuba, China, Zimbabwe, and the Palestinian governments in the West Bank and Gaza—sided with their legitimate struggle against apartheid in years past.

Yet in a hypercritical display of double-standard immorality, they will never forgive Israel for its support of Dr. Klerk's South Africa, despite the reality that most Arab and Muslim nations traded extensively with the apartheid regime. They demand a moral pass for serving as enablers of repression on the ground that these tyrants supported them, but they refuse to give Israel a pass for having supported a tyrannical regime that helped them during trying times.

Bishop Tutu's call for a boycott against the Jewish state is hypocrisy at its worst. First, a boycott is the personification of collective punishment directed against all Israelis, regardless of their individual views or actions. Second, it singles out only Israel for a boycott while encouraging "reconciliation" (and trade) with some of the world's worst human rights offenders. Third, it hurts the poorest people, mostly blacks in South Africa. Consider the recent boycott of Ben Gurion University by the University of Johannesburg, a boycott encouraged by Tutu. Ben Gurion has helped Johannesburg with research on water purification, which affects many poor South Africans. This joint research project, which helps South Africa far more than Israel, has now been ended because of the Tutu-inspired boycott.

Now Tutu has called for a worldwide cultural, academic, and economic boycott against the Jewish state, a boycott reminiscent of the Nazi boycott of Jewish goods in the 1930s. The difference, of course, is that today a total boycott of Israeli products would include cell phones, Intel processors, numerous medical technologies and pharmaceuticals, and important environmental and agricultural innovations.

I'm proud of standing up against Bishop Tutu's singular bigotry against the Jewish nations and the Jewish people. I will continue to do so until and unless he stops applying a double-standard to all things Jewish.

Yet I defend Tutu's right and those of his sycophants such as Judge Davis to express their anti-Israel views. I would never try to censor them, as they have tried to censor me and others who express views supportive of Israel. The difference is, I am not afraid of the truth, of debate, or of the marketplace of ideas. Those, like Judge Davis, who tried to ban me from speaking on university campuses are clearly afraid to have all sides of the Arab-Israeli dispute aired. They have resorted to the age-old tactic employed by those who do not trust the public to make up their own minds: censorship of opposing views. That seems to be the approach taken by South African universities when it comes to Israel.

South Africa thus joins Norway as among the nations of the world most intolerant of pro-Israel—even moderately pro-Israel—views. In at least one respect, South Africa is even worse: one major university has imposed a formal academic boycott against an Israeli university, thanks to Bishop Tutu, and another university has succeeded in preventing its students from hearing a pro-Israel speaker on their campus, thanks to Judge Davis. But in another respect, South Africa is far better: its vibrant Jewish community is willing to fight back against those who would censor pro-Israel views.

April 11, 2011
An American Academic Supports the Targeting of Innocent Israeli Civilians

The terrorists in the West Bank who murdered the Fogel family and the war criminals from Gaza who aimed sophisticated mortars at a school bus had the support of an American academic who is widely admired by Palestinians, Europeans, and radical Americans. Norman Finkelstein didn't wield the knife that slit the throat of the Fogel baby or fire the mortar that seriously injured a 16-year-old and barely missed killing 30 other students, but he might as well have. Just days after the Fogel murders, and days before the attempted school bus massacre, Finkelstein advised his Palestinian admirers that terrorist groups like Hezbollah, and presumably Hamas and Islamic Jihad "has the right to target Israeli civilians…"

This is a remarkable statement even for Finkelstein, who has compared Israel to Nazi Germany.

Targeting civilians is a universal war crime, and inciting others to kill innocent civilians is at least deeply immoral, if not arguably illegal. Finkelstein is particularly close to the Hezbollah leadership having met with Hezbollah figures in Lebanon and declaring that "we are all Hezbollah." When he tells Iran's major surrogate that they have the right to target Israeli civilians, they become emboldened, if not incited. Israeli intelligence has just concluded that Hezbollah is preparing to fire 10,000 rockets at Tel Aviv.[51] And now they have Finkelstein's blessing. And what is "right" for

Hezbollah certainly can't be wrong for Hamas and other terrorist groups that seek to kill as many Israeli civilians as possible.

Finkelstein will claim, as he always does, that he was quoted out of context and that he qualified his opinion. Here is the precise answer he gave to the question:

Do you unequivocally condemn Palestinian attacks against innocent civilians?

> *"It is impossible to justify terrorism, which is the targeting of civilians to achieve a political goal. But it's also difficult to make categorical statements of the kind you suggest. I do believe that Hezbollah has the right to target Israeli civilians if Israel persists in targeting civilians until Israel ceases its terrorist acts."*

Finkelstein is an expert at double-speak: to his American and European audiences, he emphasizes the qualifying language, but to his terrorist audiences, all that matters is his imprimatur on their right to target Israeli civilians.

Let's consider his qualifying language that terrorist groups have the right to target Israeli civilians "if Israel persists in targeting civilians until Israel ceases its terrorist acts." Putting aside the question of whether Israel targets civilians, as distinguished from targeting terrorists who hide among civilians, thereby creating the possibility that civilians will be inadvertently killed—it is still unlawful to retaliate against the deliberate killing of civilians by deliberately killing other civilians. If that were not the law, then Israel would have the perfect right to target Palestinian or Lebanese civilians for what nobody denies is the Hezbollah and Hamas policy of targeting Israeli civilians. Israel has no such policy, nor do they claim such a right—as Hezbollah, Hamas, and Finkelstein do.

Consider the implications of the "right" asserted by Finkelstein. Any time one nation or group targets another's civilians (or is falsely accused of doing so, as is the case with Israel), the other nation or group would have "the right" to retaliate indiscriminately against civilians. Such an approach to the "right" of retaliation would make civilians the legitimate, indeed the primary, target of warfare. This is precisely the opposite of the entire trend of international humanitarian law since the end of World War II, which has been to prohibit the specific targeting of civilians, while recognizing the inevitability of civilian casualties in all wars, and especially in wars fought by terrorists who fight from behind civilian shields, as does Hamas and Hezbollah.

But have no fear, Finkelstein would reject the targeting of civilians as a general matter. He did not say that all nations or groups have the right to target any civilians. He said that his favorite terrorist group, Hezbollah, has the right to target the civilians of his least favorite country, Israel. And he means to make this distinction, since he consistently applies a double standard to the Jewish state.

Consider his attack on me for having advocated the destruction of homes used by terrorists in retaliation for those terrorists murdering innocent Israeli civilians. He compared my proposal to the Nazi bombing of Lidice in which hundreds of civilians were killed, despite the fact that my proposal involved the destruction of property only in retaliation for the taking of life. Moreover, the people whose houses would be destroyed were far from innocent. He characterized my proposal as "collective punishment" of innocent Palestinians and called me a "war criminal" for even suggesting it. But now he is legitimating the murder of Israeli civilians in retaliation for the inadvertent killing of civilians by the Israeli military in its efforts to prevent terrorism and rocket attacks against its civilians.

Finkelstein's latest outrage should make him a pariah among all decent people. Yet he remains a popular speaker on American and European campuses, as well as a valued advisor to Hezbollah and a close associate of Noam Chomsky. The time has come to reject Finkelstein's pernicious views in the marketplace of ideas, and to reiterate the crucial distinction between the deliberate targeting of innocent civilians, regardless of their religion or nationality, and legitimate military actions that inadvertently kill civilians. It is this distinction on which the law and morality of just war has rested since St. Augustine.

May 13, 2011
Civil Libertarians and Academics
Who Support Censors

Should students who conspire to "shut down" an invited speaker with whom they disagree be prosecuted for the misdemeanor of conspiracy to disturb a meeting? That is the question roiling the University of California. The facts are not really in dispute. Israel's Ambassador to the United States—a moderate academic named Michael Oren—was invited to present a talk at the University of California at Irvine, a hotbed of radical Islamic hate speech against Israel. The Muslim Student Union organized an effort, in the words of one of its leaders, to "shut down" Oren's speech—that is to prevent Oren from expressing his views and to stop the audience who came to hear him from listening to them. Here is the way the dean of the law school, who opposes any criminal prosecution, described what happened.

> *"The Muslim Student Union orchestrated a concerted effort to disrupt the speech. One student after another stood and shouted so that the ambassador could not be heard. Each student was taken away only to be replaced by another doing the same thing."*

The dean's description is something of an understatement—as anyone can see by watching a video of the event, available online. This was more than a "concerted effort to disrupt the speech. It was a concerted effort to stop it completely—to "shut [it] down."

Ultimately, that effort failed and Oren managed to deliver his speech, after many long and sustained disruptions, but if the Muslim Student Union had gotten its way, Oren would have been shut down completely. The university, which is a state institution, had a constitutional obligation to protect the First Amendment rights of Oren's audience to hear what he had to say, and the state prosecutor has a legal obligation to deter future conspiracies to censor controversial speakers, by criminally prosecuting those students who conspired to deny other students their First Amendment rights.

While dissenting students have the right to express disapproval of a speaker's views by <u>episodic</u> booing, heckling, or holding signs, they have no right to conspire to shut down a speaker, which is what the Muslim Student Union students did in this case. One would think that this distinction should be clear to all civil libertarians, academics, and others who claim to care about freedom of speech on campus.

It is shocking, therefore, to see who has lined up behind the students who set out to censor Ambassador Oren. Two prominent leaders of the American Civil Liberties have joined with radical Muslims and other extremists in an effort to pressure the local District Attorney to drop misdemeanor charges against 11 student censors.

A letter supporting the censoring students was signed by Chuck Anderson, President of the Orange County ACLU, and Hector Villagra, the incoming Executive Director of the ACLU of Southern California, along with several other radical anti-Israel extremists such as the local heads of the Council on American-Islamic relations, the Muslim Public Affairs Council, the National Lawyers Guild, the Islamic Shura Council, and the West Coast Islamic Society.

The ACLU leaders have denied they support censorship and claim that the letter they signed is merely a request to the local district attorney to drop criminal charges against the students who tried to shut Oren down. But the letter goes much further and defends—indeed praises—the censorial actions those students, while condemning the actions of other students who wanted to hear the speaker.

Here is how the letter described the actions of the students who came to shut down the speaker:

"the students non-violently and verbally protested a university-invited speaker. The students left the event peacefully."

The letter then compared the actions of the censors with those who wanted to listen:

"[They] conducted themselves in less of a disruptive manner than some of the counter-protesters...."

Sounds as if the Muslim Student Union deserved a civil liberties award, while the students who came to listen to the invited speaker—"the counter-protestors"—deserve to be condemned. In a more recent letter the ACLU leaders claim that "the students' intent was not to censor the speaker...."

The problem with the ACLU account is that it is completely fictional—made up out of whole cloth—as anyone can see for themselves by viewing the video and listening to the Muslim Students Association leaders who described their aim to "shut down"—that is to <u>censor</u>—the speakers. That is why these students are being prosecuted, according to the district attorney—not for merely "protesting" the speaker's views, but because they "meant to stop [Ambassador Oren's] speech and stop anyone else from hearing his ideas." The students themselves have been more honest about their intentions than the ACLU leaders. For instance, one student leader refused to acknowledge that Mr. Oren had First Amendment rights of his own by interrupting him and shouting, "Propagating murder is not an expression of free speech!" Another student was caught on video telling a crowd assembled outside the event that "we pretty much shut them down."

Ultimately a jury will decide whether the students conspired to "shut down" Oren's talk, or whether they were merely "protesting" the content of his talk. The evidence will clearly show a conspiracy to stop Oren from speaking.[52]

Why then have the ACLU leaders distorted the facts and conveyed a totally misleading impression of what took place at the University of California? The answer seems clear. These leaders don't like Israel and they support the censorship of pro-Israel views. They would never take the same position if the shoe had been on the other foot: If the speaker were from Hamas and the students trying to shut him down were pro-Israel.

The national ACLU must investigate this matter and take action to assure that its longstanding principle of <u>neutral</u> support for freedom of expression has not been compromised by local leaders who have placed their opposition to Israel above the principles of free speech.

Another group that has sought to pressure the District Attorney to give the censors a pass is comprised of 30 Jewish Studies faculty members at the University of California. That may be surprising to some who believe that such professors would be sympathetic to students who wanted to listen to the Israeli Ambassador and history professor.

But it is not surprising to those who understand that many Jewish Studies have departments been hijacked by anti-Israeli extremists. Among the signers of this letter were academics who favor boycotts, divestment, and demonization of Israel as an Apartheid or Nazi regime.

As a lifelong civil libertarian and defender of free speech, I hope the district attorney will not succumb to these political pressures. The values of the First Amendment favor prosecution in this case, just as they would if Jewish students conspired to shut down an Anti-Israel speaker. The defense of freedom of speech must be neutral and vigorous.

[Update: Ten of the 11 students were convicted in 2011 of "shutting down" the Israeli Ambassador's speech, while an eleventh student took a plea deal. The defense appealed the decision but it was upheld. The court said: "in this case, that right of free speech extended not only to Ambassador Oren, but to the several hundred persons who had assembled to hear this presentation."]

June 14, 2011
Yale's Distressing Decision To Shut Down Its "Initiative for the Interdisciplinary Study of Anti-Semitism"

At a time of increasing—and increasingly complex—anti-Semitism throughout the world, Yale University has decided to shut down the Yale Initiative for the Interdisciplinary Study of Anti-Semitism, YIISA. Founded in 2006, YIISA is headed by a distinguished scholar, Charles Small, with an international reputation for serious interdisciplinary research. The precipitous decision to close YIISA, made without even a semblance of due process and transparency, could not have come at a worse time. Nor could it have sent a worse message.

I recently returned from a trip abroad—England, Norway, and South Africa, among other countries—where I experienced the changing face and growing acceptability of anti-Semitism. Sometimes it hid behind the facade of anti-Zionism, but increasingly the hatred was directed against Jews, Judaism, Jewish culture, the Jewish people, and the very concept of a Jewish state (by people who favor the existence of many Muslim states).

In England, a prominent and popular jazz musician rails against the Jewish people, denies the Holocaust, and apologizes to the Nazis for having once compared the Jewish state to Nazi Germany, since in his view Israel is far worse. In Norway, a prominent professor openly criticizes the Jewish people as a group and Jewish culture as a collective deviation. In Johannesburg, the university severs its ties with an Israeli university, while in Cape Town a newspaper headline welcomes me with the following words, "Dershowitz is not welcome here" and an excuse is found to cancel a scheduled lecture by me at the university.

Throughout my visits to European capitals, I hear concern from Jewish students who are terrified about speaking out, wearing yarmulkes, Stars of David, or anything else that identifies them as Jews.

In the United States, and particularly at American universities, matters are not nearly as bad. There are, of course, some exceptions, such as at several campuses at the University of California where Muslim students have tried to censor pro-Israel speakers and have been treated as heroes for doing so, while those who support pro-Israel speakers are treated as pariahs. The same is true at some Canadian universities as well.

One university that has been a model of tolerance, up until now, has been Yale, where Jewish and pro-Israel students feel empowered and comfortable, as do Muslim and anti-Israel students. Perhaps this is why the Yale administration had no hesitancy in dropping YIISA. It can easily defend itself against charges of bias by saying, "Some of my best organizations are Jewish!" But this is no excuse.

Since Yale has thus far refused to release the so-called study on which it claims to have based its decision—or even to show it to those most directly affected—it is impossible to know the real reasons behind this controversial action. The two offered by Yale do not satisfy academic criteria. The first, that there was insufficient faculty interest in the initiative, is simply not true. Many faculty members, both inside and outside of Yale, have supported the initiative and have participated in its programs. I myself have delivered a lecture and serve on an advisory board. Several distinguished academics from around the world have also participated. But even if it were true, a lack of interest by the Yale faculty in the growing problem of anti-Semitism would be a symptom of the problem and not an excuse for refusing to study it.

The second claimed reason was a lack of scholarly output from this relatively new institution. This too is doubtful since numerous articles, books, conferences, and other scholarly output have been generated over the past several years—with the promise of more to come.

I have been in and around American academic institutions for more than half a century. Never before have I seen such a lack of process and fairness in the termination of a program. Generally, if there is any dissatisfaction with the program, university administrators sit down with those in charge and seek ways of improving it. Rarely if ever is the program simply shut down, as this one has been. Yale has some explaining to do. Even better, it should reconsider its decision, solicit input from outsiders who have participated in the program and figure out a constructive way of keeping the important work of the initiative going.

One of the most important human rights issues of the 21st century is whether Israel's actions in defense of its citizens, or indeed its very existence, will provide the newest excuse for the oldest of bigotries. There has rarely been a more important time for the interdisciplinary study of the spreading phenomenon of anti-Semitism in the world today. Yale has a chance to be at the forefront of this study. Instead it has taken a cowardly step away from the controversy. It's not too late to undo its mistake.

[Addendum: On June 19, 2011, following widespread outcry, the Yale Program for the Study of Anti-Semitism (YPSA) was established to replace YIISA.]

September 21, 2011
The United Nations Should Not Recognize an Apartheid, Judenrein, Islamic Palestine

The United Nations is being asked to grant the Palestinians the status of a "state," for at least some purposes. The question arises what kind of a state will it be? In an effort to attract Western support, the Palestinian Authority claims that it will become another "secular democratic state." Hamas, which won the last parliamentary election, disagrees. It wants Palestine to be a Muslim state governed by Sharia law.

We know what the Palestinian leadership is saying to the West. Now let's look at what its saying to its own people, who will, after all, be the ultimate decision makers if Palestine is indeed a democracy.

The draft constitution for the new state of Palestine declares that, "Islam is the official religion in Palestine." It also states that Sharia law will be "the major source of legislation." It is ironic that the same Palestinian leadership which supports these concepts for Palestine refuses to acknowledge that Israel is the nation state of the Jewish people. Israel, in contrast to the proposed Palestinian state, does not have an official state religion. Although it is a Jewish state, that description is not a religious one but rather a national one. It accords equal rights to Islam, Christianity, and all other religions, as well as to atheists and agnostics. Indeed, a very high proportion of Israelis describe themselves as secular.

The new Palestinian state would prohibit any Jews from being citizens, from owning land, or from even living in the Muslim state of Palestine. The ambassador of the PLO to the United States was asked during an interview whether "any Jew who is inside the borders of Palestine will have to leave?" His answer: "Absolutely!" After much criticism, the ambassador tried to spin his statement, saying that it applied only to Jews "who are amid the occupation." Whatever that means, one thing is clear: large numbers of Jews will not be welcome to remain in Islamic Palestine as equal citizens. In contrast, Israel has more than 1 million Arab citizens, most of whom are Muslims. They are equal under the law, except that they need not serve in the Israeli army.

The new Palestine will have the very "law of return" that it demands that Israel should give up. All Palestinians, no matter where they live and regardless of whether they have ever set foot in Palestine, will be welcome to the new state, while a Jew whose family has lived in Hebron for thousands of years will be excluded.

To summarize, the new Palestinian state will be a genuine apartheid state. It will practice religious and ethnic discrimination, it will have one official religion and it will base its laws on the precepts of one religion. Imagine what the status of gays will be under Sharia law!

Palestinian leadership accuses Israel of having roads that are limited only to Jews. This is entirely false: a small number of roads on the West Bank are restricted to Israelis, but they are equally open to Israeli Jews, Muslims, and Christians alike. The entire state of Palestine will have a "no Jews allowed" sign on it.

It is noteworthy that the very people who complain most loudly about Israel's law of return and about its character as the nation state of the Jewish people, are silent when it comes to the new Palestinian state. Is it that these people expect more of Jews than they do of Muslims? If so, is that not a form of racism?

What would the borders of a Palestinian state look like if the Palestinians got their way without the need to negotiate with Israel? The Palestinians would get, as a starting point, all of the land previously occupied by Jordan prior to the 1967 War, in which Jordan attacked Israel. This return to the status quo that led to the Six Day War is inconsistent with the intention of Security Council Resolution 242, which contemplated some territorial changes.

The new boundaries of this Palestinian state would include Judaism's holiest place, the Western Wall. It would also include the access roads to Hebrew University, which Jordan used to close down this great institution of learning founded by the Jews nearly 100 years ago. The new Palestinian state would also incorporate the Jewish Quarter of Jerusalem, in which Jews have lived for 3,000 years, except for those periods of time during which they were expelled by force.

It is contemplated, of course, that Israel would regain these areas as part of a land swap with the Palestinians. But there is no certainty that the Palestinians would agree to a reasonable land swap. Palestinian leaders have already said that they would hold these important and sacred sites hostage to unreasonable demands. For example, the Western Wall covers only a few acres, but the Palestinian leadership has indicated that these acres are among the most valuable in the world, and in order for Israel to regain them, they would have to surrender thousands of acres. The same might be true of the access road to Hebrew University and the Jewish Quarter.

When Jordan controlled these areas, the Jordanian government made them Judenrein—Jews could not pray at the Western Wall, visit the Jewish Quarter, or have access to Hebrew University. There is no reason to believe that a Palestinian state would treat Jews any differently if they were to maintain control over these areas.

An apartheid, Islamic, Judenrein Palestine on the 1967 borders is a prescription for disaster. That is why a reasonable Palestinian state must be the outcome of negotiations with Israel, and not the result of a thoughtless vote by the United Nations.

The Palestinians and Israeli leaders are now in New York. Israeli Prime Minister Benjamin Netanyahu has offered to sit down and negotiate, with no preconditions, a realistic peace based on a two-state solution. President Abbas should accept that offer, which will actually get the Palestinians a viable state rather than a cheap paper victory that will raise expectations but lower the prospects for real peace.

[Addendum: On November 29, 2012, the UN General Assembly voted overwhelmingly to accord "Palestine" the status of "non-observer state." Essentially, as an "observer state," the Palestinians could join international treaties and specialized UN agencies. The Palestinian Authority has since acceded to numerous UN treaties/conventions. This is in spite of the fact that most treaties are open only to internationally recognized sovereign "states."]

November 4, 2011
Why Are John Mearsheimer and Richard Falk Endorsing a Blatantly Anti-Semitic Book?

As the discourse about Israel on university campuses continues to degenerate, there is growing concern that some of Israel's most vocal detractors are crossing a red line between acceptable criticisms of Israel and legitimizing anti-Semitism. The recent endorsements by several internationally prominent academics—including John Mearsheimer of the University of Chicago and Richard Falk of Princeton—of an overtly anti-Semitic book written by a notorious Jew-hater illustrate this dangerous trend.

The book in question is entitled *The Wandering Who?* and was written by Gilad Atzmon, a British jazz musician. Lest there be any doubt about Atzmon's anti-Semitic credentials, listen to his self-description in the book itself. He boasts about "drawing many of my insights from a man who...was an anti-Semite as well as a radical misogynist" and a hater of "almost everything that fails to be Aryan masculinity" (89-90). He declares himself a "proud, self-hating Jew" (54), writes with "contempt" of "the Jew in me" (94), and describes himself as "a strong opponent of ... Jewishness" (186). His writings, both online and in his new book, brim with classic anti-Semitic motifs that are borrowed from Nazi publications.

Throughout his writings, Atzmon argues that Jews seek to control the world:

- "[W]e must begin to take the accusation that the Jewish people are trying to control the world very seriously."
- "American Jewry makes any debate on whether the 'Protocols of the elder of Zion' [sic] are an authentic document or rather a forgery irrelevant. American Jews do try to control the world, by proxy."

Atzmon expands on this theme in *The Wandering Who?*, repeatedly conflating "the Jews" and "the Zionist.":

- He calls the recent credit crunch "the Zio-punch" (22) and says it was not "a Jewish conspiracy" because "it was all in the open" (30).
- Paul Wolfowitz, Rahm Emanuel, and other members of "the Jewish elite" remain abroad instead of moving to "Zion" because they "have proved far more effective for the Zionist cause by staying where they are" (19).
- The American media "failed to warn the American people of the enemy within" because of money (27).

Atzmon has written that Jews are evil and a menace to humanity:

- "With Fagin and Shylock in mind Israeli barbarism and organ trafficking seem to be just other events in an endless hellish continuum."
- "The Homo Zionicus quickly became a mass murderer, detached from any recognized form of ethical thinking and engaged in a colossal crime against humanity."

Atzmon rehearses many of these ideas in *The Wandering Who?*:

- "[T]o be a Jew is a deep commitment that goes far beyond any legal or moral order" (20) and this commitment "pulls more and more Jews into an obscure, dangerous and unethical fellowship" (21).
- If Iran and Israel fight a nuclear war that kills tens of millions of people, "some may be bold enough to argue that 'Hitler might have been right after all'" (179).

Atzmon regularly urges his readers to doubt the Holocaust and to reject Jewish history:

- "It took me years to accept that the Holocaust narrative, in its current form, doesn't make any historical sense...If, for instance, the Nazis wanted the Jews out of their Reich (Judenrein—free of Jews), or even dead, as the Zionist narrative insists, how come they marched

hundreds of thousands of them back into the Reich at the end of the war?"
- "[E]ven if we accept the Holocaust as the new Anglo-American liberal-democratic religion, we must allow people to be atheists."

Atzmon reprises some of this language in *The Wandering Who?*:

- Children should be allowed to question, as he did, "how the teacher could know that these accusations of Jews making Matza out of young Goyim's blood were indeed empty or groundless" (185).
- "The Holocaust religion is probably as old as the Jews themselves" (153).
- The history of Jewish persecution is a myth, and if there was any persecution the Jews brought it on themselves (175, 182).

Atzmon argues that Jews are corrupt and responsible for "why" they are "hated":

- "[I]n order to promote Zionist interests, Israel must generate significant anti-Jewish sentiment. Cruelty against Palestinian civilians is a favorite Israeli means of achieving this aim."
- "Jews may have managed to drop their God, but they have maintained goy-hating and racist ideologies at the heart of their newly emerging secular political identity. This explains why some Talmudic goy-hating elements have been transformed within the Zionist discourse into genocidal practices."

Atzmon returns to this theme repeatedly in *The Wandering Who?*:

- The "Judaic God" described in Deuteronomy 6:10-12 "is an evil deity, who leads his people to plunder, robbery and theft" (120). Atzmon explains that "Israel

and Zionism...have instituted the plunder promised by the Hebrew God in the Judaic holy scriptures" (121).
- The moral of the Book of Esther is that Jews "had better infiltrate the corridors of power" if they wish to survive (158).

Finally, Atzmon repeatedly declares that Israel is worse than the Nazis and has actually "apologized" to the Nazis for having earlier compared them to Israel:

- "Many of us including me tend to equate Israel to Nazi Germany. Rather often I myself join others and argue that Israelis are the Nazis of our time. I want to take this opportunity to amend my statement. Israelis are not the Nazis of our time and the Nazis were not the Israelis of their time. Israel, is in fact far worse than Nazi Germany and the above equation is simply meaningless and misleading."

In light of this Der Stürmer-like bigotry against Jews, it should come as no surprise that even some of the most hardcore anti-Israel activists have shunned Atzmon out of fear that his anti-Semitism will discredit their cause. Tony Greenstein, a self-styled "anti-Zionist" who recently participated in the Palestine Solidarity Campaign's unprecedented disruption of an Israel Philharmonic Orchestra concert in London (which Greenstein compared to protesting the Berlin Philharmonic Orchestra in the 1930s), denounced *The Wandering Who?* as "a poisonous anti-Semitic tome." Sue Blackwell, who co-wrote the Association of University Teachers' motion to boycott Israeli universities in 2005, removed all links to Atzmon from her website and placed Atzmon on her list of "nasties" along with David Irving and Israel Shamir. *Socialist Worker*, a website that frequently refers to Israeli "apartheid" and publishes articles with titles such as "Israel's murderous violence," removed an interview with Atzmon and called the evidence of Atzmon's anti-Semitism "damning." At least ten authors associated with the Leftist publisher that published *The Wandering Who?* have called on the publisher to distance itself from Atzmon's views, explaining that the "thrust of Atzmon's work is to normalise and legitimise anti-Semitism."

Hardcore neo-Nazis, racists, anti-Semites, and Holocaust deniers, on the other hand, have happily counted Atzmon as one of their own. David Duke, America's premier white supremacist, has posted more than a dozen of Atzmon's articles on his website over the past five years and recently praised Atzmon for "writ[ing] such fine articles exposing the evil of Zionism and Jewish supremacism." Kevin MacDonald, a professor at Cal State Long Beach whose colleagues formally disassociated themselves from his "anti-Semitic and white ethnocentric views," called Atzmon's book "an invaluable account by someone who clearly understands the main symptoms of Jewish pathology." Israel Shamir, a Holocaust denier (who has said: "We must deny the concept of Holocaust without doubt and hesitation") argues that Jews ritually murdered Christian children for their blood and that "The rule of the Elders of Zion is already upon us," refers to Atzmon as a "good friend" and calls Atzmon one of "the shining stars of the battle" against "the Jewish alliance."

But neither Atzmon's well-established reputation for anti-Semitism nor the copious anti-Semitic filth that fills *The Wandering Who?* has deterred Professors John Mearsheimer and Richard Falk from actively endorsing Atzmon's work. Mearsheimer, the Harrison Distinguished Service Professor of Political Science at the University of Chicago and a member of the American Academy of Arts and Sciences, calls *The Wandering Who?* a "fascinating" book that "should be read widely by Jews and non-Jews alike." Falk, Milibank Professor of International Law Emeritus at Princeton University and United Nations Special Rapporteur on "human rights in the Palestinian territories," calls *The Wandering Who?* an "absorbing and moving" book that everyone who "care[s] about real peace" should "not only read, but reflect upon and discuss widely." Falk's endorsement appears prominently on the cover of Atzmon's book. Mearsheimer's endorsement is featured on its first page. These professors are not merely defending Atzmon's right to publish such a book; they are endorsing its content and urging their colleagues, students, and others to read and "reflect upon" the views expressed by Atzmon. One wonders which portions of this bigoted screed Professors Mearsheimer and Falk believe their students and others "should" read and "discuss widely."

Mearsheimer has defended his endorsement (on Stephen Walt's blog) by questioning whether his critics have even read Atzmon's book. Well, I've read every word of it, as well as many of Atzmon's blogs. No one who has read this material could escape the conclusion—which Atzmon freely admits—that many of his "insights" are borrowed directly from classic anti-Semitic writings. Mearsheimer claims, however, that he has endorsed only Atzmon's book and not his other writings. But the book itself is filled with crass neo-Nazi rants against the "Jew," "World Jewry," and "Jewish bankers." He claims that "robbery and hatred is imbued in Jewish modern political ideology on both the left and the right" (123). And like other anti-Semites, Atzmon is obsessed in the book with Jewish names. It was Jews, such as Wolfowitz and Libby, who pushed the United States into war against Iraq in the "interests" of "their beloved Jewish state" (26). "How is it that America failed to restrain its Wolfowitzes?" Atzmon asks (27).

Likewise, according to Atzmon's book, it was "Jewish bankers," financiers, economists, writers, and politicians such as Greenspan, Levy, Aaronovitch, Saban, Friedman, Schiff, and Rothschild who have caused the economic and political problems of the world, ranging from the Bolshevik revolution to the wars of the 20th century to the current economic troubles (27,194). And like other classic anti-Semites, Atzmon doesn't simply fault the individual Jews he names; he concocts a worldwide Jewish conspiracy motivated by a "ruthless Zio-driven" (27) "Jewish ideology" (69) that finds its source in "the lethal spirit" (122) of the Hebrew Bible. This sort of conspiratorial drivel is borrowed almost word for word from the Protocols of the Elders of Zion—the Czarist forgery that became a staple of Nazi propaganda.

A number of other prominent academics have defended Atzmon and his endorsers. Brian Leiter, the Llewellyn Professor of Jurisprudence at the University of Chicago Law School, dismissed the reaction to the book and to Mearsheimer's "straightforward" endorsement as "hysterical" and not "advanc[ing] honest intellectual discourse," though he acknowledges not having read Atzmon's book. On the basis of having perused one brief interview with Atzmon,

Leiter is nonetheless prepared to defend him against charges that he is an anti-Semite or a Holocaust denier: "His positions [do not mark him] as an anti-Semite [but rather as] cosmopolitan. ... He does not deny the Holocaust or the gas chambers..." Leiter should read the book, especially pages 175-176, before leaping to Atzmon's defense. There Atzmon reflects "that 65 years after the liberation of Auschwitz, we must be entitled to start asking questions. We should ask for historical evidence and arguments rather than follow a religious narrative that is sustained by political pressure and laws."

James Petras, Bartle Professor of Sociology Emeritus at Binghamton University, called *The Wandering Who?* "a series of brilliant illuminations" and praised Atzmon's "courage." The list of academics who have endorsed Atzmon also includes William A. Cook, a professor of English at the University of La Verne in Southern California; Makram Khoury-Machool, a lecturer at the University of Cambridge; and Oren Ben-Dor of the University of Southampton School of Law.

These endorsements represent a dangerous step toward legitimizing anti-Semitic rhetoric on university campuses. If respected professors endorse the views contained in Atzmon's book as "brilliant," "fascinating," "absorbing," and "moving," these views—which include Jewish domination of the world, doubting the Holocaust, blaming "the Jews" for being so hated, and attributing the current economic troubles to a "Zio-punch"—risk becoming acceptable among their students. These endorsements of Atzmon's book are the best evidence yet that academic discourse is beginning to cross a red line, and that the crossing of this line must be exposed, rebutted, and rejected in the marketplace of ideas and in the academy. (Another evidence of this academic trend in Europe appeared recently on Atzmon's website, where he brags that he has been invited to "give a talk on ethics at the Trondheim University" in Norway. This is the same university whose faculty refused to invite me to speak about the Arab-Israel conflict.)

Accordingly, I hereby challenge Professors Mearsheimer and Falk to a public debate about why they have endorsed and said such positive things about so hateful and anti-Semitic a book by so bigoted and dishonest a writer. [Neither Mearsheimer nor Falk responded to my repeated offer to debate me on the merits of the argument.]

January 13, 2012
Friends Seminary Legitimates Anti-Semitism

If you want to understand why anti-Semitism seems to be increasing among young people—especially young people on the hard left—consider a recent invitation extended by a left-leaning school in New York to a self-proclaimed Jew hater.

The Friends Schools around the country are legendary. Presidents' children attend them, my own daughter and nephew were students, and they are regarded as among the most elite schools in the world. That is why it is so shocking that the Friends Seminary in New York has lent its imprimatur to a notorious anti-Semite and Holocaust denier.

Friends Seminary has a reputation for propagandizing its students against Israel, but it has now crossed a red line into legitimating anti-Semitism.

Gilad Atzmon, who was invited to be a featured performer in a celebration of Martin Luther King at the Friends Meeting House, has written an overtly anti-Semitic book titled *The Wandering Who?*, which, he acknowledges, draws...much of his "insights from a man who...was an anti-Semite as well as a radical misogynist."

Atzmon has told students that he cannot "say whether it's right or not to burn down a synagogue. I can say that it is a rational act."

It is not as if Friends School is unfamiliar with Atzmon's anti-Semitic rants. Atzmon was previously invited to make a guest appearance in a class last year and one of his essays was distributed to the students. The essay came from his website, which is replete with anti-Semitic "insights."

When I heard about this bizarre invitation, I wrote the following letter to the school's headmaster:

"Your school is now legitimating anti-Semitism by inviting a self-described Jew hater, Gilad Atzmon, to participate in events at the school. This sends a powerful message to your students,

> and to other students around the world, that Atzmon's views are legitimate and an appropriate subject for discussion in academic circles.
>
> "If you believe these views are appropriately discussed, considered and possibly accepted by your students, then you are doing the right thing by associating your school with the man who expressed them. If not, then you are doing a terrible disservice to your students and to the values for which the Friends School purports to stand.
>
> "I cannot overemphasize how serious this matter is. Legitimating the oldest form of bigotry is a moral and academic sin. I cannot remain silent in the face of complicity with bigotry. Nor should you."

The headmaster did not respond to my letter, but he had the director of development (the fundraiser) send me an email saying that Atzmon was invited "solely for his musical accomplishments" and that the invitation was extended by "the Meetinghouse Jazz Orchestra."

Atzmon performed on January 13 to honor a man—Martin Luther King—who despised anti-Semitism and would have been appalled by Atzmon's hateful words. Students cheered his performance and conversed with him.

I cannot imagine an overtly homophobic, sexist, or racist musician being invited by any group in any way associated with Friends "solely for his musical accomplishments." (I hear that David Duke, the white supremacist perennial candidate, plays a mean saxophone.)

Atzmon is famous (really, infamous) not because he is a distinguished musician, but rather because he is a notorious anti-Semite whose blogs are featured on neo-Nazi websites all over the world. He never would have been invited but for his well-publicized bigotry.

Friends Seminary is well known for inviting artists whose politics and ideology are consistent with the values of the school. Indeed, the poster advertising his featured appearance at the "22nd

Annual Martin Luther King Concert" at the "Meetinghouse at Friends Seminary" included a description of him as a "writer" and "political activist."

Moreover, when he was previously invited by the school to address a class, the teacher distributed one of his bigoted essays from his anti-Semitic website.

However the school may try to spin this invitation, the end result will be that Atzmon's bigoted views will have been given the imprimatur of the Friends Seminary. Shame on Friends.

February 2, 2012
A Victory Over Bigotry at Friends Seminary

The Friends Seminary in New York, which made the God-awful mistake in judgment of twice inviting Gilad Atzmon to meet with its students, has now acknowledged that it was wrong to do so and has promised never again to allow that bigot to set foot on its premises. It has also promised to invite me and representatives of the Anti-Defamation League to address its students about the dangers of the sort of anti-Semitic hatred spewed by Atzmon.

This dispute was never about Atzmon himself. He is just one of a number of hatemongers who crawl out from beneath the rocks of the internet. His claims that Jews may have killed "Goyim" to use their blood, his doubts about the Holocaust, his incitement to burn down synagogues as "reasonable," his claims that Jews try to control the world and are responsible for most of its evils—these are the screwball rants of pathological anti-Semites that are and should be ignored. The issue was always about the lack of judgment showed by the Friends Seminary, which legitimated this hate speech to its students by inviting Atzmon.

When I first raised these issues, the headmaster of the Friends School ignored my requests for a discussion. He obviously thought the issue would go away with time. But I would not let it simply pass. I wrote op-eds, blogs, and letters demanding that the school acknowledge its mistake. (I never sought to have his scheduled appearances cancelled.)

Finally, when I threatened to appear in front of the school and hand my essays to any of their students who were willing to read it, and when *The Wall Street Journal* decided to cover the story, the school began to take the issue seriously. By expressly promising never to allow Atzmon to darken their doorstep, the school has implicitly acknowledged that it was wrong to invite him and to assign the students to read one of his hate-filled essays. (The school has also agreed to assign my essay rebutting Atzmon to the students who were assigned his essay.) Of course it was wrong ever to welcome him, especially in light of the school's policy to invite speakers and performers who represent the school's peaceful and tolerant values. Those who invited him should have known better, and hopefully now they do.

The school's positive response to my advocacy, and to that like others like the ADL, demonstrates that silence is never an acceptable answer to bigotry. I understand why some of the parents and students in the school were afraid to risk grades and college opportunities by challenging those in power. That is precisely why those of us outside the school had a responsibility to act, and to act vigorously and firmly.

In the end, the entire experience was almost certainly a positive one in the eternal fight against bigotry. No one in the Friends community and no one who reads the media can now claim ignorance regarding Atzmon's poison pen and viperous tongue. No decent school will ever invite Atzmon again, and anyone who does invite him must be charged with the knowledge that they are legitimating a known bigot.

In a recent post, Atzmon said that he would be willing to play alongside David Duke. What a duet! But that's exactly where Atzmon belongs—in the company of neo-Nazis, Holocaust deniers, homophobes, misogynists, sexists, and other bigots. He does not belong in American schools, especially high schools, and his views—though he has a complete right to express them—should never be legitimated. They must be rejected in the marketplace of ideas. The Friends Seminary has now done that--kudos to them for learning from their mistakes.

February 26, 2012
Friends Seminary Plays Bait and Switch on Anti-Semitism

The Friends Seminary of New York, which invited the notorious anti-Semite Gilad Atzmon to one of its classes, and assigned its students to read his hate-filled writings, has now backed out of an agreement to invite me to the school to talk to the students about the evils of anti-Semitism. The headmaster of the Friends Seminary, a school that is supposed to be committed to honesty and integrity, has broken his solemn promise to me, and to members of its own community, to allow its students to hear both sides of an issue which really has only one side: namely, the illegitimacy of bringing hate mongers into high school classrooms.

After I exposed the original invitations to Gilad Atzmon—who justifies the burning down of synagogues as "reasonable" response to Jewish efforts to "control the world"—the headmaster of the school agreed to several things. First, he would speak at an assembly to the students about the evils of anti-Semitism; second, he would assign my essay to the students who were assigned Atzmon's essay; and third, he would invite me to address the students. He has now broken each of these promises.

Students who were at the assembly have confirmed that the speakers only made things worse. The teacher who invited Atzmon talked about what a great musician he was. The headmaster was defensive about how his words were manipulated and justified bringing Atzmon based on Quaker principles. Apparently the word anti-Semitism was never once mentioned during this meeting. My article was not assigned to the students; a citation was sent to them saying that <u>I</u> wanted students to read its content.

When I wrote to the headmaster complaining about these breaches, they used my letter as an excuse for canceling my appearance. The real reason was almost certainly pressure from hard-left members of his faculty and others.

Let's be clear what this means. The school was unwilling to cancel Atzmon's appearance, even <u>after</u> learning that he was a virulent anti-Semite who questions the Holocaust but believes that it may be true that Jews kill Christians to use their blood for religious purposes. But they have canceled my appearance because they didn't like the tone of a private letter that I wrote to them that was critical of the headmaster's failure to comply with his promises. I ended my letter with the following words: "Please assure me that I am wrong about my judgment about you. I really would like to see this move forward in a positive direction, but you are not helping. The ultimate sufferers are your students, who are being taught the wrong values that will serve them poorly in college and in life."

The values that headmaster Bo Lauder is imbuing to his students are deception, breach of promise, toleration of anti-Semitism, and an unwillingness to present all sides of an issue. In the end, the headmaster is showing tremendous distrust of his students by refusing to allow them to hear another side of the issue, by canceling my promised appearance, by not assigning my essay and by continuing to be defensive regarding the dreadful mistake of judgment he made in allowing Atzmon to teach his students.

The headmaster may believe that by breaking his promises, he has ended this issue. Let him be absolutely certain, that, as I wrote in my letter to him: "This issue will not go away, and nor will I. Misled once, shame on you. Misled twice, shame on me." Unless I am invited to address the students <u>inside</u> of the school, I will appear <u>outside</u> of the school, where I will hand out my essays to those students who are willing to read them and will address those students who have an interest in hearing a response to anti-Semitism. I am also considering inviting parents, students and other members of the Friends Seminary community to an event, in a venue outside of the school, where these issues can be discussed openly and candidly. Headmaster Lauder may be able to keep me physically outside of his school, but he will not be able to stop my ideas from reaching his community. The truth does not respect artificial boundaries.

The Friends Seminary, like other elite schools around the country, teaches our future leaders. Many Friends Schools around the country have espoused strongly anti-Israel policies for years. The Friends Seminary in New York itself has a rabidly anti-Israel history teacher on its faculty, who propagandizes his students against Israel in the classroom, and who has a picture of Anne

Frank wearing a Palestinian headdress on his website. The school has and is again planning to take its students on trips to the Middle East that present a one-sided perspective. Now they have crossed the line from preaching anti-Zionism to tolerating anti-Semitism. I will not remain silent in the face of the Friends Seminary's double standard and neither should you.

February 27, 2012
Should Harvard Sponsor a One-Sided Conference Seeking the End of Israel?

In order to assess whether Harvard is acting properly in relation to the upcoming student-sponsored conference entitled Israel/Palestine and the One-State Solution, I propose the following thought experiment. Ask yourself what Harvard would do if a group of right wing students and faculty decided to convene a conference on the topic, *Are the Palestinians Really a People?*, and invited as speakers only hard right academics who answered that question in the negative? Would the Provost office at Harvard help fund such a conference? Would the Kennedy School at Harvard grant such conference legitimacy by hosting it? Would Harvard's Carr Center For Human Rights Policy or Weatherhead Center for International Affairs support such a conference? Would distinguished Harvard professors agree to speak at it?

If the answers to those questions are clearly "yes," then Harvard cannot be faulted for its role in the forthcoming anti-Israel hate fest. It would mean that in the name of academic and speech freedom Harvard will host a conference on nearly any kooky idea of the hard right or hard left. If the answer is "no," then the single standard of academic freedom would demand reconsideration of the Harvard Provost's decision to help fund the anti-Israel hate fest and the decision of the Kennedy School to lend its premises to this event. If Harvard were to decide to host the anti-Israel hate fest but not the anti-Palestinian one, that would reveal either an anti-Israel or pro hard left bias unbecoming a great university.

To be fair, the dean of the Kennedy School did issue a statement that his school "in no way endorses or supports the apparent position" of the conference, and that he hopes the "final shape of the conference will be significantly more balanced." But the question remains, would he have done no more than that if an anti-Palestinian conference were being hosted on his premises and supported by "centers" associated with the Kennedy School?

I believe Harvard would probably pass the "neutrality test," but I hope the issue is never directly put to Harvard, because it would be obnoxious for there to be a conference here on the subject of whether the Palestinians are a real people. They are, and so are the Israelis. The quest for a Palestinian state is a legitimate one, as is the need to preserve Israel as the nation state of the Jewish people.

The participant is the Harvard conference will deny that there is any parallel between the subject of their conference and the subject of my hypothetical one. They will claim that the "one state solution" is a serious academic subject, whereas the question "are the Palestinians really a people?" is not. This is a pure rationalization. The question regarding the Palestinians was raised by a candidate for president of the United States and has been the subject of debate and controversy in the media and in academic writings. Both subjects are essentially political in nature and both have similarly phony academic veneers. Both conferences would be academically one-sided in their selection of speakers. Moreover, a great university committed to free speech and academic freedom does not get to pick and choose which political issues it deems sufficiently "correct" to warrant its imprimatur.

The only real difference between the two subjects is that if Harvard were to sponsor a one-sided conference against a Palestinian state, there would be massive protests, especially by some of the very academics who are willingly lending their imprimatur to the anti-Israel hate fest. But the charge of hypocrisy has never stopped these professors from applying a double standard against Israel. They should not be stopped from speaking—that would be censorship and a denial of academic freedom. But they should be shamed for participating in a one-sided academic hate conference, and for their hypocrisy in doing so in the name of academic freedom, when they would never tolerate a comparable hate conference against a Palestinian state or the Palestinian people.

Let there be no doubt that the call for a single state solution is a euphemism for ending the existence of Israel as the nation state of the Jewish people. The major proponents of this ruse acknowledge—indeed proclaim—that this is their true goal. Tony Judt, who was the academic godfather of the "one state" ploy, saw it as an alternative to Israel as the nation-state of the Jewish people, which he believed was a mistake. Many of those speaking at the Harvard conference are on record opposing the existence of Israel. Leon Weiselteir was right when he observed that the one state gambit is not "the alternative for Israel. It is the alternative to Israel."

The "one state" solution failed in the former Yugoslavia. It failed in India. And it would fail in the Middle East. That's why most Palestinians and nearly all Israelis are against it. They favor a two state solution, as does most of the rest of the world.

Many of the speakers at this conference will rail against "a Jewish State." But they will not protest the Palestinian Constitution, which establishes Islam as the only "official religion" and requires that "the principles of Islamic Sharia shall be the main source of legislation." Moreover, it establishes Arabic as the sole "official language" of Palestine. Israel, in contrast, treats Judaism, Islam, and Christianity equally, does not base its laws (except regarding family matters of Jews) on Jewish law, and has three official languages—Hebrew, Arabic, and English (with Russian constituting the 4th unofficial language and (Ethiopian) Amharic a 5th, manifesting its extensive ethnic diversity).

As this conference goes forward, and as the massive casualties mount in Syria, the resounding silence about the victims of the Assad brutality by those speakers, who use the G word (genocide) every time Israel acts in defense of its citizens, speaks louder than their hypocritical words. The extremists who will be speaking at this hate fest are so obsessed with Israel's imperfections that they ignore—indeed enable—the most serious human rights violations that are occurring throughout the world. That is the real shame of the double standard that is represented by this hateful conference.

January 1, 2013
Brooklyn College Political Science Department's Israel Problem

The international campaign to de-legitimize Israel by subjecting the Jewish state—and the Jewish state alone—to divestment, boycotts, and sanctions (BDS) has now come to the most unlikely of places: Brooklyn College. The political science department of that college has voted to co-sponsor a campaign event at which only pro-BDS speakers will advocate a policy that is so extreme that even the Palestinian Authority rejects it.

The poster for the BDS event specifically says that the event is being "endorsed by...the political science department at BC." The BDS campaign accuses Israel of "Apartheid" and advocates the blacklisting of Jewish Israeli academics, which is probably illegal and certainly immoral. The two speakers at the event deny Israel's right to exist, compare Israel to the Nazis, and praise terrorist groups such as Hamas and Hezbollah.

The president of Brooklyn College claims that this co-sponsorship does not constitute an endorsement by the college and that this is an issue of freedom of speech and academic freedom. But when a department of a university officially co-sponsors and endorses an event advocating BDS against Israel, and refuses to co-sponsor and endorse an event opposing such BDS, that does constitute an official endorsement. Freedom of speech and academic freedom require equal access to both sides of a controversy, not official sponsorship and endorsement of one side over the other. The heavy thumb of an academic department should not be placed on the scale, if the marketplace of ideas is to remain equally accessible to all sides of a controversy.

I have no problem with a BDS campaign being conducted by radical students at Brooklyn College or anywhere else. Students have a right to promote immoral causes on college campuses. Nor do I have a problem with such an event being sponsored by the usual hard left, anti-Israel and anti-American groups, such as some of those that are co-sponsoring this event. My sole objection is to the official sponsorship and endorsement of BDS by an official department of a public (or for that matter, private) college.

I was once a student at Brooklyn College, majoring in political science. Back in the day, departments did not take official positions on controversial political issues. They certainly didn't sponsor or endorse the kind of hate speech that can be expected at this event, if the history of the speakers is any guide. The president of the university says this is a matter of academic freedom. But whose academic freedom? Do "departments"—as distinguished from individual faculty members—really have the right of academic freedom? Does the political science department at Brooklyn College represent only its hard left faculty? What about the academic freedom of faculty members who do not support the official position of the department? One Brooklyn College faculty member has correctly observed that:

"[B]oycotting academics is the opposite of free speech. It symbolizes the silencing on people based on their race and religion."

Does the political science department not also represent the students who major in or take courses in that subject? I know that as a student I would not want to be associated with a department that officially supported divestment, boycott and sanctions against Israel. My academic freedom would be compromised by such an association. Also, I would worry that a department that was so anti-Israel would grade me down or refuse me recommendations if I were perceived to be pro-Israel, or even neutral. I would not feel comfortable expressing my academic freedom in such a department. I'm sure there are many students at Brooklyn College who feel the same. What can they do to express their academic freedom? Should they fight fire with fire by advocating divestment, boycotts, and sanctions against the political science department or against Brooklyn College? Would that, too, be an exercise of academic freedom?

If I were a Brooklyn College student today and an opponent of BDS against Israel, I would not major in political science. I would worry that my chances of getting into a good law school or graduate program would be put at risk. I would pick a department—or a school—that was less politicized and more academically unbiased.

Academic freedom does not include the power of department or faculty members to proselytize captive students whose grades and future depend on faculty evaluations. That's why academic departments should not take political positions that threaten the academic freedom of dissenting students or faculty.

I can understand the department of political science sponsoring a genuine debate over boycotts, divestment and sanctions in which all sides were equally represented. That might be an educational experience worthy of departmental sponsorship. But the event in question is pure propaganda and one-sided political advocacy. There is nothing academic about it. Would the political science department of Brooklyn College sponsor and endorse an anti-divestment evening? Would they sponsor and endorse me, a graduate of that department, to present my perspective to their students? Would they sponsor a radical, pro-settlement, Israeli extremist to propagandize their students? Who gave the department the authority to decide, as a department, which side to support in this highly contentious debate? What are the implications of such departmental support? Could the political science department now vote to offer courses advocating BDS against Israel and grading students based on their support for the department's position? Should other departments now be lobbied to support divestments, boycotts and sanctions against China, Venezuela, Cuba, and Russia, the Palestinian Authority or other perennial violators of human rights?

Based on my knowledge of the Brooklyn College political science department, they would never vote to sponsor and endorse an anti-BDS campaign or a BDS campaign against left-wing, Islamic, anti-Israel or anti-American countries that are genuine violators of human rights. Universities and some departments in particular, are quickly becoming more political than academic. This trend threatens the academic freedom of dissenting students and faculty. It also threatens the academic quality of such institutions.

The Brooklyn College political science department should get out of the business of sponsoring one-sided political propaganda and should stop trying to exercise undue influence over the free marketplace of ideas. That is the real violation of academic freedom and freedom of speech.

Shame on the Brooklyn College political science department for falsely invoking academic freedom and freedom of speech to deny equal freedoms to those who disagree with its extremist politics.

February 3, 2013
Does Brooklyn College Pass the "Shoe on the Other Foot" Test?

The decision by the Brooklyn College political science department to endorse the BDS campaign—which includes the boycotting of Jewish-Israeli academics—has been "justified" on freedom of speech and academic freedom grounds by the Chairman of the department. Brooklyn College's president has said that departments have the right to sponsor one-sided partisan events. Let's see if these "justifications" pass the "shoe on the other foot test."

What would these administrators say if the department of philosophy were to officially endorse the right to life and oppose a woman's right to choose abortion? What if the economics department had officially endorsed Mitt Romney during last year's election? What if the Spanish department had voted to endorse an academic boycott against Cuban or Venezuelan professors? What if the department of religion were to officially condemn homosexuality?

I can assure you that both the lyrics and the music would be very different. The chairman of the political science department, a radical leftist, would be complaining that his academic freedom is being denied by these departments officially endorsing positions with which he disagrees. The president of the college, known for her feminist views, would not likely remain silent in the face of an official departmental endorsement of the right to life. Nor would many faculty members justify a departmental condemnation of homosexuality on the ground of academic freedom or freedom of speech.

So these invocations of free speech and academic freedoms are merely a smokescreen to cover the hypocrisy of those who claim that they are committed to open dialogue and the expression of all points of view. That is so much hooey. Of course, the event should go forward, but it should be sponsored by students and outside groups, not by a department of the college. The same should be true of pro-Israel events.

The very same professors who demand the right to advocate BDS against Israel would demand the right to suppress the free speech and academic freedom of those who support Israeli settlements and the denial of statehood to the Palestinians. "Free speech for me but not for thee" has always been the hallmark of extremists on both the left and right. These extremists believe they know the Truth and that there is no reason for supporting, endorsing or even tolerating opposing viewpoints. They cannot be trusted to grade students neutrally and without bias. I know that if I were a student at Brooklyn College today, I would not major in political science for fear that my support for Israel and my opposition to BDS might make me a target in the eyes of professors whose department has officially endorsed BDS, thus discriminating against my point of view in the marketplace of ideas. How could I be sure they wouldn't discriminate against my point of view in grading or recommending students? This is the real issue in the hullabaloo over the decision by the Brooklyn College political science department to co-sponsor and endorse the BDS campaign at Brooklyn College.

Nor is this only a hypothetical or abstract fear. One political science student at Brooklyn College said she was afraid to criticize her department because "that's going to put a target on my back." Other students talked about a "chilling effect" that the department's decision would have on them. And yet another student said that she had "an uncomfortable feeling" about raising her hand and arguing "with a professor who voted for it" and who tried to justify his vote in the classroom.

The president of Brooklyn College says she believes that departments have the right to take controversial positions and to sponsor and endorse controversial events. Where is the line to be drawn? Would the Brooklyn College political science department have the right to offer a course entitled, "Why BDS against Israel is a good thing?" Would the faculty have the right to grade students based on whether their exams agree or disagree with the department's official party line on BDS? Would the department have the right to deny the request of a faculty member to teach a course on why BDS against Israel is a bad thing? Surely the answer to these questions is no and even the chairman of the political science department at Brooklyn College would probably agree.

But his department has endorsed BDS against Israel, and it would not co-sponsor or endorse an equivalent speech on the other side of the issue: namely, by a radical, pro-settlement, anti-Palestinian statehood, zealot. I doubt his department would co-sponsor and endorse a speech by a moderate pro-Israel advocate who favored the two-state solution and opposed settlement building That issue is being tested because Brooklyn College Hillel is asking the political science department to "co-sponsor" and "endorse" an anti-BDS talk by me. The shoe is now on the other foot! And it is causing painful blisters.

There are only two reasonable approaches to what departments should be entitled to do: either they should sponsor and endorse events on all sides of controversial issues, or they should get out of the business of selectively sponsoring and endorsing only one side of such issues. The approach taken by the political science department at Brooklyn College is absolutely unacceptable: namely, to endorse and sponsor only one side of a controversial issue, while refusing to co-sponsor and endorse the other side of the issue. The president of Brooklyn College is wrong when she says that departments should have the right to selectively sponsor and endorse only one side of a controversy. That is a long step on the road to turning academic departments into biased, partisan and one-sided propaganda centers, reminiscent of "political science" departments in the former Soviet Union that "encouraged" their students to follow the official party line.

February 8, 2013
The Brooklyn College BDS Debate and Me: the Critics' Real Agenda

Whenever I speak in support of Israel or in criticism of its enemies, the dogs of defamation are unleashed against me. The attacks, all from the hard left, seemed coordinated, focusing on common ad hominem themes. They accuse me of being a plagiarist, a supporter of torture, a right-wing "Zio-fascist," a hypocrite, an opponent of the two-state solution, and a supporter of Israel's settlement policies. All these allegations are demonstrably false, but this does not seem to matter to those whose job it is to try to discredit me.

Let me begin with the charge of plagiarism—a charge originally made by the academic Norman Finkelstein. In my case, the charge centered on a one-paragraph quotation from Mark Twain in my book *The Case for Israel*. I cited the paragraph to Mark Twain, but Finkelstein said that I should have cited it to a writer named Joan Peters, because he believes I found the quote in her book.

The truth is that I found the quote ten years prior to the publication of Peters' book and used it repeatedly in debates and speeches. When Finkelstein leveled his absurd charge, I immediately reported it to the Harvard University president and to the dean of the law school to ask that it be thoroughly investigated. Harvard appointed its former president, Derek Bok, to investigate the charge. After a thorough investigation, he found it to be utterly frivolous. But to the dogs of defamation, this only goes to prove that Harvard must be part of the pro-Israel conspiracy.

The second charge is that I am pro-torture, despite my repeated categorical statements in my writings that I'm opposed to all torture under all circumstances. I do believe that torture *will* be used, not *should* be used, in the event we ever experience a ticking bomb situation. Accordingly, I have suggested that no torture should ever be permitted without a court approved warrant, of the type the ACLU has demanded in targeted killing cases.

But to the dogs of defamation, this distinction is irrelevant. Because I am pro-Israel, I must be pro-torture. This is particularly ironic, since both the Palestinian Authority and Hamas routinely torture dissidents, without their leaders being called pro-torture by the same hard-left defamers who falsely accuse me.

The most recent unleashing of the dogs of defamation was stimulated by the position I took on a BDS conference at Brooklyn College. Although I support the conference going forward, and oppose any attempt to censor it, I raise troubling questions about whether the Brooklyn College political science department should be sponsoring and endorsing that advocacy event, if they would not be willing to sponsor and endorse an anti-BDS event by an equally radical anti-Palestinian right-wing group.

My position, of course, has been distorted, and I have been lumped with those who would censor the event. I have been called a hypocrite because, apparently, the political science department at UPENN once co-sponsored an anti-BDS speech I gave there, despite the fact that I was totally unaware of this sponsorship and would have been opposed if I'd known about it. I was informed, and believed until now, that the event had been sponsored by Hillel and the Jewish Federation.

Along the same lines, two members of the political science department at Brooklyn College have claimed that my speeches there were sponsored by the department and were as controversial as the BDS advocacy event. That is totally false. So far as I can remember, I have made three speeches at Brooklyn College: one, the Konefsky lecture in the late 1960s or early 1970s, which was a purely academic lecture focusing on the work of Professor Samuel Konefsky; there was nothing controversial about it. Second, a speech I was invited to give when I donated my papers to Brooklyn College: again, not very controversial. And third, a talk I gave in 2008 about my teachers at Brooklyn College and about a letter by Thomas Jefferson I had found in a book store (this can be heard online); again, not particularly controversial.

Why, then, is there such a concerted effort to attack me personally and to question my integrity every time I speak about Israel?

It has little to do with me, because my attackers know that I can fight back and that my academic standing will not in any way be influenced by their attacks. The attacks are directed at young academics, without tenure who would dare to speak up on behalf of Israel.

The message is clear: if you support Israel, we will attack you like we attack Dershowitz, but you will be hurt much more than Dershowitz would. We will damage your reputation, hurt your student evaluations, and decrease your chances for tenure.

It should come as no surprise, therefore, that so many pro-Israel young academics refuse to speak up. I know because they call and discreetly tell me about the fear they have that they will be subjected to the same kind of McCarthyite tactics to which I am subjected.

That is why I will continue to fight back and respond every time the dogs of defamation are unleashed against me.

February 12, 2013
Did Brooklyn College's Political Science Department Violate the First Amendment?

The co-sponsorship by the Brooklyn College political science department of an anti-Israel hate fest, from which pro-Israel students were excluded, may have violated the First Amendment. Had the event been sponsored only by student and outside private groups, their decision to exclude pro-Israel students and to prevent the distribution of anti-BDS leaflets would have been a private matter, that at worst may have violated the rules of the college. But the official co-sponsorship of the event by an academic department may have turned their exclusionary decisions into illegal "state action."

For purposes of the First Amendment, the political science department is Brooklyn College, which is the City University of New York, which is the State of New York. It was the State of New York, therefore, that expelled pro-Israel students who wanted to distribute constitutionally protected leaflets and wanted to pose constitutionally protected political questions. Such state action violates the First Amendment and New York law.

Accordingly, the benighted action of the political science department in taking sides in the debate over boycotting Israeli academics and institutions, may now come back to haunt the City University of New York, which is taking this situation seriously. The Chancellor issued the following statement:

> *At last week's event at Brooklyn College, sponsored by Students for Justice in Palestine and the College's Department of Political Science, allegations were made by members of the college community who attended that they were impeded from expressing views either orally or in writing. There were reports that some said they were asked without cause to leave the event. If this were true, it was wrong and we need to understand exactly*

> *what the circumstances were. At the request of President Karen L. Gould, I have asked General Counsel and Senior Vice Chancellor for Legal Affairs Frederick P. Schaffer to quickly investigate these allegations. This investigation will be coordinated by CUNY's Office of Legal Affairs, working with an independent consultant, and charged with reporting directly back to me.*

There is, apparently, strong evidence to corroborate the accounts that pro-Israel students, especially those wearing yarmulkes or "looking" Jewish, were deliberately excluded, even though they secured written permission to attend. There is also corroboration of the accusation that pro-Israel students who managed to get into the event were thrown out when they refused to turn over to the organizers anti-BDS leaflets they wished to distribute. When these students complained to an official of the college, he reportedly replied that the anti-Israel students who were running the event were "calling the shots" and he could therefore do nothing.

But once the political science department became involved as a co-sponsor, the students alone could not call the shots, when it comes to the First Amendment. The university assumed responsibility for assuring that the free speech of all students was equally protected. The First Amendment forbids the State of New York from discriminating against pro-Israel or anti-BDS speech, as it apparently did here.

What happened at Brooklyn College demonstrates the wisdom of keeping academic departments from sponsoring non-academic hate fests, such as the BDS event. When academic departments become selective sponsors, the constitutional rules change, because the imprimatur of the university—and thus the state—is placed on the event.

The radical anti-Israel students who arranged the BDS conference thought they had obtained a benefit from the political science department's co-sponsorship—and perhaps they did in the short term. But in the long term, they may rue the day they persuaded the department to become involved in what should have been a student event. Now there may be legal consequences. The sword of co-sponsorship may have become a shield to protect the First Amendment rights of the students who were prevented from handing out anti-BDS leaflets and asking anti-BDS questions. I wonder if we will hear from Mayor Michael Bloomberg and the New York Times editorial board about these violations of freedom of speech!

February 26, 2013
Pink Anti-Semitism Is No Different from Brown Anti-Semitism

The core characteristic of anti-Semitism is the assertion that everything the Jews do is wrong, and everything that is wrong is done by the Jews. For the anti-Semite every rich Jew is exploitive, every poor Jew a burden on society. For the anti-Semite, both capitalism and communism are Jewish plots. For the anti-Semite, Jews are both too docile, allowing themselves to be led to the slaughter like sheep, and too militant, having won too many wars against the Arabs. For the anti-Semite, Jews are too liberal and too conservative, too artsy and too bourgeois, too stingy and too charitable, too insular and too cosmopolitan, too moralistic and too conniving.

To the anti-Semite, every depression, war, social problem, plague must have been the fault of the Jews. Whenever the Jews appear to be doing something good—giving charity, helping the less fortunate, curing the sick—there must be a malevolent motive, a hidden agenda, a conspiratorial explanation beneath the surface of the benevolent act.

Now the very twisted illogic that has characterized classic anti-Semitism is being directed at the Jewish state, which for the anti-Semite has become "the Jew" among nations. When Israel sent help to tsunami and hurricane victims, the Jewish state was accused of merely trying to garner positive publicity calculated to offset its mistreatment of Palestinians. When Israeli medical teams save the lives of Palestinian children, they must be up to no good. When it was disclosed that the Israeli army has the lowest rate of rape against enemy civilians, radical anti-Zionists argued that this was because Israeli soldiers were so racist that they did not find Palestinian women attractive enough to rape! Nothing the Jew or the Jew among nations does can be praised, because its purpose is always to "manipulate," to "conceal," to "divert attention away from" or to "distort" the evil that inheres in all Jewish actions and inactions.

That is the bigoted thesis of a new anti-Israel campaign being conducted by some radical gay activists who absurdly claim that Israel is engaging in "pinkwashing." This burlesque of an argument first surfaced in a *New York Times* op-ed that claimed that Israel's positive approach to gay rights is "a deliberate strategy to conceal the continuing violation of Palestinians human rights behind an image of modernity signified by Israeli gay life." In other words, the Jew among nations is now being accused of feigning concern over the rights of gay people in order to whitewash—or in this case pinkwash—its lack of concern for Palestinian people.

How this pinkwashing is supposed to work, we aren't told. Is the media supposed to be so obsessed with Israel's positive policies toward gays that it will no longer cover the Palestinian issue? If so, that certainly hasn't worked. Are gays around the world supposed to feel so indebted to Israel that they will no longer criticize the Jewish nation? That surely hasn't worked, as evidenced by increasingly rabid anti-Israel advocacy by several gay organizations.

Well, to the unthinking anti-Semite, it doesn't matter how the Jewish manipulation works. The anti-Semite just knows that there must be something sinister at work if Jews do anything positive. The same is now true for the unthinking anti-Israel bigot.

In Israel, openly gay soldiers have long served in the military and in high positions in both government and the private sector. Gay pride parades are frequent. Israel is, without a doubt, the most gay friendly country in the Middle East and among the most supportive of gay rights anywhere in the world. This occurs despite efforts by some fundamentalist Jews, Muslims, and Christians to ban gay pride parades and legal equality for gays. In contrast to Israel are the West Bank and Gaza, where gays are murdered, tortured, and forced to seek asylum—often in Israel. In every Arab and Muslim country, homosexual acts among consenting adults are criminal, often punishable by death. But all this doesn't matter to the "growing global gay movement" against Israel, which according to

The New York Times op-ed, regards these positive steps as nothing more than a cover for malevolent Israeli actions.

The pinkwash bigots would apparently prefer to see Israel treat gays the way Israel's enemies do, because they hate Israel more than they care about gay rights. Nor do these pink anti-Semites speak for the majority of gay people, who appreciate Israel's positive steps with regard to gay rights, even if they don't agree with all of Israel's policies. Decent gay people who have themselves been subjected to stereotyping, recognize bigotry when they see it, even—perhaps especially—among other gay people. That's why so many prominent gay leaders and public officials have denounced this "pinkwashing" nonsense.

Now this pinkwashing campaign is coming to the City University of New York. A pinkwashing conference is being sponsored by the Gay and Lesbian Studies Center at The Graduate Center on April 10-11, 2013. It will be yet another hate-fest against Israel, but this time it will cross the line into classic anti-Semitic tropes. Don't be fooled by its benign pink hue, or its academic pretext. At its core, the newly fashioned charge of pinkwashing is little different from the old-fashioned charges leveled by brown-shirted anti-Semites—namely, that neither the Jews nor the Jewish state ever does good things without bad motives. And this time, the hate conference is being co-sponsored by the Philosophy and Psychology Departments and The Graduate Center of the City University of New York, as well as by the Center for The Study of Gender and Sexuality at New York University.[53]

Shame on anyone who exploits his or her sexual orientation to promote anti-Semitic bigotry. And shame on anyone who sponsors those who practice pink anti-Semitism.

June 24, 2013
Alice Walker's Crass Bigotry Exposed

In her most recent book, *The Cushion in the Road*, Pulitzer Prize-winning author Alice Walker writes about how her "own work has been banned a lot." She writes about book banning in the context of criticizing Israel and applauding an Israeli writer named Uri Avnery, whose criticisms of Israel, she implies, have also been banned: "He's been kept away from most of the uncurtained windows of Israel into which curious outsiders might look."

This juxtaposition of her own experiences with those of Uri Avnery encapsulates Walker's approach to writing about Israel. She tells half-truths, omits salient facts, finds fault with everything Israel does, suggests false comparisons, and paints a cartoonish absurd picture of the Israeli-Palestinian conflict. Worst of all, she opposes peace talks, the two-state solution, and any rational approach to the Israeli-Palestinian conflict.

Let's begin with Alice Walker's own work being banned. It is true that one cannot read *The Color Purple*, Walker's most famous book, in Hebrew. But that's because Alice Walker herself has banned it.

She has adamantly refused to allow *The Color Purple* to be translated into Hebrew, because she advocates a cultural boycott of Israel, of Jewish Israeli artists, and of films made by Jewish Israelis. Half-truth number one.

Now let's turn to Uri Avnery, whose writings are widely available both in Hebrew and in English and whose works have never, to my knowledge, been banned. Indeed, it is fair to say that few countries in the world publish more self-critical books, magazines, and newspapers than does Israel. Half-truth number two.

The half-truths and outright lies go on and on. Even the most strident critics of Israeli policies and/or actions do not believe many of the bizarre and counter-factual assertions made by Walker.

According to Walker in her new book, Israel routinely tortures innocent nine- and ten-year-old Palestinian children.

According to Walker, Rachel Corrie was "murdered," just like three civil rights workers who were kidnapped, tortured, and murdered in cold blood.

According to Walker, there are roads that are for "Jews only," rather than for Israelis of all religions and ethnicities.

According to Walker, the big ugly security wall runs all through Israel and the Palestinian territories—"it is everywhere"—rather than through roughly 5% of those areas. Moreover, she suggests that the wall was put up solely to colonize the West Bank, and not to protect Israelis from terrorism.

According to Walker, the Turkish flotilla terrorists who attacked the Israeli sailors who had boarded their ship were "assassinated" and "massacre[d]."

According to Walker, no rockets were ever fired at Israeli civilians from Gaza and Israel's attacks against Gaza were unprovoked and constitute "genocide."

According to Walker, there has never been a more brutal occupation in the history of the world.

According to Walker, what Israel is doing to the Palestinians is the equivalent of what Hitler did to the Jews.

According to Walker (as quoted by The Simon Wiesenthal Center) Israel may someday launch a nuclear attack against the United States, "because the United States and Israel, working together have done terrible things to others [and] it is the nature of thieves to eventually have a grand falling out."

According to Walker, anyone who is "not Jewish" suffers "dehumanizing treatment" when trying to cross the border into Israel.

According to Walker, the Jews learned how to rape, murder, pillory, steal, and occupy from their Torah. (She learned this from her former husband, who is Jewish and whose family she hated, and she advocates black churches teach this anti-Jewish version of Biblical and modern history.)

According to Walker, there is no Palestinian terrorism, only Israeli terrorism, and there is no threat to Israel's survival—only "nonviolent" Palestinian protest in the spirit of Gandhi. She dedicates a poem to Palestinian suicide bombers who murdered innocent Israeli children.

According to Walker, Jews first came to Palestine after a "holocaust" (her quote marks), that "so many future disasters would resemble." They were welcomed by the Palestinians, who then had their land stolen by their ungrateful guests.

According to Walker, Israel has no right to be the nation state of the Jewish people. Instead the Jews should live as a minority in a Muslim, Christian, and Jewish Palestine from the river to the sea. She has never "believed in the Israeli-Palestinian peace talks."

According to Walker, there should be no Israel.

Putting aside the plausible claim made by Abe Foxman and others that Alice Walker has crossed the line from fervent anti-Zionist to rancid anti-Semitism (which she denies because Palestinians are Semites too), the question remains why anyone would take seriously her ignorant rants about the Israeli-Palestinian conflict.

Critics who have any ability and willingness to think in a nuanced way, understand that there are rights and wrongs on both sides, and that comparisons between Nazi Germany and today's Israel can be motivated only by crass bigotry. Nor will peace come to the area from those, like Walker, who don't "believe...in the Israeli-Palestinian peace talks." Yet because she has written well-received works of fiction about the American South, there are some who think she may have something worthwhile to say about the Middle East. They are wrong.

Reasoned debate about Israeli policies is essential to democratic governance and the peace process. That is why I dedicated my book *The Case Against Israel's Enemies* to:

"Israel's constructive and nuanced critics, whose rational voices are too often drowned out by the exaggerations, demonizations, and hate-filled lies put forth by Israel's enemies. Criticism is the lifeblood of democracy and a sure sign of admiration for an imperfect democracy seeking to improve itself."

Unfortunately, for both Palestinians and Israelis, Alice Walker is part of the problem, not part of the solution.

December 17, 2013
Boycotting Israeli Universities: A Victory for Bigotry

The American Studies Association has just issued its first ever call for an academic boycott. No, it wasn't against China, which imprisons dissenting academics. It wasn't against Iran, which executes dissenting academics. It wasn't against Russia, whose universities fire dissenting academics. It wasn't against Cuba, whose universities have no dissenting academics. It wasn't against Saudi Arabia, whose academic institutions refuse to hire women, gay, or Christian academics. Nor was it against the Palestinian Authority, whose colleges refuse to allow open discourse regarding the Israeli-Palestinian conflict. No, it was against only academic institutions in the Jewish State of Israel, whose universities have affirmative action programs for Palestinian students and who boast a higher level of academic freedom than almost any country in the world.

When the association was considering this boycott, I issued a challenge to its members, many of whom are historians. I asked them to name a single country in the history of the world faced with threats comparable to those Israel faces that has had a better record of human rights, a higher degree of compliance with the rule of law, a more demanding judiciary, more concern for the lives of enemy civilians, or more freedom to criticize the government, than the state of Israel.

Not a single member of the association came up with a name of a single country. That is because there are none. Israel is not perfect, but neither is any other country, and Israel is far better than most. If an academic group chooses to engage in the un-academic exercise of boycotting the academic institutions of another country, it should do it in order of the seriousness of the human rights violations and of the inability of those within the country to seek redress against those violations.

By these standards, Israeli academic institutions should be among the last to be boycotted.

I myself disagree with Israel's settlement policy and have long urged an end to the occupation. But Israel offered to end the occupation twice in the last 13 years. They did so in 2000–2001 when Prime Minister Ehud Barak offered the Palestinians a state on approximately 95% of the occupied territories. Then it did so again in 2008 when former Prime Minister Ehud Olmert offered an even more generous deal. The Palestinians accepted neither offer and certainly share the blame for the continuing occupation. Efforts are apparently underway once again to try to end the occupation, as peace talks continue. The Palestinian Authority's President Mahmoud Abbas himself opposes academic boycotts of Israeli institutions.

China occupies Tibet, Russia occupies Chechnya, and several other countries occupy Kurdish lands. In those cases, no offers have been made to end the occupation. Yet no boycotts have been directed against the academic institutions of those occupying countries.

When the president of the American Studies Association, Curtis Marez, an associate professor of ethnic studies at The University of California, was advised that many nations, including all of Israel's neighbors, behave far worse than Israel, he responded, "One has to start somewhere." This boycott, however, has not only started with Israel. It will end with Israel.

You would think that historians and others who belong to the American Studies Association would understand that in light of the history of discrimination against Jews, you can't just pick the Jewish State and Jewish universities as the place to "start" and stop.

The American Studies Association claims that it is not boycotting individual Israeli professors, but only the universities at which they teach. That is a nonsensical word game, since no self-respecting Israeli professor would associate with an organization that singled out Israeli colleges and universities for a boycott. Indeed, no self-respecting American professor should in any way support the bigoted actions of this association.

Several years ago, when a similar boycott was being considered, a group of American academics circulated a counter-petition drafted by Nobel Prize physicist Steven Weinberg, and I read as follows:

"We are academics, scholars, researchers and professionals of differing religious and political perspectives. We all agree that singling out Israelis for an academic boycott is wrong. To show our solidarity with our Israeli academics in this matter, we, the undersigned, hereby declare ourselves to be Israeli academics for purposes of any academic boycott. We will regard ourselves as Israeli academics and decline to participate in any activity from which Israeli academics are excluded."

More than 10,000 academics signed this petition including many Nobel Prize winners, presidents of universities, and leading scholars from around the world.

Shame on those members of the American Studies Association for singling out the Jew among nations. Shame on them for applying a double standard to Jewish universities. Israeli academic institutions are strong enough to survive this exercise in bigotry. The real question is, will this association survive its complicity with the oldest and most enduring prejudice?

December 27, 2013
Israel and the Myopic BDS Campaign

The so-called boycott, divestment, and sanctions (BDS) campaign against Israel, which was recently energized by the decision of the American Studies Association to boycott Israeli academic institutions, is actually making it harder for Israel and the Palestinian Authority to negotiate a reasonable resolution to the Israeli-Palestinian conflict. That is why Mahmoud Abbas, the head of the Palestinian Authority, has come out against boycotting Israel and Israeli academic institutions. As he put it in an interview while attending the service for Nelson Mandela:

"[W]e don't ask anyone to boycott Israel itself. We have relations with Israel, we have mutual recognition of Israel."

The leaders of the BDS campaign understand Abbas's point, but they persist in the demand for BDS. Some seem to be against a peaceful resolution of the Israeli-Palestinian dispute based on a two-state solution. The BDS campaign is not only directed against Israel's occupation of the West Bank. Judging from the rhetoric of some of its leaders, it is directed against the very existence of the state of Israel.

Abbas understands this. The BDS leaders understand this. Israeli leaders understand this. But some of the naive academics who sign onto BDS because they oppose Israel's settlement and occupation policies do not seem to understand this. BDS leaders exploit that confusion to lull ivory tower professors into thinking that by signing onto BDS they are demonstrating opposition to the occupation, rather than to Israel itself.

The BDS campaign places pressure on the Palestinian Authority to reject Israel's compromise peace offers, as the authority did in 2001 and 2008. Abbas understands that radical elements within his constituency play the BDS card as a way of pressuring him into seeking an unrealistically better deal. That is, a deal he will never get. The end result may well be a continuation of the untenable status quo.

This is not to deny that there are some within the BDS campaign, particularly those who would limit it to products and institutions on the West Bank (which Abbas would do), who honestly believe that the threat of BDS will push Israel toward changing its settlement policy and moving toward peace. They are simply wrong. Israel will never submit to the blackmail of BDS, and the Palestinians will never agree to a compromise peace if they erroneously believe that the pressure of BDS will force Israel into offering a better deal.

There is nothing good about the BDS campaign. It is hypocritical, for singling out the nation state of the Jewish people for BDS, while ignoring other occupations (such as those by Turkey, China, and Russia), as well as far worse violations of human rights and academic freedom, such as those committed by Cuba, Saudi Arabia, the Palestinian Authority, Russia, China, and nearly all the countries of Africa. It is ineffective, because its impact on Israel is minuscule and its impact on the Palestinian Authority is to make it more difficult for its leadership to accept a reasonable peace offer. It may also be illegal, since it discriminates on the basis of religion (it applies only to Jewish academics and business people in Israel, and not to Muslims), national origin, and ethnicity. Moreover, BDS constitutes collective punishment, since it targets Jewish Israelis who oppose Israel's settlement policies as well as those who favor them.

That is why so few world leaders and responsible individuals support BDS. That is why so many academic institutions, such as Harvard, condemn academic boycotts. That is why more than 10,000 American academics have signed a petition declaring themselves to be "Israelis" for purposes of any academic boycott against Israeli academics. BDS is largely a plaything of the hard left. It is an irresponsible gambit being promoted by irresponsible people who are more interested in being politically correct and feeling good than in helping to bring about a reasonable resolution to a complex problem, the fault for which is widely shared.

It is important, therefore, that opponents of this bigoted foolishness fight back. Dissenting members of academic organizations that support BDS should resign in protest. Colleges and universities should stop giving financial support to organizations that promote hypocritical and possibly illegal boycotts. Alumni should "divest" from any universities that divest from Israel, and peace-loving people should denounce those organizations and individuals who are hindering the peace process by promoting BDS.

While small ivory tower academic institutions debate BDS, Secretary of State John Kerry, Israeli Justice Minister Tzipi Livni, and Palestinian chief negotiator Saeb Erekat continue the hard work of trying to negotiate permanent borders for a Palestinian state, land swaps, a complex division of Jerusalem, a resolution of the double refugee problem (Palestinian refugees as well as Jewish refugees from Arab states), and security arrangements along the Jordan River. Some progress is in evidence. Let peace not be made more difficult by the leaders of the BDS campaign who oppose the two-state solution and by their naive followers who think they are doing good while actually violating the important principle of morality: "First, do no harm."[54]

March 11, 2014
Europe's Alarming Push to Isolate Israel

Why are so many of the grandchildren of Nazis and Nazi collaborators who brought us the Holocaust once again declaring war on the Jews?

Why have we seen such an increase in anti-Semitism and irrationally virulent anti-Zionism in western Europe?

To answer these questions, a myth must first be exposed. That myth is the one perpetrated by the French, the Dutch, the Norwegians, the Swiss, the Belgians, the Austrians, and many other western Europeans: namely, that the Holocaust was solely the work of German Nazis aided perhaps by some Polish, Ukrainian, Latvian, Lithuanian, and Estonian collaborators.

False.

The Holocaust was perpetrated by Europeans—by Nazi sympathizers and collaborators among the French, Dutch, Norwegians, Swiss, Belgians, Austrians, and other Europeans, both Western and Eastern.

If the French government had not deported to the death camps more Jews than their German occupiers asked for; if so many Dutch and Belgian citizens and government officials had not cooperated in the roundup of Jews; if so many Norwegians had not supported Quisling; if Swiss government officials and bankers had not exploited Jews; if Austria had not been more Nazi than the Nazis, the Holocaust would not have had so many Jewish victims.

In light of the widespread European complicity in the destruction of European Jewry, the pervasive anti-Semitism and irrationally hateful anti-Zionism that has recently surfaced throughout Western Europe toward Israel should surprise no one.

"Oh no," we hear from European apologists. "This is different. We don't hate the Jews. We only hate their nation-state. Moreover, the Nazis were right-wing. We're left-wing, so we can't be anti-Semites."

Nonsense.

The hard left has a history of anti-Semitism as deep and enduring as the hard right. The line from Voltaire, to Karl Marx, to Levrenti Beria, to Robert Faurisson, to today's hard-left Israel bashers is as straight as the line from Wilhelm Mars to the persecutors of Alfred Dreyfus to Hitler.

The Jews of Europe have always been crushed between the Black and the Red—victims of extremism whether it be the ultra-nationalism of Khmelnitsky to the ultra-anti-Semitism of Stalin.

"But some of the most strident anti-Zionists are Jews, such as Norman Finkelstein and even Israelis such as Gilad Atzmon. Surely they can't be anti-Semites."

Why not? Gertrude Stein and Alice Toklas collaborated with the Gestapo. Atzmon, a hard leftist, describes himself as a proud self-hating Jew and admits that his ideas derive from a notorious anti-Semite.

He denies that the Holocaust is historically proved but he believes that Jews may well have killed Christian children to use their blood to bake Passover matzah. And he thinks it's "rational" to burn down synagogues.

Finkelstein believes in an international Jewish conspiracy that includes Steven Spielberg, Leon Uris, Eli Wiesel, and Andrew Lloyd Webber!

"But Israel is doing bad things to the Palestinians," the European apologists insist, "and we are sensitive to the plight of the underdog."

No, you're not! Where are your demonstrations on behalf of the oppressed Tibetans, Georgians, Syrians, Armenians, Kurds, or even Ukrainians? Where are your BDS campaigns against the Chinese, the Russians, the Cubans, the Turks, or the Assad regime?

Only the Palestinians, only Israel? Why? Not because the Palestinians are more oppressed than these and other groups.

Only because their alleged oppressors are Jews and the nation-state of the Jews. Would there be demonstrations and BDS campaigns on behalf of the Palestinians if they were oppressed by Jordan or Egypt?

Oh, wait! The Palestinians were oppressed by Egypt and Jordan. Gaza was an open-air prison between 1948 and 1967, when Egypt was the occupying power. And remember Black September, when Jordan killed more Palestinians than Israel did in a century? I don't remember any demonstration or BDS campaigns—because there weren't any.

When Arabs occupy or kill Arabs, Europeans go ho-hum. But when Israel opens a soda factory in Ma'ale Adumim, which even the Palestinian leadership acknowledges will remain part of Israel in any peace deal, Oxfam parts ways with Scarlett Johansson for advertising a soda company that employs hundreds of Palestinians.

Keep in mind that Oxfam has provided "aid and material support" to two anti-Israel terrorist groups, according to the Tel Aviv-based Israeli Law Group.

The hypocrisy of so many hard-left Western Europeans would be staggering if it were not so predictable based on the sordid history of Western Europe's treatment of the Jews.

Even England, which was on the right side of the war against Nazism, has a long history of anti-Semitism, beginning with the expulsion of the Jews in 1290 to the notorious White Paper of 1939, which prevented the Jews of Europe from seeking asylum from the Nazis in British-mandated Palestine. And Ireland, which vacillated in the war against Hitler, boasts some of the most virulent anti-Israel rhetoric.

The simple reality is that one cannot understand the current Western European left-wing war against the nation-state of the Jewish people without first acknowledging the long-term European war against the Jewish people themselves.

Theodore Herzl understood the pervasiveness and irrationality of European anti-Semitism, which led him to the conclusion that the only solution to Europe's Jewish problem was for European Jews to leave that bastion of Jew hatred and return to their original homeland, which is now the state of Israel.

None of this is to deny Israel's imperfections or the criticism it justly deserves for some of its policies. But these imperfections and deserved criticism cannot even begin to explain, must less justify, the disproportionate hatred directed against the only nation-state of the Jewish people and the disproportionate silence regarding the far greater imperfections and deserved criticism of other nations and groups—including the Palestinians.

Nor is this to deny that many western European individuals and some Western European countries have refused to succumb to the hatred against the Jews or their state. The Czech Republic comes to mind. But far too many western Europeans are as irrational in their hatred toward Israel as their forbearers were in their hatred toward their Jewish neighbors.

As author Amos Oz once aptly observed: the walls of his grandparents' Europe were covered with graffiti saying, "Jews, go to Palestine." Now they say, "Jews, get out of Palestine"—by which is meant Israel.

Who do these Western European bigots think they're fooling? Only fools who want to be fooled in the interest of denying that they are manifesting new variations on their grandparents' old biases.

Any objective person with an open mind, open eyes, and an open heart must see the double standard being applied to the nation-state of the Jewish people. Many doing so are the grandchildren of those who lethally applied a double standard to the Jews of Europe in the 1930s and 1940s.

For shame!

October 21, 2014
Metropolitan Opera Stifles Free Exchange of Ideas About a Propaganda Opera

On Monday night I went to the Metropolitan Opera. I went for two reasons: to see and hear John Adams' controversial opera, *The Death of Klinghoffer*; and to see and hear what those protesting the Met's judgment in presenting the opera had to say. Peter Gelb, the head of the Met Opera, had advised people to see it for themselves and then decide.

That's what I planned to do. Even though I had written critically of the opera—based on reading the libretto and listening to a recording—I was also critical of those who wanted to ban or censor it. I wanted personally to experience all sides of the controversy and then "decide."

Lincoln Center made that difficult. After I bought my ticket, I decided to stand in the Plaza of Lincoln Center, across the street and in front of the protestors, so I could hear what they were saying and read what was on their signs. But Lincoln Center security refused to allow me to stand anywhere in the large plaza. They pushed me to the side and to the back, where I could barely make out the content of the protests. "Either go into the opera if you have a ticket or leave. No standing." When I asked why I couldn't remain in the large, open area between the protestors across the street and the opera house behind me, all I got were terse replies: "security," "Lincoln Center orders."

The end result was that the protestors were talking to and facing an empty plaza. It would be as if the Metropolitan Opera had agreed to produce *The Death of Klinghoffer*, but refused to allow anyone to sit in the orchestra, the boxes, or the grand tier. "Family circle, upstairs, side views only."

That's not freedom of expression, which requires not only that the speakers be allowed to express themselves, but that those who want to see and hear them be allowed to stand in an area in front of, and close to, the speakers, so that they can fully participate in the marketplace of ideas. That marketplace was needlessly restricted on the opening night of *The Death of Klinghoffer*.

Unable to see or hear the content of the protest, I made my way to the opera house where I first registered a protest with the Met's media person and then sat down in my fourth row seat to listen to and watch the opera.

I'm an opera fanatic, having been to hundreds of Met performances since my high school years. This was my third opera since the beginning of the season, just a few weeks ago. I consider myself something of an opera aficionado and "maven." I always applaud even flawed performances and mediocre operas. By any standard, *The Death of Klinghoffer* is anything but the "masterpiece" its proponents are claiming it is. The music is uneven, with some lovely choruses—more on that coming—one decent aria, and lots of turgid recitatives. The libretto is awful. The drama is confused and rigid, especially the weak device of the captain looking back at the events several years later with the help of several silent passengers. There are silly and distracting arias from a British show girl who seems to have had a crush on one of the terrorists, as well as from a woman who hid in her cabin eating grapes and chocolate. They added neither to the drama nor the music of the opera.

Then there were the choruses. The two that open the opera are supposed to demonstrate the comparative suffering of the displaced Palestinians and the displaced Jews. The Palestinian chorus is beautifully composed musically, with some compelling words, sung rhythmically and sympathetically. The Jewish chorus is a mishmash of whining about money, sex, betrayal, and assorted "Hasidism" protesting in front of movie theaters. It never mentions the six million Jews who were murdered in the Holocaust, though the chorus is supposed to be sung by its survivors. The goal of that narrative chorus is to compare the <u>displacement</u> of 700,000 Palestinians—some of which was caused by Arab leaders urging them to leave and return victoriously after the Arabs murdered the Jews of Israel—with the systematic genocide of six million Jews. It was a moral abomination.

And it got worse. The Palestinian murderer is played by a talented ballet dancer, who is portrayed sympathetically. A chorus of Palestinian women asks the audience to understand why he would be driven to terrorism. "We are not criminals," the terrorists assure us.

One of the terrorists—played by the only black lead singer—is portrayed as an overt anti-Semite, expressing hateful tropes against "the Jews." But he is not the killer. Nor, in this opera, is Klinghoffer selected for execution because he is a Jew. Instead, he is picked because he is a loudmouth who can't control his disdain for the Palestinian cause.

At bottom, *The Death of Klinghoffer*—a title deliberately selected to sanitize his brutal murder—is more propaganda than art. It has some artistic moments but the dominant theme is to create a false moral equivalence between terrorism and its victims, between Israel and Palestinian terrorist groups, and between the Holocaust and the self-inflicted Nakba. It is a mediocre opera by a good composer and a very bad librettist. But you wouldn't know that from the raucous standing ovations received not only by the performers and chorus master, who deserved them, but also by the composer, who did not. The applause was not for the art. Indeed, during the intermission and on the way out, the word I heard most often was "boring." The over-the-top standing ovations were for the "courage" displayed by all those involved in the production. But it takes little courage to be anti-Israel these days, or to outrage Jews. There were, to be sure, a few brief expressions of negative opinion during the opera, one of which was briefly disruptive, as an audience member repeatedly shouted "Klinghoffer's murder will never be forgiven." He was arrested and removed.

What would require courage would be for the Met to produce an opera that portrayed Mohammad, or even Yassir Arafat, in a negative way. The protests against such portrayals would not be limited to a few shouts, some wheelchairs, and a few hundred distant demonstrators. Remember the murderous reaction to a few cartoons several years ago.

November 10, 2014
How Amnesty International Suppresses Free Speech

Last month the Columbia University chapter of Amnesty International invited me to deliver a talk on human rights in the Middle East. I accepted the invitation, anxious to present a balanced view on human rights, focusing on the Israeli-Arab-Palestinian issue. As a supporter of the two-state solution and an opponent of many of Israel's settlement decisions, I regard myself as a moderate on these issues. That was apparently too much for the national office of Amnesty International to tolerate. They demanded that the Columbia chapter of Amnesty International disinvite me. They did not want their members to hear my perspective on human rights.

The excuse they provided were two old and out-of-context quotes suggesting that I favored torture and collective punishment. The truth is that I am adamantly opposed to both. I have written nuanced academic articles on the subject of torture warrants as a way of minimizing the evils of torture, and I have written vehemently against the use of collective punishment of innocent people—whether it be by means of the boycott campaign against all Israelis or the use of collective punishment against Palestinians. I do favor holding those who facilitate terrorism responsible for their own actions.

The real reasons Amnesty International tried to censor my speech to its members is that I am a Zionist who supports Israel's right to exist as the nation-state of the Jewish people. As such, I have been somewhat critical of Amnesty International's one-sided approach to the Israeli-Palestinian conflict. For example, I wrote an article criticizing Amnesty International's report on honor killings in the West Bank. An honor killing occurs when a woman has been raped and her family then kills her because of the shame her victimization has brought. Despite massive evidence to the contrary, Amnesty International mendaciously claimed that honor killings had increased in the West Bank since the Israeli occupation, and that the fault for this increase in Arab men killing Arab women lies with Israel. The reality is that there are far fewer honor killings in the West Bank than there are in adjoining Jordan, which is not under Israeli occupation, and that the number of honor killings in the West Bank has been reduced dramatically during the Israeli occupation. But facts mean little to Amnesty International when Israel is involved.

The national office of Amnesty International did not want their members to hear my criticisms of their organization, despite the fact that I was a strong supporter in its early days, before it became so one sided and anti-Israel. They were afraid to have their members hear the truth. They feared an open marketplace of ideas, so they tried to shut me down.

Fortunately, another Columbia student group immediately invited me to give my talk, and some members of Columbia Amnesty, to their credit, came to listen. They asked me hard questions, which I tried to answer with fact and logic. Some agreed with me, while others disagreed. That is the nature of open dialogue that Amnesty International claims to champion—except when it comes to their own organization, in which case it tries to censor speech critical of its policies.

In general, Amnesty International—especially its European branch located in London—has abandoned its commitment to human rights in preference for an overtly political and ideological agenda. Its position on the Israeli-Palestinian conflict has become particularly troubling. In addition to providing an abuse excuse to Palestinian honor killers in the West Bank, it has demonized Israel for its attempts to protect its citizens from Hamas war crimes. In a recent report, it condemns Israel for its military actions in Gaza without even mentioning the Hamas terror tunnels that provoked Israel's defensive actions. These tunnels—I was in one of them just before the war—were built for one purpose and one purpose only: to kill and kidnap Israeli citizens. The tunnel I was in exited right near an Israeli kindergarten with more than 50 children. The sole purpose of the tunnel was to send Hamas death squads into Israel to kill and kidnap as many of these children as possible.

No country in the world would tolerate the existence of such tunnels, and international law permits defensive actions to shut them down. Yet Amnesty International never mentions the tunnels and makes it seem that Israel sent troops into Gaza simply to kill as many Palestinians as possible.

Amnesty International has become an apologist for terrorism and an enemy of democracy. Its failed effort to stifle my free speech and the rights of Columbia students to listen to me is symbolic of what a once great organization has become: a cheerleader for human wrongs rather than human rights.

December 19, 2014
Harvard's President Stops an Anti-Israel Boycott

Harvard University Dining Services [HUDS] has been rebuffed in its efforts to join the boycott campaign against Israel. A group of radical anti-Israel Harvard students and faculty had persuaded the dining service to boycott Sodastream, an Israeli company that manufactures soda machines that produce a product that is both healthy and economical. But Harvard President Drew Faust rebuffed this boycott and decided to investigate the unilateral action of the Harvard University Dining Services.

I have visited the Sodastream factory and spoken to many of its Palestinian-Arab employees, who love working for a company that pays them high wages and provides excellent working conditions. I saw Jews and Muslims, Israelis and Palestinians, working together and producing this excellent product.

The Sodastream factory I visited is in Ma'ale Adumim—a suburb of Jerusalem that Palestinian Authority leaders acknowledge will remain part of Israel in any negotiated resolution of the conflict. I was told this directly by Palestinian president Mahmoud Abbas and by former Prime Minister Salam Fayyad. Moreover, in all the negotiations about borders and land swaps, the Palestinians have acknowledged that Ma'ale Adumim will remain within Israel's borders.

Accordingly, although the factory is in an area beyond the Armistice lines of 1949, it is not really disputed territory. Nor does it pose any barrier to a two-state solution. Moreover, Israel offered to resolve its conflict with the Palestinians in 2000–2001 and in 2008, but the Palestinian Authority did not accept either offer. Had these generous offers been accepted, the dispute would have ended and Ma'ale Adumim would have been recognized as part of Israel. So the Palestinian leadership shares responsibility for the continuation of the conflict and the unresolved status of the area in which Sodastream operates. Punishing only Israel—and Israeli companies—for not resolving the conflict serves only to disincentivize the Palestinian Authority from accepting compromise solutions.

The students and faculty who sought the boycott of Sodastream invoked human rights. But it is they who are causing the firing of more than 500 Palestinian workers who would like to continue to earn a living at Sodastream. As a result of misguided boycotts, such as the one unilaterally adopted by Harvard University Dining Services, Sodastream has been forced to move its factory to an area in Israel where few, if any, Arabs can be employed. This is not a victory for human rights. It is a victory for human wrongs.

I have no doubt that some students and other members of the Harvard community may be offended by the presence of Sodastream machines. Let them show their displeasure by not using the machines instead of preventing others who are not offended from obtaining their health benefits. Many students are also offended by their removal. Why should the views of the former prevail over those of the latter? I'm sure that some students are offended by any products made in Israel, just as some are offended by products made in Arab or Muslim countries that oppress gays, Christians, and women. Why should Harvard University Dining Services—or a few handfuls of students and professors—get to decide whose feelings of being offended count and whose don't?

In addition to the substantive error made by Harvard University Dining Services, there is also an important issue of process. What right does a single Harvard University entity have to join the boycott campaign against Israel without full and open discussion by the entire university community, including students, faculty, alumni and administration? Even the president and provost were unaware of this divisive decision until they read about it in the *Crimson*. As Provost Garber wrote:

"Harvard University's procurement decisions should not and will not be driven by individuals' views of highly contested matters of political controversy."

Were those who made the boycott decision even aware of the arguments on the other side, such as those listed above? The decision of the HUDS must be rescinded immediately and a process should be instituted for discussing this issue openly with all points of view and all members of the university community represented.

The end result should be freedom of choice: those who disapprove of Sodastream should be free to drink Pepsi. But those who don't disapprove should be free to drink Sodastream.

Economic boycotts should be reserved for the most egregious violations of human rights. They should not be used to put pressure on only one side of a dispute that has rights and wrongs on both sides.

December 27, 2014
Hard Leftists Are as Guilty of Censorship as North Korea's Dictator

Nobody should be surprised that the dictatorial ruler of North Korea would want to censor a film that offended him, or even that he would feel entitled to break the law by threatening reprisals against the offenders. His actions emulate those of hard-left feminists, radical Muslims, university administrators, and others who seek to prevent the publication or distribution of material they deem offensive.

I recall an incident several years ago when radical feminists fired bullets through the windows of a Harvard Square bookstore to protest its sale of *Playboy* magazine. I also recall being physically threatened by a group called "Dykes on Bikes"—a feminist motorcycle gang—for providing legal representation to alleged pornographers.

Then there is radical Islamic censorship that has become far more deadly. When some radical Muslims were offended by Theo van Gogh's film *Submission*, which exposed Islam's demeaning views toward women, van Gogh was murdered in cold blood and his co-producer's life threatened by a *fatwa*. Salman Rushdie had to go into hiding when a *fatwa* was issued against him and his book *The Satanic Verses*. Yale University Press, fearful of threats of violence, censored the actual cartoons depicting Mohammed from a book about that subject, following violent reactions to the publication of the cartoons in Scandinavia.

More recently, radical anti-Israel students tried to get SodaStream products banned from Harvard dining halls, because they were offended by the "micro-aggression" represented by the location of the company's factory beyond Israel's Green Line[55]. So instead of simply not drinking the product themselves, they tried to prevent everyone else from drinking it or even seeing its name!

Hard-left students, and even some on the soft left, have tried to ban sexist jokes and offensive classroom discussion on university campuses. Speech codes on many campuses are designed to prevent students from being offended by the comments of others.

The national office of Amnesty International recently rescinded an invitation I had received from the Columbia University branch of the organization because they were offended by some of my views. And several universities, including Brandeis, rescinded offers of honorary degrees from proposed recipients because some students regarded their views as offensive. Other deserving candidates have been passed over for fear of offending some.

We live in an age in which censoring material that is deemed offensive by some is becoming widely accepted, especially among young people on the left.

There are, of course, major differences between using criminal means (violence, hacking, threats) and using arguably lawful means (speech codes, rescinding invitations) to achieve the censorship of offending material, but the results may be similar: self-censorship.

In my book *Taking the Stand: My Life in the Law*, published last year, I predicted that "self-censorship that results from fear of violent responses" will give "those who threaten violence an effective veto over what can be published in the United States." Unfortunately, events since I wrote those words have confirmed their accuracy.

So why are we surprised when a foreign dictator tries to achieve what mainstream Americans—and indeed mainstream leftists around the globe—are trying to achieve: namely the "right" to be free from being offended.

This alleged "right" is, of course, in direct conflict with the most basic of rights in any democracy: the right to express views deemed offensive by some, and the corollary right to hear or see such views.

There are at least two ways a person can be offended by freedom of expression. The first is by actually having to read the offending book or see the offending film. In totalitarian dictatorships, citizens are indeed required to read and see what the dictator wants them to be exposed to. Not so in democracies, where we are free to choose our book and films.

The second is by simply knowing that others, who are not offended, may choose to read or see the offending work.

The first has a simple solution: don't read the book; don't see the movie; change the channel; drink Pepsi instead of SodaStream.

The second way has no legitimate claim to acceptance in a diverse democracy. Citizen A should not be able to prevent Citizen B from reading or seeing something that would offend Citizen A if he were required to read or see it.

There are also cases in which the material in question reveals private information about Citizen A or portrays him or her in an unsavory light. In those cases, there are appropriate legal remedies—such as the law of defamation—for those who are harmed by what others read about them. Beyond that, being offended should never be the basis for censoring.

So if we really want any right to de-legitimize what the North Korean dictator is ostensibly trying to do to us, we should begin at home: by de-legitimizing the efforts of our own citizens to censor material that they find offensive.

December 28, 2014
A Brandeis Student Refuses to Show Sympathy for Assassinated Policemen— and Her Critic Is Attacked

As I watched, with tears in my eyes, the funeral of police officer Rafael Ramos who was ambushed along with fellow officer, Wenjian Liu, in revenge for the deaths of two black young men who were killed by policemen, I could not help thinking of the following horrible words tweeted by a bigoted young woman named Khadijah Lynch, on the day the police officers were murdered in cold blood, and the day after:

"i have no sympathy for the nypd officers who were murdered today." (December 20, 2014) "lmao, all i just really dont have sympathy for the cops who were shot. i hate this racist f...ing country." (December 21, 2014)

Khadijah Lynch is a Brandeis University junior who at the time she wrote the tweet was the undergraduate representative in the Brandeis African and Afro-American studies department.

Nor was this her first bigoted tweet. She has apparently described her college as "a social themed institution grounded in Zionism. Word. That a f...ing fanny dooly." And she cannot understand why "black people have not burned this country down...." She describes herself as "in riot mode. F... this f...ing country." She has apparently said that she would like to get a gun and has called for an intifada: "Amerikkka needs an intifada. Enough is enough." "What the f... even IS 'non-violence.'"

Ms. Lynch is certainly entitled to express such despicable views, just as Nazis, Klansmen, and other bigots are entitled to express theirs. But when another Brandeis student, named Daniel Mael, decided to post her public tweets on a website, Lynch threatened to sue him for "slander." Republishing someone's own published words could not possibly constitute slander, libel, or any other form of defamation, because you can't be slandered by your own words. You can, of course, be embarrassed, condemned, ostracized, or "unfriended" due your own words, as Donald Sterling, the former owner of the LA Clippers, was. But Sterling's bigoted words were never intended to be public, whereas Lynch's tweets were publicly circulated.

People, even students, are responsible for the words they write, speak or tweet in public. They should not be able to hide behind absurd claims of slander. Moreover, other students have the right to know that one of their classmates is advocating intifada against America and is considering getting a gun. They are entitled to have this information in order to judge the character of those with whom they associate. Lynch has now apparently made her Twitter profile private, which may be even more dangerous because she can continue to express her incendiary views to those who support them, without others being made aware of her dangerous advocacy.

Mael had the right—and was right—to expose Lynch's words for public assessment and criticism. Now hard left students at Brandeis are calling for Mael's head—or at least, his expulsion—

for exercising <u>his</u> freedom of expression. He has been accused of "stalking," "cyberbullying," and "inciting racial hatred and oppression" for merely republishing what Lynch published.

The most remarkable statement came from the Brandeis Asian American Society. One of the assassinated officers was Asian American. Yet the Asian American Society "stands by" Lynch, who in their view has been "wrongfully targeted and harassed" for essentially expressing lack of sympathy for the two assassinated police officers. They asserted Lynch's right to speak freely—a right no one has disputed—but not Mael's right to republish her tweets, which is also a form of free expression.

So welcome to the topsy-turvy world of the academic hard left, where bigoted speech by fellow hard leftists is protected, but counter-expression is labeled as "embarrassment," "incitement," and "bullying."

I hope Brandeis will do the right thing this time, as it certainly did not do when it caved to hard left pressures to withdraw an honorary degree from Ayaan Hirsi Ali. Free speech for me but not for thee cannot become the operative motto of a great university. There is every indication that Brandeis will be according protection to Mael and defending his freedom of expression, and that it will guarantee the safety of all of its students against other students who go beyond advocacy of violence and try to bring guns onto the campus. I would hope that Brandeis would also express opposition to the kind of bigotry expressed by Khadijah Lynch and those who support her views.

January 12, 2015
Prager University: Are Israeli Settlements the Barrier to Peace?

Is Israel's policy of building civilian communities in the area known as the West Bank the reason there is no permanent peace between Israel and the Palestinians?

The answer to that question, despite all the sound and fury regarding the so-called settlement issue, is no.

The Israeli settlements in the West Bank are not the major barrier to a peace agreement.

A little historical context will make this clear.

For two decades before June 1967, the West Bank, including much of Jerusalem, was controlled by Jordan. During that time—a time when Israel did not have a single settlement—there were numerous Palestinian terror attacks against the nation state of the Jewish people. In other words, Palestinians committed terror attacks against Israel when there were no settlements and they committed terror attacks against Israel when there were settlements. If Israel were to pull out of every single settlement in the West Bank tomorrow, it's unlikely that anything much would change. In fact, if history is any indicator, Israel could be worse off.

In 2005, Israel abandoned every single community, every house, every farm, every structure it had built in the Gaza Strip. How did the Palestinians of Gaza react? They launched thousands of rockets and numerous other terror attacks against the nation state of the Jewish people. The attacks continue to this very day. And every year the range of these rockets get longer and their payloads more lethal. Only a very sophisticated Israeli anti-missile defense keeps the country secure. Can you blame Israel for not wanting to risk a two-front rocket war?

But Israel has no right to be in the West Bank at all, many say. So, permit me, a law professor at Harvard, to say that on the basis of international law this position is incorrect.

Military occupations are clearly permitted under international law following an aggressive attack by a neighboring state. Jordan, Israel's neighbor to the east, attacked Israel in 1967, despite Israel's repeated efforts to keep Jordan out of the Six Day War.

In defending itself against Jordan, Israel captured the West Bank and the eastern part of Jerusalem. Under international law, until a meaningful peace is achieved and all terrorism against it ceases, Israel has every right to retain military control over this area. Since no peace treaty has been reached and the terrorism continues with new attacks threatened almost daily, Israel is under no legal obligation to leave. Given the danger that Israel would be putting itself in if it did leave the West Bank—exposing its major cities and international airport to rocket attacks—it would be irresponsible to do so, which is why Israel is still there.

Nevertheless, I fully acknowledge that a military occupation is significantly different, both as a matter of law and politics, from building civilian settlements even in a territory that is legitimately subject to a military occupation. That's why I have long opposed the building of settlements in the West Bank. I believe it has caused resentment and has given enemies of Israel an excuse to attack the legitimacy of the occupation in general.

It is also why I have always supported Israel's efforts to exchange land for peace as it has done on multiple occasions over the last few decades. So, while the settlements may have contributed to the difficulty of making peace, it has not been the major barrier that Israel's enemies claim it to be. It is not the reason there has been no peace agreement between Israel and the Palestinians. The reason has always been and remains the unwillingness of Palestinian leaders—and, according to Palestinian polls, much of the Palestinian population—to recognize Israel's right to exist as the nation state of the Jewish people. Until and unless the Palestinian leadership and the Palestinian people acknowledge that the State of Israel has the right to be free from military assault, from terrorism from rocket attacks, and from diplomatic warfare, there will be no resolution to the Middle East dispute.

If these conditions, which must be the basis of any two-state solution, meaning a nation state for the Jewish people and a Palestinian state, are met, the occupation will end, the settlement issue will be resolved, and the blessings of a mutual peace will finally be achieved.

January 12, 2015
Brandeis University: Both Pro-Israel and Pro-Free Speech

Brandeis University, like many other academic institutions, is experiencing a wave of vicious, irrational, and extremist hatred of Israel, the nation state of the Jewish people, and Zionism, which is the national liberation movement of the Jewish people. On many campuses, anti-Israel zealots among the faculty often misuse the classroom to promote bigotry, hate speech, and extremism. Much of their venom is directed not only against Israel, but also against Western democratic values, and especially the United States. These hateful attitudes often influence young students who identify with popular radical professors. Sometimes the students come to the university with these views already formed.

Based on my experience, I believe that the numbers of faculty and students who express such views are relatively small, but their influence exceeds their numbers because they often speak more openly and loudly than those who support Western values, the United States, and Israel. On some university campuses, student groups such as Students for Justice in Palestine are well funded by questionable sources and have the resources to magnify their views.

None of this is surprising, since universities have often been the focal points of radical groups, both left and right. What surprises many is that Brandeis University has joined the ranks of academic institutions with a small but significant number of faculty and students who hate Israel, America, and Western values. Brandeis was the first university in America to be established under Jewish auspices. Though it is not a religious school or a school with institutional affiliations to Jewish organizations, it has always proudly reflected its Jewish heritage. Its motto is the Hebrew word "*emet*," which means "truth." Its founding generation consisted largely of American Zionists, some of whom played active roles in the establishment of Israel. The university is named after the most prominent Zionist in American history, Justice Louis Brandeis.

So when the name Brandeis is in the news, associated with vocal faculty or students who express anti-Israel bigotry, it comes as a shock to many. Some mistake the individual views of some faculty and students with the institutional views of the university. Moreover, in addition to Brandeis's commitment to specifically Jewish and Zionist values, it is also long been committed to universal principles of academic freedom, open inquiry and the marketplace of ideas.

Enter Fred Lawrence, Brandeis's current president, who is both a deeply committed Jewish Zionist, and a constitutional scholar deeply committed to free expression, academic freedom, and the open exchange of ideas. His unwillingness to censor rabidly anti-

Zionist speech—speech with which he fundamentally disagrees—has sometimes been misunderstood as placing Brandeis's imprimatur, or brand, on such expression. Nothing could be further from the truth.

Hateful speech against Israel, America, and Western values must be responded to in the marketplace of ideas. It cannot be defeated by the censor. It must win the battle for the minds and hearts of open-minded students and faculty.

President Lawrence has a difficult job, but in my view, he is doing it well. Reasonable people can disagree with specific decisions, such as the withdrawal of an honorary doctorate from Ayaan Hirsi Ali. I do. But that was not so much a matter of free speech—she was not prevented from expressing her views on the campus. It was a question of whom the university should honor. With regard to other issues, President Lawrence has expressed strong personal support for Israel and Zionism while defending the rights of those who disagree with him to express contrary views.

There are few more difficult jobs today than being a university president. They must balance so many conflicting principles and values. President Lawrence has tried hard to strike the appropriate balance under challenging circumstances. In my view, both he and the university have done a commendable job.

Brandeis, as an institution, remains deeply committed to the Jewish and Zionist principles of its founders and namesake. It has close connections to Israel. It presents a safe environment for supporters, detractors and critics of both Israel and its enemies.

As an institution, and through the words and deeds of its president, Brandeis University is supportive of the nation state of the Jewish people. I would be both proud and comfortable sending my own children and grandchildren to Brandeis University, knowing that they will have a safe and intellectually challenging experience, in an environment supportive of Jewish, Zionist and free speech values.

[Addendum: As a result of mounting pressure over the free speech debate, Fred Lawrence was forced out of his position in May 2015. Ron Leibowitz took over as president of Brandeis University in the summer of 2016.]

January 23, 2015
The Case Against the International Criminal Court Investigating Israel

In 2012, my friend and colleague, Luis Moreno Ocampo, who was then the Chief Prosecutor of the International Criminal Court ruled correctly that "Palestine could not be recognized as a 'State.'" He now appears to agree with his successor's conclusion that "Palestine could now join the Rome statute," presumably as a state. I respectfully disagree.

How can an entity become a state, for purposes of joining the ICC, without boundaries? The assumption seems to be that the pre-June 1967 armistice lines now constitute the de jure, if not the de facto, boundaries of the Palestinian state, despite the reality that even the Palestinian authority seems to understand that there will never be a return to those artificial boundaries. If the Palestinian "state," as accepted by the Rome statute, were to be defined by the pre-1967 truce lines, it would follow that the Western Wall and its plaza, Judaism's most sacred area, is "occupied territory" and any Israeli who moved into that area would be a war criminal, as would Israeli leaders who allowed Israeli Jews to pray at this holy place. The same would be true of Hebrew University, on Mt. Scopus, because its access road was captured by Jordan during Israel's war of independence and was thus not a de facto part of Israel before June 1967. Likewise with the Jewish quarter of Jerusalem, in which Jews have lived for thousands of years, but which was captured and viciously destroyed by Jordan during the 1948 war. The same is true of Gilo, Ma'ale Adumin, and other suburbs of Jerusalem, which Palestinian leaders have long acknowledged would remain part of Israel in any negotiated resolution, despite being beyond the Green Line. Moreover, land swaps, which will be part of any negotiated solution, would make some areas that are now part of pre-1967 Israel, part of a Palestinian state, and some areas that are now outside the Green Line, part of Israel. These shifting boundaries pose an especially daunting problem in the context of Palestinian claims—which they have vowed to bring to the ICC—that it is a war crime to allow Israelis to live in occupied areas, when so many areas of alleged occupation are disputed, fluid, and subject to future land swaps. Moreover Resolution 242 of the Security Council contemplated that Israel would retain some—though how much was never decided—of the land it lawfully captured in the defensive war against Jordan in 1967.

These practical problems simply illustrate the difficulties of recognizing a "state" that has no agreed upon boundaries and whose ultimate borders will be shifting in the future if peace is to be achieved. It is not even clear whether the Palestinian state currently encompasses the Gaza Strip, which has not been contiguous with the West Bank since the UN proposed the division of what remained of British Mandatory Palestine after the creation of Jordan. Gaza is now under the de facto control of Hamas, which is widely regarded as a terrorist group lacking any semblance of legality or any commitment to the rule of law. Would leaders of the Palestinian Authority in the West Bank be held legally culpable for the terrorist acts of Hamas, even though they have no control over what occurs in Gaza? Would Hamas military commanders be held accountable even if they refuse to recognize the authority of ICC over them?

In addition to the practical problems that would be posed by recognizing a "Palestine" without boundaries as a "state," there are important technical and legal reasons why the recent symbolic actions of several parliaments and the UN General Assembly do not change the legal status of what was correctly deemed a non-state as recently as 2012. Several of the "recognitions" adopted by national parliaments were not accepted by their government and were conditional on a negotiated resolution in the future. So, too, the General Assembly's recognition. The issue of what constitutes a state involves more than symbolic, contingent, or aspirational votes designed more for domestic political considerations than serious diplomatic and legal consequences.

Beyond these practical and technical reasons for not recognizing Palestine at this time are the moral considerations. Israel accepted, and the Palestinians rejected, the two-state solution in 1938 and 1948. It offered land for peace in 1967, only to be greeted with the three "nos": no peace, no negotiation, and no recognition. It offered generous proposals in 2000–2001, 2008, and most recently in 2014, none of which was accepted. To now reward this intransigence with unilateral recognition is both immoral and not conducive to a negotiated peace. If the Palestinians believe they can secure unilateral recognition without negotiation and compromise, they will have less of an incentive to accept a negotiated compromise resolution.

Moreover, regardless of Ocampo's good faith belief that the Palestinian decision to bring Israeli leaders before the ICC "should not be construed as an assault on Israel," that is surely how the Palestinian leadership construes it, referring to this "card" as a "weapon." And it is a weapon, because it seeks to create a false moral equivalence between a vibrant democracy that is governed by the rule of law; and a loose assortment of groups—Fatah, Hamas, Islamic Jihad, and others—that do not accept the results of elections, that murder dissenters with no semblance of due process, and that allow their official media organs to incite violence against civilians based on their religion. It also seeks to create a false moral equivalence between an army that seeks to defend its civilians from rocket attacks, suicide bombers, and terror tunnels and a terrorist group that murders civilians in their beds, kidnaps and kill children, and targets civilians from behind human shields.

It is telling that Hamas has expressed satisfaction with the decision of the ICC to open an investigation of Israel's military action during the recent war in Gaza. The hypocrisy of a terrorist group that boasts of its multiple war crimes expressing satisfaction that the victims of these war crimes are being investigated for trying to stop rocket and tunnel attacks, should be evident to any reasonable person.

More significant is the response of the U.S., which issued the following statement, "We strongly disagree with the ICC prosecutor's action. The place to resolve the differences between the parties is through direct negotiation, not unilateral actions by either side."

Ocampo acknowledges that the principle of "complementarity" precludes an ICC investigation of Israel unless "there are no genuine national investigations of the crimes committed under its jurisdiction." I am familiar with the Israeli legal system and its mechanisms for investigating alleged war crimes. There is no country in the world with a legal system that is more responsive to claims made by victims of war crimes. At the apex of the Israeli legal system is its Supreme Court, which is widely admired by lawyers around the world. If it were to be ruled that the Israeli legal system does not provide the required complementarity to deny the ICC institution jurisdiction as "a court of last resort," then no nation would pass that test. The United States will never, and should never, submit itself to the jurisdiction of an international court that does not regard the Israeli legal system as a satisfactory fulfillment of the principle of complementarity.

On balance, the decision to open an investigation against Israel at this time will harm prospects for a peaceful resolution of the conflict and will harm the credibility of the ICC. It is a serious mistake and should be rescinded.[56]

January 30, 2015
Confronting European Anti-Semitism

I just completed a three-day visit to Prague and the former Terezin concentration camp. I was there to speak at a conference commemorating the 70th anniversary of the liberation of the Nazi death camps. Many European speakers talked about the efforts they are making to confront the rising tide of anti-Semitism throughout Europe. But before one can decide how to confront a sickness like anti-Semitism, one must first describe and diagnose the pathology.

There are several distinct, but sometimes overlapping, types of anti-Semitism. The first is traditional, right wing, fascist Jew hatred that has historically included theological, racial, economic, social, personal, and cultural aspects. We are seeing a resurgence of this today in Greece, Hungary, and other European countries with rising right-wing parties that are anti-Muslim as well as anti-Jewish.

The second is Muslim anti-Semitism. Just as not all Greeks and Hungarians are anti-Semitic, so too, not all Muslims suffer from this malady. But far too many do. It is wrong to assume that only Muslims who manifest Jew hatred through violence harbor anti-Semitic views. Recent polls show an extraordinarily high incidence of anti-Semitism—hatred of Jews as individuals, as a group, and as a religion—throughout North Africa, the Middle East, and Muslim areas in Europe. This hatred manifests itself not only in words, but in deeds, such as taunting Jews who wear yarmulkes, vandalizing Jewish institutions, and occasional violence directed at individual Jews. Among a small number of extremists, it also results in the kind of deadly violence we have seen in Toulouse, Paris, Brussels, and other parts of Europe. Several decades ago it manifested itself in attacks on synagogues by Palestinian terrorists, including some operating on behalf of the Palestine Liberation Organization.

Third, there is hard left anti-Zionism that sometimes melds into subtle and occasionally overt anti-Semitism. This pathology is seen in the double standard imposed on everything Jewish, including the nation state of the Jewish people. It is also reflected in blaming "Jewish power," and the "pushiness" of Jews in demanding support for Israel. I'm not referring to criticism of Israeli policies or actions. I'm referring to the singling out of Israel for extreme demonization. The ultimate form of this pathology is the absurd comparison made by some extreme leftist between the extermination policies of the Nazis and of Israel's efforts to defend itself against terrorist rockets, tunnels, suicide bombers, and other threats to its civilians. Comparing Israel's actions to those of the Nazis is a not-so-subtle version of Holocaust denial. Because if all the Nazis really did was what Israel is now doing, there could not have been a Holocaust or an attempt at genocide against the Jewish people. A variation on this perverse theme is apartheid denial: by accusing Israel—which accords equal rights to all its citizens—of apartheid, these haters deny the horrors of actual apartheid, which was so much more horrible than anything Israel has ever done.

Fourth, and most dangerous, is eliminationist anti-Zionism and anti-Semitism of the kind advocated by the leaders of Iran, Hezbollah, Hamas, and ISIS. Listen to Hassan Nasrallah:

> *"If [the Jews] all gather in Israel, it will save us the trouble of going after them worldwide"* or *"If we search the entire world for a person more cowardly, despicable, weak and feeble in psyche, mind, ideology and religion, we would not find anyone like the Jew. Notice I didn't say the Israeli."*

These variations on the theme of anti-Semitism have several elements in common. First, they tend to engage in some form of Holocaust denial, minimization, glorification, or comparative victimization. Second, they exaggerate Jewish power, money, and influence. Third, they seek the de-legitimation and demonization of Israel as the nation state of the Jewish people. Fourth, they impose a double standard on all things Jewish.

Finally, they nearly all deny that they are anti-Semites who hate all Jews. They claim that their hatred is directed against Israel and Jews who support the nation state of the Jewish people.

This common form of the new anti-Semitism—we love the Jews, it's only their nation state that we hate—is pervasive among many European political, media, cultural, and academic leaders. It was evident even among some who came to commemorate the liberation of the death camps. A recent poll among Germans showed a significant number of the children, grandchildren, and great-grandchildren of Nazi supporters didn't want to hear about Nazi atrocities, but believed what Israel was doing to the Palestinians was comparable to what the Nazis had done to the Jews.

This, then, is the European problem of anti-Semitism that many European leaders are unwilling to confront because they have a built-in excuse! It's Israel's fault—if only Israel would do the right thing with regard to the Palestinians, the problem would be solved.

Tragically, it won't be solved, because the reality is that hatred of Israel is not the cause of anti-Semitism. Rather, it is the reverse: anti-Semitism is a primary cause of hatred for the nation state of the Jewish people.

February 23, 2015
Prager University: Israel's Legal Founding

Of all the countries that have come into existence in the last century, no country's birth certificate is more legitimate than that of Israel. One reason is that many of the men who founded the country—Theodore Herzl, Ze'ev Jabotinosky, David Ben Gurion,

Menecham Begin, and Yitchak Shamir—were either lawyers or had legal training. They were obsessed with "making it legal."

Unlike almost every other country, lawyers, not generals, were the midwives of Israel's birth—or more accurately re-birth, since it had existed as an independent country twice before in history.

Step by legal step Israel moved legally toward nationhood—from the Balfour Declaration in 1917, to the San Remo Agreement in 1920, the League of Nations Resolution in 1922, to the Anglo-American Convention on Palestine in 1924, to the partition of land ordained by the United Nations in 1947, into a nation state for the Jewish people and an Arab state.

Yet, immediately upon its lawful establishment in 1948 as the nation state of the Jewish people, Israel was illegally attacked by all the surrounding Arab states as well as by elements of the local Arab population. In defending its right to exist during that war, Israel lost one percent of its population, including many civilians and Holocaust survivors. It also lost some of the land assigned to it by the United Nations. It captured other land from the aggressors that was originally assigned to the Arab state. The end result of that war against Israel was an armistice line that prevailed until 1967, when Israel was once again attacked by Jordan during Israel's war with Egypt and Syria.

Between 1948 and 1967, despite the armistice, Arab terrorists continued to infiltrate Israeli borders and to injure and kill Israeli citizens. This was part of an official policy by the surrounding governments and by leaders of local Palestinian groups. All of it was in obvious violation of international law.

Following the establishment of Israel, a transfer of populations occurred. Several hundred thousand Arabs who fled from Israel during the War of Independence were not allowed to return. Some had chosen to leave, assured by their Arab leaders that the fledging country would not last a week. Others were forced to leave. At that time, approximately the same number of Jews were forced to leave Arab countries—another violation of international law—where they had lived for thousands of years. The difference was that Arab countries kept the Arabs who left Israel in refugee camps, where many of them still live more than half a century after leaving Israel. And Israel, on the other hand, fully integrated all the Jewish refugees from Arab countries into Israeli society, where many of their descendants now serve in the highest positions of Israeli life.

Israel's establishment as the nation state of the Jewish people by entirely lawful means is quite remarkable for several reasons. First, there is no country in the world that is as surrounded by hostile enemies as is Israel. It's been that way since 1948. Yet Israel sought the way of the pen rather than of the sword. It has needed the sword to survive. But its preference has always been for the pen, that is, for peaceful negotiations. Its peace treaty with Egypt in 1978, its peaceful abandonment of Gaza in 2005, and its many attempts to reach a peace agreement with the Palestinians are examples.

Yet despite its entirely lawful origins, Israel is the only country in the world today whose origins—and therefore its very legitimacy—have been questioned by the General Assembly of the United Nations, by numerous member nations, and by many organizations that claim the mantle of human rights and the rule of law. Ironically, current attacks on Israel's legitimacy have taken the form of "lawfare"—the use of international law as a weapon. Any fair tribunal that judged Israel by universal standards would reject such attacks out of hand. But, alas, international courts, like the UN itself, have been packed by those bitterly antagonistic to the nation state of the Jewish people. For example, the misnamed International Court of Justice refuses to acknowledge that Israel, a country that deals with terror attacks and the threats of terror attacks on a regular basis, has any special security needs.

As I've demonstrated, this phenomenon—questioning the very right of Israel to exist as the nation-state of the Jewish people—cannot be explained on legal grounds or on any other rational basis, for that matter.

So, then, how can this worldwide attack on Israel alone be explained? In only one way: It is pure bigotry. And there's a word for this bigotry. Anti-Semitism.

If you have a better explanation for why the one country in the world whose right to exist is denied is also the one country that is the nation state of the Jewish people, I ask you, what is it?

March 20, 2015
Guess Who's Not Speaking at the J Street Conference?

J Street—the lobby group that claims to be "pro-Israel" and "pro-peace"—is anything but "open" to centrist views that are critical of its policies. It has invited several prominent anti-Israel speakers to address its national conference, including Saeb Erekat, one of the Palestinian Authority's chief negotiators, who has repeatedly accused Israel of war crimes and committing massacres in the West Bank. It has also invited speakers who are generally pro-Israel but who strongly oppose the current Israeli government. The one group of pro-Israel advocates who never get invited to J Street conferences are those of us who are somewhat critical of J Street, particularly with regard to its policies toward Iran and other issues involving Israel's security. I know this because I have repeatedly sought an opportunity to address the J Street conference. I have personally implored Jeremy Ben-Ami, the head of J Street, either to allow me to address the conference, or to sit down with me for a public conversation in front of the group's members. He has adamantly refused. We have publicly debated and discussed our differences in front of non-J Street audiences, but he has never allowed me to engage him in the marketplace of ideas in front of his own followers.

This is more than ironic. It is hypocritical, especially in light of J Street's demands that other organizations, such as Hillel and AIPAC, be open to speakers who are critical of Israel. What's good for Hillel and AIPAC, is apparently not good for J Street—at least by J Street's own standards.

Why then is J Street so determined to deny its members the opportunity to hear divergent views from center-leftists like me? Because its leaders are afraid that if I were allowed to address its conference, I would tell its members the truth about J Street—a truth they try hard to conceal, particularly from college students who are lured into the J Street fold under false pretenses. The key to J Street's success in increasing its membership rolls is its ability to speak out of both sides of its mouth. To those on the hard left, it offers anti-Israel and pro-BDS speakers support for the mendacious Goldstone Report, and opposition to keeping the military option on the table as a last resort in preventing Iran from developing nuclear weapons.

To the soft left, it focuses on its opposition to Israeli settlements and its support for a two-state solution—positions with which I and many supporters of Israel agree. But it hides its controversial, hard left positions that endanger Israel's security—positions with which most supporters of Israel disagree. It also hides the financial support it has received from anti-Zionists such as George Soros, as well as the anti-Zionist statements made by some of its founders and activists.

Two summers ago, I spoke to a mixed group of pro- and anti-J Street people in the Martha's Vineyard Hebrew Center. When I read from some of J Street's positions on Israel's security, some of the J Street supporters were shocked. They were unaware that J Street has expressed opposition to any use of military force against Iran, even as a last resort in preventing Iran from developing or even deploying nuclear weapons. This is even weaker than the position of the Obama administration, which has refused to take the military option off the table, if all other options fail to stop Iran's quest for nuclear weapons.

Without distinguishing between an Israeli and an American military attack, J Street mendaciously claims that "top Israeli security experts and former officials warned about the inefficacy and disastrous consequences of a military strike against Iran's nuclear facilities" and that "many in the American and Israeli intelligence and security establishments believe that a strike on Iran would fail to end Iran's nuclear program and may even accelerate it...."

While this may be true of a unilateral *Israeli* strike, it is untrue of an *American* or *joint* attack, which many of these experts acknowledge would wreak havoc on the Iranian nuclear weapons program. Many of these same experts have explicitly called for the United States to maintain its military option as a last resort. But J Street, on its website, expressly "oppose[s] legislation authorizing, encouraging or in other ways laying the groundwork for the use of military force against Iran."[57] Such legislation refers exclusively to an *American*, not an Israeli, attack. But *"laying the groundwork for the use of military force against Iran" by the United States* is precisely what is needed to deter Iran from going forward with its nuclear weapons program, regardless of whether or not a deal is struck. By credibly laying such groundwork, the United States reduces the chances that it will actually need to employ its military option. By undercutting the threat of employing the military option, J Street increases the likelihood that it will have to be used.

J Street, in addition to undercutting mainstream Israeli and American policy toward Iran, has also mischaracterized the views of those it cites in support of its position, including former Mossad chiefs Meir Dagan and Efraim Halevy. It cites these two Israeli security experts as opposing an *American* strike and an *American* threat to strike. Both Dagan and Halevy have repeatedly said, however, that the American military option "must always be on the table." Indeed, the vast majority of Israeli security experts, as well the Israeli public, wants the United States to maintain the military threat against Iran. J Street, which purports to be pro-Israel, wants the United States to eliminate that deterrent military threat. But many centrist J Street members are not aware of this hard-left position because its leadership will not allow critics of this and other J Street positions to tell its members the truth.

Finally, J Street is now calling for an end to bipartisan political support for the government of Israel, telling Democrats, including the woman at "the forefront" of the Democratic Party that "everyone is now going to have to pick a side."

So I call for "open J Street." Let its members hear all sides of the issues, not only those carefully screened and vetted by its leaders.

May 28, 2015
Universities Should Be Unsafe for Political Correctness

The current code word being tossed around to protect political correctness from competition in the marketplace of ideas is "unsafe."

"I feel unsafe" has become the argument stopper on many university campuses. Efforts have been made to shut down controversial events or speakers, some of which have succeeded, at

MIT, the University of Michigan, Northeastern University, Oxford, Hampshire College, Smith College, and other great universities, on the grounds that students would feel "unsafe." Students must, of course, be and feel physically safe in their dorms, classrooms, and campuses. That's what university and city police are for: to protect against physical assaults and threats. But no one on a university campus should be or feel safe or protected when it comes to the never-ending war of ideas.

An important role of a university is to challenge every idea, every truth, every sacred notion, even if challenge makes students (or faculty) feel intellectually uncomfortable, unsettled, or unsafe. There must be no safe spaces in the classroom or auditorium that protect members of the university community from dangerous, disturbing, or even emotionally unsettling ideas.

There can be rules of civility that prevent shouting down opposing views, but these rules must be content-neutral, applicable in equal measure to politically correct and politically incorrect speech. Universities must not have acceptable ideas that are given greater protection that unacceptable ones. All ideas must compete on an equal footing in open marketplaces.

But what about ideas that really do make certain individuals or groups feel intellectually or emotionally unsafe—ideas such as opposition to gay marriage, to a woman's right to choose abortion, to race-based affirmative action, to religion in general or to particular religions or religious practices, to Zionism or anti-Zionism? It is especially these unpopular ideas—some of which were quite popular in the recent past—that today need protection against the forces of political correctness that seek to stifle dissent in the name of safety.

So long as there is no realistic, imminent threat to physical safety—such as an incitement to commit violence against gays, women, blacks, Jews, and so forth—the university must assure the safety of the politically incorrect speaker, student, faculty member, administrator, or employee. The answer to bad speech must be good speech; the response to false ideas must be true ideas; the protection against dangerous ideas is effective rebuttal, not censorship.

The university should be an uncomfortable place for comfortable ideas. It should be a dangerous place for all deeply felt ideologies. It should be an unsafe place for political correctness or incorrectness. Ideas must live and die on their merits and demerits, so long as those espousing them are kept safe from physical intimidation or threats.

The line between physical safety, on the one hand, and intellectual or emotional safety, on the other hand, will not always be clear or easy to administer, but doubts must always be resolved in favor of freedom of expression, even against claims of unsafety, because it is far too easy to argue that safety is being endangered in ambiguous circumstances. For example, one professor has talked about "the violence of the word"—a metaphorical concept that could spell the end of controversial speech on campus. I don't doubt that some people really do feel subjectively unsafe when their conventional wisdom and deeply felt worldviews are challenged, but freedom of expression is too valuable to surrender to subjective feelings. Before speech may be stifled in the name of safety, rigorous objective standards should have to be met.

Freedom of dissent on many university campuses is quickly becoming an endangered species. Many constituent groups support free speech "for me but not for thee." Ideas that they express come within the ambit of free expression, but opposing ideas that make them feel unsafe are now included in the amorphous category of "harassment."

The real world into which students graduate is not always a safe place. Students must be prepared to face the cruel realities of obnoxious views that make them feel uncomfortable and unsafe. Sexism, racism, homophobia, anti-Semitism, Islamophobia, and other awful "isms" still exist in many parts of our own country and in the world. We have the right to try to defeat these pernicious and dangerous ideas in the marketplace. But we cannot censor them in the real world. Nor should we try to protect our students from them as they prepare to enter that world. Instead, members of the university community must learn the best ways to respond to ideas they detest within the framework of a free and open marketplace.

July 1, 2015
A Jurisprudential Framework for Defending Israel

Another recent United Nations report once again condemned Israel for defending its civilians against rockets fired by Hamas from densely populated civilian areas. Once again Israel responded by releasing information compiled by independents experts. This article attempts to put these issues in a broader jurisprudential context.

The aspiration of every legal system is to be governed by the objective rule of law rather than the ad hoc decisions of biased human beings. What then is the rule of law, as distinguished from the rule of men and women, since all law must, in practice, be administered by fallible humans. The essence of the rule of law—from the Bible, the Codes of Hammurabi, and Lipit-Ishtar, to the Magna Carta, to the United States Constitution, to the Geneva Accords—is advanced codification: that is a series of written rules that are designed to be applied equally to all, without knowing in advance who will be perpetrators, who victims and who bystanders.

The great legal philosopher John Rawles made the principle an important part of the legal cannon, where he coined the phrase "veil of ignorance." In his abstract conception, rules must be written in a netherworld by those veiled in ignorance in what their status will be in the real world to be governed by the rules.

In other words, the writers cannot know whether they will be male or female, gay or straight, white or black, handicapped or fully able, Jew or gentile, handsome or ugly, strong or weak, smart or not so smart, poor or rich, healthy or unhealthy, etc. etc., when they draft the rules that will govern their future conduct.

In this way, they will be incentivized to enact laws that will be fair to all.

This idea was not original with Rawles, though he deserves credit for formulating it in a clever and accessible manner. The idea underlying Rawles's conception is an ancient as codification, and finds expression in such Biblical concepts as "be kind to strangers, for you were once strangers in the land of Egypt," with the implication that you may be strangers once again in other lands.

In the United States Constitution, this idea is manifested in the prohibition against Bills of Attainder, which preclude Congress from enacting laws punishing named individuals. All criminal laws must be a general nature, equally applicable to all who come within its prohibitory language. No one is above the law, as courts have repeatedly stated. The principle is also reflected in the prohibition against "common law crimes," applied retroactively to conduct that was not specifically codified in advance.

How then do these general principles, about which there is universal agreement in theory, apply to the subject of our discussion today? Directly!

The way Israel is being judged today is a dramatic exception to the rule of law and the principles articulated above. Under the current approach, the international community first considers Israel's actions, in isolation from the actions of other nations; it judges them to be imperfect, when evaluated against abstract rules; it then creates specific rules applicable only to the nation state of the Jewish people, and to no other nation.

This has clearly been the case with the Goldstone Report, the more recent report by Mary McGowan Davis, the decisions of the International Court of Justice, the resolutions of numerous United Nations bodies, especially the misnamed Human Rights Council, and even the reports of Israeli NGOs such as B'tselem and Breaking the Silence.

These so-called applications of the rules of international law all share a common modus operandi: they begin with Israel's actions rather than with neutral principles of law designed to govern the actions of <u>all nations</u> and groups. They then judge Israel's actions against unrealistic, anachronistic, and abstract principles that could not be, and have never been, applied to other nations or groups. They then condemn Israel, without articulating rules of general applicability.

Consider the following relevant examples: What is the international law governing nations whose civilians are being targeted by rockets being deliberately fired from densely populated civilian areas? One can search the various codes of law without finding a definitive answer to this question. Must the victim nation simply accept the casualties and fear that accompany such rocket fire? May it try to stop the launch of future rockets, even if its preventive actions will inevitably kill some civilians? How many potential civilian deaths are permissible to prevent how many rockets, under the rules of "proportionality?"

What about the risk from terror tunnels dug under its territory with intended exits near civilian areas? Can the known entrances to these terror tunnels that are built in or near civilian homes, mosques, schools, hospitals, or United Nations facilities, be destroyed preventatively? Or must the victim nation wait until the terrorists exit the tunnels at unknown locations?

May a nation that is repeatedly threatened with non-negotiable demands for its complete destruction take preemptive or preventive military action to destroy nuclear facilities that may soon give the threatening nation the ability to carry out its threats with nuclear weapons? Or must they depend on negotiations from which they are excluded.

The international community refuses to address these general issues of great and immediate relevance. They refuse to apply the Rawlsian test veiled in ignorance of whether they will be the aggressor nation or the victim nation. They prefer instead to enact Bills of Attainder against only one specifically named country: the nation state of the Jewish people.

Well you can't just talk about Jews, or any other specific groups, when you apply the rule of law. Nor can you talk only about the nation state of the Jewish people. You must talk about all groups, all nations, and all people when you enact or apply rules of law.

The same analysis is applicable to BDS. As far as I'm aware, none of the advocates of BDS, nor any of the institution that have adopted it, have asked what general criteria should have to be met before BDS is directed against any country. The principle of the "worst first," is never applied by BDSers. Instead they apply the President Lawrence approach: "We're talking only about the Jews now." (See the introduction, page 5.) If general principles were applied to the worst first no boycott campaign would reach Israel until the very end of the list.

I suggest, therefore, the following approach to BDS: whenever and wherever BDS is proposed, an effort ought to be made to apply BDS to the worst first. A document should be provided to the institution, listing the human rights violators in order of the seriousness of their violation and of the inability of its victims to achieve redress from institutions within the state, especially an independent judiciary and media. Topping this list would be nations such as China, Cuba, Iran, Russia, Turkey, Venezuela, Saudi Arabia, Egypt, Pakistan, Belarus, Syria, Lebanon, and Libya. The list goes on and on, well before it would reach Israel. The idea of singling out Israel for BDS is as incompatible with the rule of law as is the focus of the international community on Israel's alleged war crimes.

Those who support Israel should not be defending every Israeli action but merely demanding that Israel's imperfections be assessed in a comparative context, as Learned Hand demanded that President Lawrence do of Harvard students, and as the Bill of Attainder clause and the prohibition against common law crimes demands in the context of the rule of law. Justice must not only be done, but it must be seen to be done and treating Israel differently from other similarly situationed nations—and from nations that are far worse by any reasonable standards—undercuts both the rule of law and the quest for justice.

August 24, 2015
Tablet Magazine: A Conversation with Alan Dershowitz

TABLET: What sparked the fire to write your new book, *The Case Against the Iran Deal*?

DERSHOWITZ: I've been very concerned about this deal and the Iranian nuclear program since 2005 when I started to write about it. I expected it to be a deal that was not acceptable but I didn't think it would be as bad as this one. I expected that the deal would continue to not cross Obama's own red lines—namely that the deal would be forever not just ten years. Secondly, I expected that there would be very rigorous, 24/7, instantaneous inspections [and] that those rules—those red lines—would not be crossed.

I also didn't think Obama would be naive enough to take the military option off the table during the negotiations, and that's what he did and led the Iranians to believe that they wouldn't face the tiger and could negotiate with us as equals. So when the deal was announced, I had a sleepless night. Then I woke up and sent an email to my publisher. I said 'I want to write a book about the Iran deal.' He said, 'If you can get it in in two weeks, we can do it.' So I sent it to him in 11 days.

TABLET: My bottom line understanding of your book is this: Regardless of political inclination, if you are pro-Israel then you have to oppose the Iran deal.

DERSHOWITZ: I would put it a little differently: If you are pro-Israel, you have to understand that this is not a good deal for Israel, not a good deal for America. Even the people who are in Congress ratifying the deal don't think that this is a good deal. So the question isn't whether this is a good deal or a bad deal; it's a bad deal. Could we have gotten a better deal? Yes. That's not the issue. The issue is: Is the alternative worse? That is, would rejecting the deal be worse, would it be worse for Israel, would it be worse for peace, or would it make war more likely?

So we're presented with two bad choices—a bad deal and, according to the president, an even worse outcome if the deal is rejected. I think that's where the debate has turned in the last month or so. I think reasonable people can disagree about that second question about whether rejecting would be worse, and that's why I pose a third alternative in my book.

The third alternative is only for those people who are going to vote for the deal. If you are going to vote for the deal, at the very least vote conditionally on the preliminary part of the deal being integral to the deal itself. Namely, Iran's commitment that it will never, under any circumstances, seek to develop nuclear weapons. And put some teeth behind that by authorizing the president to implement that part of the deal if it becomes necessary. And that's not only my proposal, it's Tom Friedman's perspective—that even people who support the deal want to see that kind of commitment or teeth put into that specific part of the deal.

TABLET: How can a Democratic liberal Jew oppose the deal without being accused of dual loyalty to Israel, and therefore not be considered a "true" American?

DERSHOWITZ: It doesn't even bother me one bit. I'm as patriotic and as American as Obama or any member of his administration. Was Obama any less patriotic when he opposed the Iraq war? He opposed his president and I opposed my president; me and Obama were on the same side when it comes to being against the Iraq war. Was it not patriotic of me to oppose the Vietnam war?

If Jews in America are considered to be first class citizens—and I insist that we are first class citizens—[then] we have the right to express any views without being accused of having dual loyalties. I will never ever be deterred by that accusation. I will say what I think and put my loyalty and patriotism on equal footing as anyone else's, including the president of the United States.

TABLET: Speaking of the president, one thing that came across very clearly in your book is your satisfaction with Obama's initial stance on Iran compared to some members of his administration. I was wondering: At this moment what are your feelings on Obama?

DERSHOWITZ: Well, I'm very disappointed. I'm very disappointed in John Kerry. John Kerry is a friend, I've known him for years, and I've known Obama for a long time. I think they've undercut American power in the world. I think it is they who have to answer questions as to whether they are as supportive of America as they could be. I'm extremely disappointed. And I do think now that governor Romney would have done a better job with in dealing with Iran than President Obama has. I'm personally disappointed with President Obama because he looked me in the eye and he essentially promised me he wouldn't do this, and he did it.

TABLET: Who are you backing in the 2016 presidential election?

DERSHOWITZ: At the moment, I'm supporting Hillary Clinton. I'm a liberal democrat. I've known Hillary Clinton for a long time and I've discussed [the Iran Deal] with her. But my vote can't be taken for granted, obviously. I have to get a feel of what the candidates look like and what their positions are on this and other issues. I vote as an American for the candidate who I think would be best for America and the values that I support so my vote can never be taken for granted. But I'm a presumptive liberal and a presumptive supporter of Hillary Clinton.

TABLET: What are your thoughts on presidential hopeful Bernie Sanders?

DERSHOWITZ: I like him personally. We both come from Brooklyn, both went to Brooklyn College for a while. We share some values but he's not going to be the president of the United States, and he's not going to be a third party candidate who will hurt the Democrats. I wish he'd be a little bit more supportive of Israel. He's been as supportive as leftists like him can be, but I wish he could be a little bit closer to mainstream pro-Israel views. But I think he serves an important function as a leftist, supporting the Jewish right to a state and a two-state solution. In general, I'm not unhappy with Bernie Sanders. [I became unhappy with him when he appointed anti-Israel extremists to the DNC platform committee.]

TABLET: One section that was very interesting in the book was about J Street.

DERSHOWITZ: I think J Street has been the most damaging organization in American history against Israel. It has been the most damaging, more damaging than Students for Justice in Palestine [and] more damaging than the early anti-Zionist Council for Judaism. J Street has done more to turn young people against Israel than any organization in the whole of history. It will go down in history as one of the most virulent, anti-Israel organizations in the history of Zionism and Judaism. It has given cover to anti-Israel attitudes on campus and particularly its approach to Israel's self-defense.

Now I agree with some of J Street's approaches to the two-state solution, and the settlements. But when it comes to Israel's war against Hamas, and when it supports the Goldstone report, and when it accepts money from anti-Zionists, and when it puts all its support and money behind this deal, it becomes very hard to describe it as anything but anti-Israel. I used to say J Street can't call itself pro-Israel. I've now changed my mind and say that J Street has to reveal itself as a major anti-Israel organization.

TABLET: The BDS campaign has been in the news a lot recently. What are your thoughts on efforts to boycott Israel?

DERSHOWITZ: Well, it will never work in the United States. No American college or university will survive if it supports BDS. It's major area of impact is in Europe. We saw what happened in Spain last week with Matisyahu. [Europe] has become more dangerous. That's why I'm going to Oxford [University] in November to debate at the Oxford Union against BDS.

TABLET: What are your arguments against BDS proponents?

DERSHOWITZ: The issue is not BDS, it's BDS against Israel. One can have a reasonable argument that a BDS "movement" might be moral if directed against China, if directed against Russia, if directed against Cuba, if directed against Hamas, if directed against a hundred countries in the world that have horrible human rights records. The question isn't BDS, it's why should be applied only to the nation state of the Jewish people. A campaign like that hurts human rights around the world because it singles out Israel and singles out the Jewish people. So there's nothing positive about the BDS campaign. Moreover, it won't work against Israel, and helps to generate anti-Israel sentiments among young people.

Let me go back to J Street. I renew here my challenge to J Street. J Street has refused me to speak at any J Street event. They've invited every hard left opponent of Israel. They've invited BDS supporters. They've invited supporters of terrorism. But they will never ever invite me to a J Street convention because it doesn't want people to hear my point of view. They want an open tent [in order] to enter into the mainstream of pro-Israel groups but it will not allow mainstream supporters of Israel to speak at their events. It's extraordinarily hypocritical.[58]

TABLET: Speaking of hypocrisy, there's a section of your book devoted to reporting on Israel, Netanyahu, and the Iran Deal. Can you elaborate on that section?

DERSHOWITZ: Take *The New York Times*. The *Times* published an editorial that stated that it is wrong for a member of Congress to listen to a foreign leader over our commander-in-chief. That is so wrong. First of all, he's not our commander-in-chief, he's only the commander-in-chief of the armed forces; he's not the commander-in-chief of the senate and he's not the commander-in-chief of the American people. We've always listened to foreign leaders. Certainly, President Obama listened to foreign leaders when he opposed the war in Iraq. Foreign leaders were telling him not to get involved in that war and our leaders were telling us to get involved in that war. So was he being unpatriotic when he didn't listen to his predecessor, our commander-in-chief? Of course not. So the reporting has been very skewed.

TABLET: One final thing I wanted to ask you was about the Iranian threat to annihilate Israel. How much substance is there behind that threat?

DERSHOWITZ: We don't know. We didn't know how much the threat was behind Hitler's *Mein Kampf*. His threat was to annihilate the Jews. Let's assume there's a 1-in-6 chance that Iran means it—that's Russian roulette. Would anybody put a bullet in a gun and spin it if there was a 1-in-6 chance of blowing their head off? What if it's only a 1-in-6 chance Iran would use a nuclear weapon against Israel? That's much too high a risk for any democracy to take. And especially for the nation state of the Jewish people to take.
  It's a gamble.
  It's a gamble and that's why the cover of my book has two dice on it—one coming up showing the peace symbol, the other coming up showing the nuclear symbol. It's a roll of the dice and we should expect more from our leaders than requiring the leader of the free

world to roll the dice with its own security and the security of its primary allies in the Middle East.

November 3, 2015
Debating Against BDS—and Winning

When I was invited to debate in favor of the motion "Is BDS Wrong?" at the Oxford Union, I fully expected to lose the vote of the 250 or so students and faculty who are members of the oldest debating society in the world.

"Israel always loses at Oxford," I was warned by colleagues who had debated other Israel-related issues. Nonetheless I decided to participate, hoping to change some minds.

I proposed as my opponent Omar Barghouti, the Qatari-born, Israeli-educated, co-founder and spokesperson of the BDS campaign, but he refused to debate me. The Union then selected Noura Erekat, a Palestinian-American human rights attorney, who has been a vocal supporter of BDS.

When she backed out at the last minute, I began to get suspicious: Was the BDS tactic boycotting me? After all, BDS advocates have called for "common sense" academic boycotts against individuals who they feel are too vocal in their support for Israel, in addition to a blanket boycott of all Israeli academic institutions.

After speaking with the organizers of the debate at Oxford, I continue to believe that I was in fact being boycotted.

The Union then selected Peter Tatchell, a distinguished and popular British human rights activist who has participated in 30 Union debates, most of which he has won. I knew I was in for a difficult time, especially when the audience applauded his points more loudly than mine and when many of the questions seemed hostile toward Israel, though polite.

Mr. Tatchell's main argument was that BDS was a nonviolent form of protest against Israel's occupation and settlement policies that mirrored the boycott campaign against apartheid South Africa, and followed the principles of Mahatma Gandhi and Martin Luther King. He was articulate in arguing that boycott tactics generally were a nonviolent alternative to war and terrorism.

The force of his argument was somewhat weakened by the recent spate of terrorist knife attacks by Palestinians against Israelis, which leaders of the BDS campaign such as Barghouti have justified as resistance to the "decades-old regime of occupation."

I argued that BDS was not an alternative to war but rather an alternative to peaceful negotiations by the Palestinian leadership. This is because the BDS campaign is firmly opposed to the two-state solution. Barghouti confirmed as much when he said "definitely, most definitely, we oppose a Jewish state in any part of Palestine." Thus, the BDS campaign makes it more difficult for the Palestinian leadership to accept the kind of painful compromises that both sides must agree to if there is to be a negotiated resolution.

Together with other efforts to de-legitimize and isolate Israel, BDS also sends a false message to the Palestinian street: namely, that international economic and political pressure can force Israel to capitulate to all Palestinian demands, without any compromise on territorial issues. In turn, this dis-incentivizes the Palestinian leadership from accepting Prime Minister Benjamin Netanyahu's offer to begin immediate negotiations with no preconditions.

Such discussions are particularly important now, to halt the gruesome cycle of violence that has intensified in recent weeks. Both sides must return to the negotiations table, and both must be willing to make concessions.

For the Israelis, this means rolling back settlements, and granting greater autonomy to the West Bank; for the Palestinian Authority, it means renouncing violence against Israeli civilians, disavowing Hamas and other terrorist organizations, and accepting the need for territorial compromise with land swaps.

BDS opposes any effort at negotiation that isn't premised on the recognition that Israel is an apartheid state.

Indeed, many of its leaders refuse to recognize the right of Israel to exist as a nation-state for the Jewish people. In so doing, they are empowering radicals on both sides of the issue who have no desire to see a peaceful resolution to the conflict.

Many liberal activists such as Mr. Tatchell—whose advocacy on behalf of LGBT rights I greatly admire—have made common cause with BDS, hoping to pressure Israel to end the occupation, and afford greater self-determination to Palestinians in the West Bank.

They seem to believe that a campaign advocating nonviolent tactics is necessarily the best way to achieve a lasting peace. But BDS is radically opposed to any negotiated settlement, and has increasingly begun to regroup bigots of all stripes who feel comfortable with the language used by its leaders, such Mr. Barghouti.

Mr. Tatchell and many pro-BDS academics also feel that Israel has committed human rights violations both in the occupation of the West Bank, and in its prosecution of the armed conflicts in Gaza.

During the course of the debate I issued the following challenge to the audience and to my opponent: name a single country in the history of the world, faced with threats comparable to those faced by Israel, that has a better record of human rights, compliance with the rule of law and seeking to minimize civilian casualties.

I invited audience members to shout out the name of a country. Complete silence. Finally, someone shouted "Iceland," and everyone laughed.

When the best is treated as the worst, in the way the BDS campaign singles out Israel for accusation, the finger of blame must be pointed at the accusers rather than the accused.

In the end, the case against BDS won not because of the comparative skill of the debaters but because I was able to expose the moral weakness of the BDS campaign itself. [59]

November 10, 2015
The Global Community Is to Blame for Palestinian Obstinance

Why should the Palestinian leadership make peace with Israel, when the international community seems willing to recognize a Palestinian state without requiring its leaders to make the kinds of compromises that are essential to a viable two-state solution?

The Israelis offered the Palestinians a generous two-state solution under the leadership of then-prime ministers Ehud Barak and Ehud Olmert. Now, Prime Minister Benjamin Netanyahu is urging them to sit down and begin unconditional negotiations. The Palestinian leadership have accepted none of these offers, because they foolishly believe they can get what they want without giving what they must.

The major fault for this impasse lies squarely on the shoulders of the international community, including the United Nations, the International Criminal Court, the International Court of Justice, the international media, and many individual governments. They have led the Palestinian leadership to believe that if they can maintain the impasse with Israel by refusing to make the kinds of compromises required for a two-state solution, the international community would come to their rescue and impose such a solution on Israel.

The international media, the BDS (boycott, divestment, and sanctions) campaign and student protests against Israel all contribute to dis-incentivizing the Palestinians from entering into real negotiations that will require compromise.

Even this newspaper, *Haaretz*, by placing virtually all the blame for the impasse on Israel, discourages the Palestinians from coming to the negotiating table. Because they believe they are winning the war of public opinion, they do not believe they need to compromise.

The time has come for the world to point a harsh finger at the Palestinian leadership, and to make clear to them that they will not be rewarded for their intransigence. The Palestinians must know that the only way they will get a viable state is to sit down and negotiate on such an entity with the Israeli government. This will require painful compromises on both sides, not just the Israeli one.

Skewed Against Israel

The Palestinian leadership must also learn that violence will not get them a state, although it may win them positive press in some parts of the world. The Palestinian tactic of initiating terrorist and rocket attacks against Israel, knowing that Israel will retaliate, and expecting that the international community will either condemn Israel or describe the ensuing events as "a cycle of violence," has scored points for the Palestinian side. But this is not a game where the team with the most points wins. The Palestinians may be winning in the court of public opinion, because the court of public opinion is skewed against Israel, but they are no closer to achieving statehood than they were when they rejected previous offers.

This is not to say that Israel is blameless for the current situation. Its policies of settlement building, particularly in areas that will probably become part of a Palestinian state, have been a mistake from the very beginning. But the primary fault for the current impasse lies squarely at the feet of the Palestinian leadership. The time has come for the international community, the media, and those who truly want peace to begin putting pressure on the Palestinian leadership to come to the negotiating table and agree to the kinds of compromises that are essential if a two-state solution is to be achieved. The Palestinians must give up their so-called "Right of Return." They must agree to an essentially demilitarized Palestinian state. They must agree that Israel has the right to defend itself against rocket and terrorist attacks. They must agree to territorial compromises, with land swaps that recognize the realities on the ground.

Israel must make compromises as well, especially with regard to settlements in areas that will be part of a Palestinian state.

The way forward is through bilateral, unconditional negotiations between the Palestinian Authority and the Israeli government. For the moment, there are no prospects for a peaceful resolution of the Gaza situation. The best that can be hoped for is a long-term cease-fire between Hamas and Israel. If a Palestinian state in the West Bank emerges from negotiations, the people in Gaza may well come to recognize that their interests would be better served by aligning themselves with those who seek peace rather than continued warfare. When the United Nations partitioned Mandatory Palestine, it explicitly contemplated a nation state for the Jewish people alongside a nation state for the Arab people. The two-state solution requires that each side recognize the legitimacy of the other.

The Palestinian Authority must acknowledge that Israel is the legitimate and authentic nation-state of the Jewish people, in which all citizens are equal under the law. Israel must recognize that Palestine is the nation-state of the Palestinian people, hopefully with equal rights for all its citizens and residents. Only then can the dream of enduring peace be fulfilled.

If this were to come to pass, the peace dividend—not only for Israelis and Palestinians, but for the entire world—would be incalculable. So let us all incentivize both sides to negotiate a real peace that will endure, and that can serve as a model for other conflicts.

November 12, 2015
Selective Outrage on Campus

Following the forced resignations of the president and provost of the University of Missouri, demonstrations against campus administrators has spread across the country. Students—many of whom are black, gay, transgender, and Muslim—claim that they feel "unsafe" as the result of what they call "white privilege" or sometimes simply privilege. "Check your privilege" has become the put-down du jour. Students insist on being protected by campus administrators from "micro-aggressions," meaning unintended statements inside and outside the classroom that demonstrate subtle insensitivities towards minority students. They insist on being safe from hostile or politically incorrect ideas. They demand "trigger warnings" before sensitive issues are discussed or assigned. They want to own the narrative and keep other points of view from upsetting them or making them feel unsafe.

These current manifestations of a widespread culture of victimization and grievance are only the most recent iterations of a dangerous long-term trend on campuses both in the United States and in Europe. The ultimate victims are freedom of expression, academic freedom and the free exchange of ideas. Many faculty members, administrators and students are fearful of the consequences if they express politically incorrect or dissident views that may upset some students. So they engage in self-censorship. They have seen what had happened to those who have expressed unpopular views, and it is not a pretty picture.

I know, because I repeatedly experience this backlash when I speak on campuses. Most recently, I was invited to deliver the

Milton Eisenhower lecture at Johns Hopkins University. As soon as the lecture was announced, several student groups demanded that the invitation must be rescinded. The petition objected to my mere "presence" on campus, stating that my views on certain issues "are not matters of opinion, and cannot be debated" and that they are "not issues that are open to debate of any kind." These non-debatable issues include some of the most controversial concerns that are roiling campus today: sexual assault, academic integrity, and the Israel-Palestine conflict. The protesting students simply didn't want my view on these and other issues expressed on their campus, because my lecture would make them feel unsafe or uncomfortable.

The groups demanding censorship of my lecture included Hopkins Feminists, Black Student Union, Diverse Sexuality and General Alliance, Sexual Assault Resource Unit, and Voice for Choice. I have been told that two faculty members urged these students, who had never heard of me, to organize the protests, but the cowardly faculty members would not themselves sign the petition. The petition contained blatant lies about me and my views, but that is beside the point. I responded to the lies in my lecture and invited the protesting students to engage me during the Q and A. But instead, they walked out in the middle of my presentation, while I was discussing the prospects for peace in the Middle East.

According to the *Johns Hopkins News-Letter*, another petition claimed that "by denying Israel's alleged war crimes against Palestinians," I violated the university's "anti-harassment policy" and its "statement of ethical standards." In other words, by expressing my reasonable views on a controversial subject, I harassed students.

Some of the posters advertising my lecture were defaced with Hitler mustaches drawn on my face. Imagine the outcry if comparably insensitive images had been drawn on the faces of invited minority lecturers.

I must add that the Johns Hopkins administration and the student group that invited me responded admirably to the protests, fully defending my right to express my views and the right of the student group to invite me. The lecture went off without any hitches and I answered all the questions—some quite critical, but all polite—for the large audience that came to hear the presentation.

The same cannot be said of several other lectures I have given on other campuses, which were disrupted by efforts to shout me down, especially by anti-Israel groups that are committed to preventing pro-Israel speakers from expressing their views.

The point is not only that some students care less about freedom of expression in <u>general</u> than about protecting <u>all</u> students from "micro-aggressions." It is that many of these same students are perfectly willing to make other students with whom they disagree with feel unsafe and offended by their own micro- and macro-aggressions. Consider, for example, a recent protest at the City University of New York by Students for Justice in Palestine that blamed high tuition on "the Zionist administration [of the University that] invests in Israeli companies, companies that support the Israeli occupation, hosts birthright programs and study abroad programs in occupied Palestine [meaning Israel proper] and reproduces settler-colonial ideology throughout CUNY though Zionist content of education."

Let's be clear what they mean by "Zionist": they mean "Jew." There are many Jewish administrators at City University. Some are probably Zionists. Others are probably not. Blaming Zionists for high tuition is out and out anti-Semitism. It is not micro-aggression. It is in-your-face macro-aggression against City University Jews.

Yet those who protest micro-aggressions against other minorities are silent when it comes to macro-aggressions against Jews. This is not to engage in comparative victimization, but rather to expose the double standard, the selective outrage, and the overt hypocrisy of many of those who would sacrifice free speech on the altar of political correctness, whose content they seek to dictate.

November 22, 2015
Safe Spaces for Hypocrisy:
The Dangerous Sensitivity Double-Standards at Play on America's College Campuses

Student activists recently staged protests at Dartmouth University library, both to demonstrate against the vandalism of a Black Lives Matter display, and to show solidarity with similar initiatives held on various college campuses.

Activists verbally harassed onlookers, shouting racially charged epithets and expletive-laden slogans at students who were trying to study. And while Dartmouth administrators have dismissed reports of physical violence, there is no doubt that the tone of protests on college campuses has grown increasingly vitriolic. Two weeks ago, for example, protesters allegedly spat on attendees of an event at Yale held to highlight the importance of free speech.

One of the central demands repeated by protesters at campuses across the country has been for university administrators to transform campuses into "safe spaces," where students are protected not only from physical violence but also from ideas that they find threatening or offensive. However, the "safe spaces" envisioned by these protesters seem to matter only when the interests of those who share their political persuasions are affected.

There has been conspicuously little attention paid to incidents of anti-Semitism reported, for example, at Hunter College, where students supportive of Israel were chased away from a rally blaming high tuition fees on "Zionist administrators," and where protestors shouted "Zionists out of CUNY" (the City University of New York), by which they meant Jews.

At Vassar, Jewish students have repeatedly stated that they feel forced to self-censor pro-Israel views out of fear of retribution from peers and faculty alike. This year in a survey at Vassar, students responded that it was best not to advertise that you were Jewish on campus. At UC-Berkeley and the University of Texas, Jewish students have been frightened by shouts of "Long live the Intifada." The Intifada they were referencing involved the stabbing of Jews. [And most recently, in March 2017, at the University of Illinois, flyers were posted across the campus calling for "an end of Jewish privilege" and stating in bold letters that, "ending white privilege starts with ending Jewish privilege."]

Where are the cries for safe spaces for Jewish students faced with such blatant intimidation?

Instead, "safe spaces" rhetoric has been used by students to insulate themselves from ideas that they deem offensive. In 2015 at Columbia, the Multicultural Affairs Advisory Board objected to the inclusion of material by the Roman poet Ovid on the ground that "like so many texts in the Western Canon, it contains triggering and offensive material that marginalizes student identities in the classroom." Last month, an event hosted by a student group at Williams College, called Uncomfortable Learning, was cancelled due to security concerns when protestors subjected organizers to severe online abuse.

Moreover, "safe spaces" activists demanded that a Yale residential hall administrator resign for daring to suggest that banning certain Halloween costumes might raise a freedom of speech issue, and that the university should not act as a heavy-handed censor.

At Smith, meanwhile, students successfully pushed administrators to ban reporters from covering a protest, unless they expressed support for the Black Lives Matters agenda.

The hypocrisy of protestors demanding protection from potentially offensive ideas while simultaneously insulting and harassing people who fail to demonstrate adequate levels of enthusiasm for their agenda should be obvious to all. But too few university administrators and faculty call out these hypocritical students for their double standard.

Let's be clear: All students should be made to feel physically safe on campus. They should also be protected from verbal abuse. Colleges should attempt to foster an inclusive and tolerant environment that allows individuals of varied backgrounds to feel comfortable discussing a wide range of intellectual, social and political topics.

As such, school administrators should condemn racist incidents, such as those that occurred at the University of Missouri. They should address allegations of anti-Semitic abuse at places like CUNY and Vassar with equal seriousness.

Students subjected to abuse or intimidation should be offered support services, and that may even entail setting aside "safe spaces" where they can find peace and quiet, access peer support groups and counseling services.

However, such safe spaces must not be extended to campuses as a whole. Classrooms in particular must not become intellectually sterile environments, where ideas are subjected to censorship based on the fact that they make some students feel uncomfortable. To the contrary, universities should foster discussions of controversial ideas, subversive ideas, ideas that provoke and challenge students to question their beliefs and preconceptions. That process is central to learning and intellectual progress more generally. Safe spaces rhetoric must not be allowed to undermine it.

March 17, 2016
A Visit to the Old and New Hells of Europe Provides a Reminder of Israel's Importance

I just returned from a week-long journey through Hell! It began with a visit to the site of the Auschwitz and Birkenau death camps in Poland (built by Nazi Germany during its occupation of the country), as a participant of the March of the Living, following a conference commemorating the 80th anniversary of the Nuremberg Laws and the 70th anniversary of the Nuremberg Trials. My week was consumed with recurring evidence of the worst crime ever perpetrated by human beings on other human beings—the Holocaust.

I traveled from the death camps to several small Polish towns from which my grandparents emigrated well before the Holocaust, leaving behind relatives and friends. During the course of my travels, I discovered the fate of two of my relatives. Hanna Deresiewicz (an original spelling of my family name) was a 16-year-old girl living in the small town of Pilzno when the Nazis arrived; she was separated from her siblings and parents. "The soldiers took several of the most beautiful Jewish girls for sex, and then killed them. [Among those] taken [was] Hanna Deresiewicz, 16."

I also learned that another Deresiewics, named Benjamin, survived, though his wife and five children, along with his parents and siblings were all murdered. He may have been Hanna's father, although I can't document that. In the book *Schindler's Ark*, on which the movie *Schindler's List* was based, the following account is given: "[The Commandant of Auschwitz] suspended his 15-year-old orderly, Poldek Dereshowitz, from the ringbolts in his office..." Although the book is fictionalized account, it is based on the recollections of an eyewitness. I cannot, therefore, be sure of the veracity of that episode. But seeing the name Dereshowitz associated with Auschwitz had an impact on me.

This is not the first time I have visited Nazi death camps. I was fully familiar with the statistical evidence of how six million Jews were systematically murdered. I was also familiar with how the Nazi death machine searched out Jews in the farthest corners of Nazi occupied Europe, even as far as the island of Rhodes in the Aegean Sea, and transported them to Auschwitz to gas them. I also knew that this was the only time in human history when people were brought from far distances to camps designed for one purpose only—to kill every possible Jew they could, find no matter where they lived. And I knew that because this was part of a planned genocide of the Jewish people, it was most important to kill every child, woman, and man capable of producing future Jews.

But this visit, during which I learned the fate of members of my own family, brought the horrors home to me in a manner more personal than any statistic could provide. I was traveling with my wife and daughter, and I repeatedly imagined what it must have felt like for the parents and spouses of the murdered Jews to realize that everything precious to them was being annihilated, and that there would be no one left to mourn them or to carry their seed to future generations.

From the old hell, Poland, I traveled to a new hell, called Hungary. Budapest is a beautiful city, but it, too, provided a hellish end to its Jewish residents in the final months of the Second World War, when Hungarian Nazis turned the Blue Danube into a red mass grave. They shot their Jewish neighbors and dumped their bodies into the Danube River, even as the Nazis were retreating. And now in modern-day Budapest, I was told of the resurgence of Nazism among many ordinary Hungarians. An increasingly popular fascist party, Jobbik[60], boasts of its anti-Semitism and of its desire to rid Hungary of its few remaining Jews. The Jobbik party in Hungary also hates Israel and everything else that is a manifestation of Jewishness.

I ended my trip meeting with a Jewish man of Greek background who told me that his grandfather was murdered by the Nazis and that he was now being targeted by Greek fascists for his outspoken defense of Israel and the Jewish people. Athens, too, has become a hotbed of Jew-hatred, with its popular fascist Golden Dawn party[61].

There was not a moment during my visit to Europe that I was not reminded of that continent's sordid history with regard to the Jewish people. Now, many Europeans—the children, grandchildren, and great-grandchildren of those who were complicit in the murder of six million Jews—have turned against the nation state of the Jewish people with a vengeance. This time the bigotry emanates mostly from the hard left, but has the support of many on the new fascist hard right. The British Labour Party is as rife with hatred of the Jewish people and Jewish nation[62] as is the Hungarian fascist Jobbik party. Once again, European Jews are caught between the extremes of the Black and the Red. Extremists on both sides seek the demise of Israel, arguing that there is no place in this world for one state that is overtly Jewish in its character, despite the universal acceptance of multiple Muslim and Christian nations. Other Europeans seek to boycott Israel's products, its professors, and its performers. While still others simply apply a double standard to its actions—a standard they apply to no other nation, including their own.

My visit to Europe made one thing unmistakably clear: If there is any group in the world that needs a safe homeland—a sanctuary from bigotry and hatred—it is the Jewish people. When Hitler was willing to expel them from Europe, before deciding to exterminate them, no country, not even the United States or Canada, would give them asylum. Britain closed the doors of what is now Israel to them. They had no place to go. So they were murdered by the

Nazis and their willing executioners throughout Europe. There is no group whose history entitles it to a safe and secure homeland more than the Jewish people.

For reasons that are difficult to explain, the hatred of the Jewish people and its nation defies rationality, but it is as real as the gas chambers of Auschwitz-Birkenau and the emerging fascist parties of Greece and Hungary. Jews today continue to be scapegoated in many parts of the world, and their nation state is demonized at the United Nations, on university campuses, in the media, and in legislative assemblies. Following the Holocaust, there seemed to be an understanding that Jews would no longer be victimized. Now, less than a century after the Nazis came to power, that moratorium on Jew-hatred seems to have expired, as the memory of the Holocaust grows dim in most parts of the world.

My week-long visit to hell reaffirmed my commitment to defend Israel's right to exist, to speak out for Israel when it is unfairly attacked, and to defeat its enemies in the marketplace of ideas. We owe nothing less to the victims of the worst crime in the history of humanity—a crime that could not have occurred without the complicity of most of the world. And a crime that will not recur if there is a strong and secure Israel.

April 13, 2016
Bernie Sanders Must Clarify Where He Stands on Israel

Bernie Sanders' ignorance and bias with regards to Israel have been on full view lately. In an interview with the *New York Daily News* editorial board, Sanders grossly misstated the number of Palestinian civilians killed during Israel's intervention in the Gaza strip in August and September 2014, generally referred to as Operation Protective Edge.

Here's what he said:

Sanders: "Help me out here, because I don't remember the figures, but my recollection is over 10,000 innocent people were killed in Gaza. Does that sound right?"

Daily News: "I think it's probably high, but we can look at that."

Sanders: "I don't have it in my number…but I think it's over 10,000. My understanding is that a whole lot of apartment houses were leveled. Hospitals, I think, were bombed. So yeah, I do believe and I don't think I'm alone in believing that Israel's force was more indiscriminate than it should have been."

Even, the United Nations—whose bias against Israel is well documented—put the number of civilians killed during Operation Protective Edge at 1,462, while the Israeli Defense Forces counted 761.

Mr. Sanders' campaign has since attempted to clarify his remarks by claiming that the media distorted Mr. Sanders's comments, and that he was in fact referring to the total number of casualties sustained by the Palestinians over the course of the conflict.

Regardless of whether Mr. Sanders was referring to total casualties or to the death toll, he should apologize for propagating this blatant mistruth. His comments seemed to confirm the wild delusions of anti-Israel zealots, who often seek to de-legitimize the nation state of the Jewish people by accusing its military of deliberately murdering large numbers of innocent Palestinians.

While the media has focused on Bernie Sanders' egregious overstatement of the specific number of innocent Palestinians killed in Operation Protective Edge, the more revealing aspect of what he told the *Daily News* is his generalization that Israel indiscriminately leveled hospitals and apartment buildings. Although he did not explicitly say that the Israeli Defense Forces deliberately targeted civilians and civilian structures, his canard can certainly be understood that way by those Israel haters who are actively supporting his campaign. The word "indiscriminate," especially applied to Israeli military actions, has acted as a code word among Israel bashers for war crimes and even genocide. The reality is that the Israeli military's efforts to stop Hamas from indiscriminately killing Israeli citizens with rockets and through terror tunnels has been the opposite of indiscriminate, as Colonel Richard Kemp and other military experts have attested. No other country in history has gone to such lengths trying to distinguish between military and civilian targets, even in the face of an enemy that regularly uses its own population as human shields, and that hides military equipment in schools and hospitals. Israel's efforts to protect its citizens compare favorably to the U.S. and NATO led military bombing campaigns in Iraq, Syria, and other areas, in which civilians have also been used as human shields.

At best, Mr. Sanders's comments on Operation Protective Edge reflect a disappointing lack of interest in the specifics of what happened during the course of the seven-week war. As has been noted by several commentators, Senator Sanders is a long-term elected official who deals with some frequency with the Israeli-Palestinian conflict, and who should be expected to avoid gross misstatements on the topic. Mr. Sanders has done nothing to assuage these concerns: in two recent interviews, Mr. Sanders mistakenly put the number of civilians killed at "over 2,000" and again described the Israeli response as "disproportionate."

In one of those same interviews, it emerged that, apparently, Mr. Sanders had never heard of Michael Oren, the well-known Israeli ambassador to the United States during President Obama's first term. Mr. Sanders would be well advised to seek out the assistance of experts such as Mr. Oren, instead of the group of radical left-wing ideologues who currently advise him on Middle East policy. Among them, Mr. James Zogby of the Arab American Institute once described the motivations behind Israel's interventions in Gaza as "putting the natives back in their place." Professor Cornel West, who is a strong advocate of the Boycott Divestment Sanctions campaign directed against Israel, has acted as a Sanders surrogate on the campaign trail. Other aspects of Mr. Sanders' approach to Israel also seem influenced by far-left organizations. I was disappointed by Mr. Sanders' decision not to attend AIPAC this year, following pressure by far-left groups like Move On. I also thought his refusal to listen in person to Prime Minister Netanyahu's address to Congress in March of last year was a serious mistake.

That said, and in spite of some of the suggestions by the right-wing punditry, I do not believe that Mr. Sanders himself is anti-Israel. He may yearn for the Israel of the 1960s and 1970s, dominated by Labour governments, and defined by the Kibbutz. He is also clearly opposed to new Israeli settlements in the West

Bank, and to the politics of Prime Minister Netanyahu. However, I have no doubt that Mr. Sanders is sincere when he says that he is a friend of Israel. At various points during his career, he has condemned Hamas, rejected BDS, refused to endorse Palestinian attempts to prosecute Israel in front of the International Criminal Court, backed legislation calling on the United Nations to rescind the hopelessly biased Goldstone report, and stated that Israel's security concerns are paramount to restarting negotiations between the parties.

But in an obvious effort to avoid alienating those among his supporters who are rabidly anti-Israel, he has remained studiously ambiguous during the campaign about these and other contentious issues regarding the Israeli-Palestinian conflict. The time has come for Bernie Sanders to be unambiguous on where he stands, so that voters can accurately assess his Middle East policies.

April 22, 2016
Obama Meddles in Brexit but Shuns Netanyahu when He Speaks Up About Iran

At a joint press conference Friday with British Prime Minister David Cameron, President Obama defended his intrusion into British politics in taking sides on the controversial and divisive Brexit debate.

In an op-ed, Obama came down squarely on the side of Britain remaining in the European Union—a decision I tend to agree with on its merits. But he was much criticized by the British media and British politicians for intruding into a debate about the future of Europe and Britain's role in it.

Obama defended his actions by suggesting that in a democracy, friends should be able to speak their minds, even when they are visiting another country: "If one of our best friends is in an organization that enhances their influence and enhances their power and enhances their economy, then I want them to stay in. Or at least I want to be able to tell them 'I think this makes you guys bigger players.'"

Nor did he stop at merely giving the British voters unsolicited advice, he also issued a not-so-veiled threat. He said that "The UK is going to be in the back of the queue" on trade agreements if they exit the EU.

President Obama must either have a short memory or must adhere to Emerson's dictum that "foolish consistency is the hobgoblin of little minds." Recall how outraged the same President Obama was when the prime minister of a friendly country, Benjamin Netanyahu, spoke his mind about the Iran Deal.

There are, of course, differences: first, Israel has a far greater stake in the Iran deal than the United States has in whatever decision the British voters make about Brexit: and second, Benjamin Netanyahu was representing the nearly unanimous view of his countrymen, whereas there is no evidence that Americans favor or oppose Brexit in large numbers.

Another difference, of course, is that Obama was invited to speak by Cameron, whereas, Netanyahu was essentially disinvited by Obama. But under our tripartite system of government, that fact is monumentally irrelevant.

Netanyahu was invited by a co-equal branch of the government, namely Congress, which has equal authority over foreign policy with the president and equal authority to invite a friendly leader. Moreover, not only are the British voters divided over Brexit, but the conservative party itself is deeply divided.

Indeed, the leading political figure in opposition to Britain remaining in the EU is a potential successor to Cameron as leader of the Conservative party. So these differences certainly don't explain the inconsistency between Obama's interference in British affairs and his criticism of Netanyahu for accepting an invitation from Congress to express his country's views on an issue directly affecting its national security.

So what is it Mr. President? Should friends speak their minds about controversial issues when visiting another country, or should they keep their views to themselves? Or is your answer that friends should speak their minds only when they agree with other friends, but not when they disagree? Such a view would skew the market place of ideas beyond recognition.

A wit once observed that, "hypocrisy is the homage vice pays to virtue." It is also the currency of diplomacy and politics. That doesn't make it right.

The president owes the American people, and Benjamin Netanyahu, an explanation for his apparent hypocrisy and inconsistency.

Let there be one rule that covers all friends—not one for those with whom you agree and another for those with whom you disagree. For me the better rule is open dialogue among friends on all issues of mutual importance. Under this rule, which President Obama now seems to accept, he should have welcomed Prime Minister Netanyahu's advocacy before Congress, instead of condemning it.

May 2, 2016
The Holocaust: Many Villains, Few Heroes

As we commemorate the 70th anniversary of the Nuremberg trials, at which selected Nazi leaders were placed in the dock, we must ask some disturbing questions about those who were never tried for their complicity in the world's worst genocide. It would have been impossible to carry out the mass murder of so many people without the complicity of so many governments, groups, and individuals. Perhaps there were too many guilty parties to put them all on trial, but it is not too late to hold the guilty morally accountable for what they did and failed to do.

To be sure, the guiltiest individuals were the Nazi leaders who directly planned and implemented the final solution. Their goal was to in gather Jews from all over the world in order to kill them and to destroy what they regarded as the "Jewish race." They came very close to succeeding, wiping out nearly all of Europe's Jews in a relatively brief period of time. These Nazi leaders had the help of many "willing executioners," both in Germany and in the countries under its control. Among the worst culprits were individual Lithuanians, Latvians, Hungarians, Slovaks, Poles, Ukrainians, and others. There were some heroes among these groups and they are justly remembered and honored. But the number of villains far exceeded the number of heroes.

Then there were the guilty governments that cooperated and helped facilitate the deportations and round-ups. The French government deported more Jews than the Nazis demanded. Other governments, including those of Norway, Holland, Hungary and Austria (which had become part of Nazi Germany), also helped the Nazis achieve their genocidal goal. Bulgaria, on the other hand, declined to cooperate with the Nazi genocide, and its small Jewish population was saved. Denmark, too, rescued its Jews, many of whom were ferried to neutral Sweden.

There were also the countries that refused to accept Jews who might have escaped the Nazis had they been permitted to enter. These countries include the United States, Canada, and many other potential places of asylum that shut their doors. In the United States and Canada too, there were heroes who pressed their leaders to do more, but for the most part they failed.

Many Arab and Muslim leaders also played ignoble roles, siding with the Nazis and conducting their own pogroms against local Jews. The leading villain in this regard was the Grand Mufti of Jerusalem, who joined Hitler in Berlin and played a hands-on role in sending Jews to their deaths and in keeping the doors of Palestine closed to Jewish refugees.

Could more have been done by Britain and the United States to end the genocide? Could they have bombed the rail lines to Auschwitz and other death camps? These are complex questions that have been asked but not satisfactorily answered since 1945.

There were also the actions of those who pardoned and commuted the sentences of Nazis convicted at Nuremberg, and those who helped Nazis escape prosecution after the war ended. That list too is long and disturbing.

The Nuremberg trials, by focusing narrowly on Nazi leaders and their direct henchmen, implicitly exculpated those who played important, but less direct, roles by their actions and inaction. By their nature, courts are limited in what they can do to bring to justice large numbers of individuals who belong on a wide continuum of legal and moral guilt. But historians, philosophers, jurists, and ordinary citizens are not so limited. We may point fingers of blame at all who deserve to be blamed, whether or not they were placed on trial at Nuremberg, or at subsequent legal proceedings.

There will never be perfect justice for those who helped carry out the Holocaust. Most of the guilty escaped prosecution, lived happy lives and died in their beds, surrounded by loving family members. West Germany prospered as a result of the Marshall Plan, and many German industrialists, who had benefited from slave labor, continued to benefit as a result of the perceived needs of the Cold War. The scales of justice remain out of balance. Perhaps this helps to explain why more than 6 million people have been murdered in preventable genocides—in Cambodia, Rwanda, Darfur, and other places—since the world pledged "never again."

There is, of course, the risk that by blaming all, we blame none. It is important to calibrate the responsibility of those who played very different roles in the Holocaust. This is a daunting task, but it must be undertaken if future genocides are to be deterred.

May 4, 2016
The Mixed Legacy of Nuremberg

This year commemorates the 80th anniversary of the notorious Nuremberg Laws, the Nazi racist enactments that formed the legal basis for the Holocaust. Ironically, it also marks the 70th anniversary of the Nuremberg Trials, which provided the legal basis for prosecuting the Nazi war criminals who murdered millions of Jews and others following the enactment of the Nuremberg Laws.

There is little dispute about the evil of the Nuremberg Laws. As Justice Robert H. Jackson, who was America's chief prosecutor at the Nuremberg Trials, put it: "The most odious of all oppressions are those which mask as justice."

There is some dispute, however, about the Nuremberg trials themselves. Did they represent objective justice or, as Hermann Göring characterized it, merely "victor's justice"? Were the rules under which the Nazi leaders were tried and convicted ex post facto laws, enacted after the crimes were committed in an effort to secure legal justice for the most immoral of crimes? Did the prosecution and conviction of a relatively small number of Nazi leaders exculpate too many hands-on perpetrators? Do the principles that emerged from the Nuremberg Trials have continued relevance in today's world?

Following the Holocaust, the world took a collective oath encapsulated in the powerful phrase "never again," but following the Nuremberg Trials, mass murders, war crimes, and even genocides have been permitted to occur again and again and again and again. Cambodia, Rwanda, Darfur, the former Yugoslavia and now Syria. Why has the promise of "never again" been so frequently been broken? Why have the Nuremberg principles not been effectively applied to prevent and punish these unspeakable crimes? Will the International Criminal Court, established in 2002, be capable of enforcing the Nuremberg principles and deterring future genocides by punishing past ones?

Whether the captured Nazi leaders—those who did not commit suicide or escape—should have been placed on trial, rather than summarily shot, was the subject of much controversy. Even before the end of the war, Secretary of the Treasury Henry Morgenthau had proposed that a list of major war criminals be drawn up, and as soon as they were captured and identified, they would be shot. President Roosevelt was initially sympathetic to such rough justice, but eventually both he and President Truman were persuaded by Secretary of War Henry Stimson that summary execution was inconsistent with the American commitment to due process and the rule of law.

It was decided, therefore, to convene an international tribunal to sit in judgment over the Nazi leaders. But this proposal was not without considerable difficulties. Justice must be seen to be done, but it must also be done in reality. A show trial, with predictable verdicts and sentences, would be little better than no trial at all. Indeed, Justice Jackson went so far as to suggest, early on, that it would be preferable to shoot Nazi criminals out of hand than to discredit our judicial process by conducting farcical trials.

The challenge of the Nuremberg tribunal, therefore, was to do real justice in the context of a trial by the victors against the vanquished—and specifically those leaders of the vanquished who had been instrumental in the most barbaric genocide and mass slaughter of civilians in history. Moreover, the blood of Hitler's millions of victims was still fresh at the time of the trials. Indeed, the magnitude of Nazi crimes was being learned by many for the first time during the trial itself. Was a fair trial possible against this emotional backdrop?

Even putting aside the formidable jurisprudential hurdles—the retroactive nature of the newly announced laws and the jurisdictional problems posed by a multinational court—there was a fundamental question of justice posed. Contemporary commentators wondered whether judges appointed by the victorious governments—and politically accountable to those governments—could be expected to listen with an open mind to the prosecution evidence offered by the Allies and to the defense claims submitted on behalf of erstwhile enemies.

A review of the trial nearly 70 years after the fact leads to the conclusion that the judges did a commendable job of trying to be fair. They did, after all, acquit three of the twenty-two defendants, and they sentenced another seven to prison terms rather than hanging. But results, of course, are not the only or even the best criteria for evaluating the fairness of a trial. Furthermore, it is impossible to determine with hindsight whether the core leaders, such as Göring, von Ribbentrop, and Rosenberg, ever had a chance, or whether the acquittals and lesser sentences for some of the others was a ploy to make it appear that proportional justice was being done.

In the end, it was the documentary evidence—the Germans' own detailed record of their aggression and genocide—that provided the smoking guns. Document after document proved beyond any doubt that the Nazis had conducted two wars: One was their aggressive war against Europe (and eventually America) for military, political, geographic, and economic domination. The other was their genocidal war to destroy "inferior" races, primarily the Jews and Gypsies. Its war aim was eventually crushed by the combined might of the Americans and the Russians. Their genocidal aims came very close to succeeding. Nearly the entire Jewish and Gypsy populations within the control of the Third Reich were systematically murdered while the rest of the world—including those nations sitting in judgment—turned a blind eye.

The Nuremberg tribunal and those that followed it administered justice to a tiny fraction of those guilty of the worst barbarism ever inflicted on humankind. The vast majority of German killers were eventually "de-Nazified" and allowed to live normal and often productive lives.

It is necessary to ask whether, on balance, the Nuremberg Trials did more good than harm. By convicting and executing a tiny number of the most flagrant criminals, the Nuremberg tribunal permitted the world to get on with business as usual. The German economy was quickly rebuilt, unification between East and West Germany became a reality, and anti-Semitism is once again rife through Europe.

Perhaps Henry Morgenthau was asking for too much when he demanded that Germany's industry and military capacity be destroyed "forever," and that Germany must be "reduced to a nation of farmers." But perhaps the Nuremberg tribunal asked too little when it implicitly expiated those guilty of thousands of hands-on murders by focusing culpability on a small number of leaders who could never have carried out their wholesale slaughter without the enthusiastic assistance of an army—both military and civilian—of wholesale butchers.

The Nuremberg trial was an example of both "victor's justice" and of the possible beginning of a "new legal order" of accountability. Trying the culprits was plainly preferable to simply killing them. But trying so few of them sent out a powerful message that the "new legal order" would be lenient with those who were "just following orders."

The reality that, following Nuremberg, the world was to experience genocide again and again demonstrated that trials alone cannot put an end to human barbarity. But the fact that tribunals were established to judge at least some of these crimes against humanity also demonstrates a willingness to at least attempt to prevent and punish evil using the rule of law.

These and other issues have challenged and continue to challenge thinking. That is why a major conference of judges, academics, prosecutors, victims, and government officials is convening today, May 4, 2016, at the Jagiellonian University in Krakow, Poland, to consider the dual legacies of the Nuremberg Laws and the Nuremberg Trials. We plan to explore all sides of these enduring issues in a series of talks, panels, and visual presentations. The goal of the conference is symbolized by Santayana's famous dictum:

"Those who fail to learn from history are doomed to repeat it." The world cannot afford to repeat the tragedies of the Holocaust and so we must learn from the duel legacies of Nuremberg.

One of the most important lessons of history is that for genocide and other mass killings to be carried out requires the active participation of numerous individuals, from those who do the actual killing to those who incite, organize, and provide the means. The Holocaust itself required hundreds of thousands of active co-conspirators and millions more of morally complicit people who remained silent while it was being carried out around them. Not only were most of these guilty participants immunized from prosecution, but many were rewarded with good jobs and other economic benefits. It should come as no surprise, therefore, that the Nuremberg trials did not effectively deter subsequent mass killings. Indeed, the use of civilians as weapons of war—victims of genocide, mass rapes, and human shields—has continued, with only a few handfuls of leaders and perpetrators prosecuted and punished. The challenge of Nuremberg is to construct an effective, ongoing, legal regime that punishes not just the leaders, but each and every guilty participant in the most egregious of war crimes.

June 6, 2016
New York Is Right to Counter-Boycott Anti-Israel Boycotters

Pundits and commentators on Sunday proclaimed New York Governor Andrew Cuomo's executive order "unconstitutional" and "McCarthyite." Such verdicts are wrong, and somewhat ironic given the McCarthyite aspects of the BDS campaign itself.

The executive order Cuomo signed on June 5, declaring a New York State counter-boycott against businesses that single out Israel for commercial, artistic, academic, and cultural boycott, divestment, and sanctions, sends a strong message that New York stands opposed to the broader campaign to de-legitimize, demonize, and discriminate against the nation state of the Jewish people, and to efforts that undermine any reasonable prospect of a negotiated peace between Israelis and Palestinians.

Israel is far from perfect—and I and other supporters of Israel have been critical of its flaws—but it has internal mechanisms for addressing its imperfections. There is no legitimate reason for singling it out for the kind of external discrimination represented by BDS.

It is important to understand that there is no such thing as a *generalized* BDS campaign. If there were, it would target first the worst human rights offenders and those regimes which permit no dissent or access to justice. But the so-called BDS campaign does not target Iran, China, Belarus, Saudi Arabia, Cuba, or other such offenders (indeed, many advocates seek to increase ties with Iran, Cuba, and China despite their horrid records on human rights). The BDS campaign that is the object of Cuomo's executive order targets only one nation: the democratic nation state of Israel which, despite being subjected to terrorist attacks virtually on a daily basis, has a free press and an independent judiciary. No country faced with comparable threats has had a better record on human rights, compliance with the rule of law, and of efforts to reduce civilian casualties in armed conflicts.

Israel has also offered to end the occupation—as it did in Gaza—on numerous occasions in exchange for peace based on a two-state solution, but those offers have not been accepted by the Palestinian leadership, or by hardliners like Omar Bargouti, one of the leaders of BDS, who declared "I am completely and categorically against bi-nationalism because it assumes there are two nations with equal moral claims to the land."

One of BDS's core components—the Palestinian Campaign for the Academic and Cultural Boycott ("PACBI")—encourages participants to disassociate from Israeli cultural, artistic, and scientific institutions—and to blacklist individuals who are deemed too supportive of Israel. I recently learned that I feature on this blacklist when Omar Barghouti refused to debate me in front of the Oxford Union.

The PACBI guidelines endorse boycotting individuals who cross the BDS "picket lines" by cooperating with Israeli academic institutions or blacklisted individuals. They also encourage the boycott of all cultural and academic institutions or artists that promote "Brand Israel," including, for example, the singer Matisyahu. Even more egregiously, PACBI calls for the boycott of institutions that promote "normalization projects" that do not sufficiently emphasize the injustice of the occupation, even if those projects aim for Israeli-Palestinian dialogue and reconciliation. The BDS campaign also implicitly opposes a two-state solution by explicitly endorsing the so-called Palestinian right of return, which would in effect unwind nearly 40 years of negotiations, and destroy Israel as the nation state of the Jewish people.

In short, BDS is an anti-Israel and anti-peace tactic with which New York State should refuse to be complicit, and which thoroughly merits targeting by counter-boycott measures such as those passed in over a dozen states across the country.

Florida, for example, now requires the State Board of Administration to "identify all companies that are boycotting Israel," to divest all public funds from those entities, and further prohibits "a state agency or local governmental entity from contracting services" from those companies.

Other states have embraced more general provisions. California, for example, passed into law a measure that forbids the state from doing business with companies that discriminate on the basis of nationality or national origin.

Similarly, Alabama has passed a bill divesting from companies that boycott U.S. allies or, nations enjoy "normal trade" with the United States.

There are merits to both approaches. On the one hand, the obvious target of these laws is the anti-Israel BDS campaign. After all, there is no significant boycott campaign against another U.S. ally.

Including reference to Israel in the text of the bill helps cement the purpose of the legislation, and prevents state resources from being wasted identifying and combatting small-scale boycott campaigns.

On the other hand, legislation with non-specific language may have some benefits as well, namely that it more directly reflects the legal principle at the heart of anti-BDS measures—that it is generally wrong to discriminate on the basis of nationality or national origin.

In some ways, Governor Cuomo's anti-BDS executive action mirrors those of several states that refused to do business with North Carolina when that state passed legislation that discriminated against the LGBTQ community. It also emulates the counter boycotts of the 1930s against the Nazi boycott of Jewish businesses.

Moreover—and contrary to the shrill claims of the pro-BDS punditry—there is longstanding precedent for anti-boycott regulations. Since the mid-1970s, for example, the U.S. has enforced a number of anti-boycott laws through the Export Administration Act ("EAA") and the Executive Administration Regulations ("EAR"). Among other provisions, the EAA and EAR penalize individuals and companies that participate in boycotts based on race, religion, sex, national origin, or nationality. They have been repeatedly applied to companies participating in the now-defunct Arab League boycott of Israel, and to boycotts targeting other U.S. allies.

To call such regulations McCarthyite is to insult the victims of real McCarthyism who were punished for their ideas, speeches, and associations, not for their actions in refusing to do business based on national origin. Yes, there will be a list of companies that discriminate against Israel, just as there are lists today of store and building owners who refuse to do business with, for example, African-Americans, LGBTQ, or Muslims. There will have to be proof that a business engaged in a discriminatory boycott by singling out Israeli entities, or individuals based on their national origin, or political convictions, and a process for challenging inclusion on any list.

The only McCarthyist blacklist is that which has been compiled by BDS enforcers—a list I am proud to be on—of supporters of Israel and of those who seek to "normalize" relations between Israelis and Palestinians.

To be clear: Governor Cuomo's executive order should go no further than this. No one, not even the most rabid BDS-activist, should face legal recriminations for expressing an opinion that is supportive of BDS, or for encouraging others to participate in BDS activities. Political speech—even bigoted, misguided political speech—is clearly protected by the Constitution. I am confident that New York State officials and courts will construe the governor's order to apply only to discriminatory business activities and not to speech or advocacy.

So applied, Governor Cuomo's counter boycott will promote political, artistic, and cultural freedoms by imposing economic sanctions on those BDS bigots who are seeking to suppress such freedoms by discriminating against Israeli, and pro-Israeli advocates, artists, cultural figures, and businesses.[63]

July 3, 2016
A Tribute to Humanity's Teacher

Elie Wiesel was my teacher, my "rabbi," my mentor, my colleague, and my dear friend. Over the past 50 years, we worked together on numerous human rights projects. Elie did more to bring the word "human" into human rights than any person in modern history. For him, it did not matter whether the victims of genocide were Jews, Christians, Muslims, black, white, from the left, or from the right. Human rights were equally applicable to all.

Elie was deeply involved in campaigns on behalf of the victims of genocide in Darfur, Rwanda, the former Yugoslavia, Cambodia, and the Middle East. My last substantive conversation with him was about the genocide currently taking place in Syria, where hundreds of thousands of Muslims are being slaughtered by both sides of an intractable conflict. He bemoaned the unwillingness of the international community to stop the slaughter. "Have we learned nothing?" he asked rhetorically. For Elie Wiesel, the worst sin was silence in the face of evil. The worst crime was indifference to genocide, and the worst people were those who stand idly by the blood of their neighbors. Though he and his family were victims of the Holocaust, he never dwelled on his personal pain, but rather on the pain of those currently being victimized.

I first met Elie after the publication of his book *The Jews of Silence*, which dealt with the plight of Soviet Jews who were being persecuted in the Soviet Union. He inspired me to go to the Soviet Union with a legal team in order to defend those who were being criminally prosecuted for doing nothing more than practicing their religion. We continued to work together on matters involving non-

Jewish victims of persecution around the world. I began as his student, then became his colleague, and finally his friend. We shared a world view and a commitment to repairing a badly damaged planet. He would call me on the phone frequently to complain that we were not doing enough. He always wanted to do more.

Elie Wiesel was one of the most important people in the post-World War II period. He spoke truth to power, regardless of who was in power. He loved and respected President Ronald Reagan, and yet he lectured him and urged him not to go to Bitburg, Germany, to commemorate the Nazi killers who were in the SS. He spoke up when others were silent. He spoke up for those for whom no one else championed. For that he justly received the Nobel Peace Prize.

I was honored to be among those who nominated him for that prize, which he used as a platform to rail against injustice. He spoke softly—so softly that one had to lean forward to hear his hushed tones. But what he said inspired, stimulated, and produced results. He saved many lives by his quiet advocacy. He called world leaders on the phone and persuaded them to act, taking no credit for their life-saving actions.

Among his most enduring contributions will be his great memoir, *Night*, which has become required reading in many schools around the world and has influenced many young people to join the enduring battle against injustice.

Elie did so many things in his life. He wrote books, he advocated for justice, he ran a foundation for humanity with his wonderful wife, Marion. But whenever he was asked what his job was, he would reply, "I am a teacher." He loved to teach more than anything else. He loved his students and his students loved him. He saw the world as a large classroom, with his role as one of its teachers. Shortly before his final illness, Elie and I agreed to teach a course together at Boston University. We had scheduled the first preliminary joint lecture, but his illness required a postponement. It was never to be. But even in death, professor Elie Wiesel will continue to teach generations of students through his passionate writing and by his uncompromising example.

I will miss my friend Elie every day of my life. The world will miss Elie Wiesel for as long as the quest for justice continues.

July 13, 2016
Who Do Bigots Blame for Police Shootings in America? Israel, of Course!

In response to the tragic deaths of Philando Castile and Alton Sterling at the hands of police officers in Minnesota and Louisiana, the New York University chapter of Students for Justice in Palestine (SJP) posted the following on its Facebook page:

> *"In the past 48 hours another two black men have been lynched by the police.... We must remember that many US police departments train with #IsraeliDefenceForces. The same forces behind the genocide of black people in America are behind the genocide of Palestinians. What this means is that Palestinians must stand with our black comrades. We must struggle for their liberation. It is as important as our own. #AltonSterling is as important as #AliDawabsheh. Palestinian liberation and black liberation go together. We must recognize this and commit to building for it."*

Even in moments of national mourning such as these, SJP bigots cannot help but exploit the deaths of innocent Americans to further their own anti-Semitic political agenda, namely to delegitimize and demonize the nation state of the Jewish people.

By implicating Israel in these killings, SJP is engaging in the old trope of blaming Jews for systemic and far-reaching societal problems. This practice was anti-Semitic when some Christian communities used it to blame Jews for plagues, poisonings, and murders; it was anti-Semitic when the Nazis used it to blame Jews for the failing German economy; and it is still anti-Semitic today. There is no more evidence that any of the police who killed Mr. Castile and Mr. Sterling were, in fact, trained in Israel than there was that Jews were responsible for any of the other crimes that formed the basis for traditional blood libels.

The oppression of black Americans long predates the founding of the state of Israel; contrary to the claims of SJP and like-minded groups, Zionism did not beget racism, nor is Zionism a reflection of racism. It is the national liberation movement of the Jewish people. But the twisted logic on the part of SJP should come as no surprise, given that the same organization blamed Zionism for rising tuition costs in the City University of New York college system. The essence of anti-Semitism is the bigoted claim that if there is a problem, then Jews—and now Zionists—must be its cause.

Addressing the structural causes of racism in the United States will take more than scapegoating Israel—it will require the type of far-reaching legislative action of which our current Congress seems incapable. By morphing the discussion about criminal justice reform and systemic racism in the United States into a polemic against Israel, SJP makes progress even more difficult.

That said, the reaction by SJP is reflective of a broader trend in hard left politics. Increasingly, groups such as Black Lives Matter (BLM), MoveOn, Code Pink, and Occupy Wall Street have embraced intersectionality—a radical academic theory, which holds that all forms of social oppression are inexorably linked.

This radical concept has led to the linking of disparate left-wing causes, no matter how tenuous their connections. Some intersectional feminist activists, for example, insist that feminists must oppose drone strikes (and by extension, Hillary Clinton), because they negatively impact women in the developing world. Even more absurdly, Jill Stein—the Green Party candidate for president—has come out in favor of the bigoted Boycott Divestment Sanctions (BDS) tactic against Israel, partly on the grounds that support for Israel furthers the interests of the military-industrial complex, and by extension the fossil fuel industry.

Those activists who do not sufficiently embrace the new intersectional orthodoxy, meanwhile, have been targeted by protests: the 2016 Gay Pride parade in Toronto, for example, was broken up by Black Lives Matter for including a police float, and for not sufficiently prioritizing the concerns of black Trans women. Similarly, a gay rights event in Chicago was broken up by activists, who insisted on the exclusion of an Israeli organization, which they claimed was co-opting the gay rights agenda and "pinkwashing" Israeli crimes against Palestinians.

Intersectionality seems to be driving hard left activists towards a "No True Scotsman" worldview; increasingly, they insist on a package of unrelated left-wing causes that must be embraced by anyone claiming the label of progressive—including the demonization of Israel as a racist, apartheid state.

Perhaps more worryingly, intersectionality tends towards the conclusion that the existing social, political, and economic system is flawed in so many profound ways, that any attempt at remaking it through democratic means is unacceptable. Activists have become increasingly obsessed with "Shut it Down" protest tactics, and a proud politics of "disrespectability," that prioritizes resistance to a "corrupt," "rigged" socio-economic system over respectful discourse and political compromise.

This helps to explain the sympathetic attitude of Black Lives Matter activists towards groups like Hamas, which embrace terror as a mode of "resistance" (in their view) against Israel. Indeed, Black Lives Matter activists have visited Gaza to express solidarity with Palestinians oppressed by so-called racist Israeli self-defense measures. While Black Lives Matter claims to disavow violence in securing its political objectives, many of its most prominent members are far more eager to criticize the "Israeli genocide of Palestinians" than to criticize Hamas for using rockets to target Israeli civilians. Black Lives Matter and other hard left groups have been notably silent about other oppressed ethnic groups such as Tibetans, Chechens, and Kurds. The only alleged "oppressors" they single out for condemnation are the Jews. This double standard raises legitimate questions about their real motivations.

Moreover, the conflation of police actions in American cities with Israeli military actions in Gaza raises a disturbing question: if the so-called oppression of Palestinians in Gaza and the oppression of people of color in the United States are two sides of the same coin—as the SJP implied in its tweet—are the violent tactics employed by Hamas, and perversely supported by many on the hard left, an appropriate model to emulate in the United States? One hopes that the answer is *no*, and that the intersectionality radicals will make that clear to their followers.

July 28, 2016
The New York Times Makes a Shocking Mistake

In a recent article "Amid Push to Curb Police Abuse, Some Act on Fringe," *The New York Times* quoted Malik Zulu Shabazz's call to kill all Zionists in Israel, including their "old ladies" and "little babies."

Those words alone are shocking and reprehensible but the *Times* reporters failed to properly identify Shabazz. They said he was "a former New Black Panther leader." It is odd to identify someone by reference to his "former" role, when his current role is more important and more relevant to the story. Shabazz is the current president of Black Lawyers for Justice, an organization that assists plaintiffs with police abuse cases and frequently organizes rallies with notorious hate groups, such as Nation of Islam.

A 30-second Google search revealed Shabazz's current role in an organization with "justice" hypocritically in its title. Why did the *Times* choose to identify him by reference to his former, rather than current role?

I know enough about the *Times'* fact-checking process to be certain that the reporters were aware of his present role. If they made an explicit editorial decision to omit it, the readers are entitled to know why.

Was it in order to artificially widen the distance between violent radical "fringe" groups and more mainstream groups that are seeking to curb police abuse? Why not include the current role of this hateful inciter of genocide and let the reader judge his proximity to the mainstream.

The *Times* didn't even identify Shabazz as a member of the bar—a practicing lawyer—who, together with his fellow members of Black Lawyers for Justice, gives legal advice to some of those mainstream groups the *Times* was focusing on in the article.

As president of Black Lawyers for Justice, Shabazz has called for genocide against the Jews of Israel: "Kill every goddamn Zionist in Israel! Goddam little babies, goddam old ladies? Blow up Zionist supermarkets." And, he has not limited his hateful vitriol to Zionists. He had blamed Jews for blowing up the World Trade Center: "They got their people out." He has accused the Jews of "[k]illing Christ," and said that "God condemns you." He has said that "Jews" set up the death of Martin Luther King. He blames "[t]he Jewish rabbis" and "the Talmud" for "the African holocaust." He has said that "the European Jews have America under control, lock stock and barrel, the media, foreign policy."

This bigoted inciter of genocide is a member of the bar of the District of Columbia—despite having been disciplined by that bar for numerous acts of unprofessional conduct. Those acts include "failing to provide competent representation" to clients, "failing to safe-keep his client's property," and "knowingly assisting another to violate the Rules of Professional Conduct." Applicants for admission to the bar have been excluded for expressing racist ideas far less virulent than the genocidal incitements attributed to Shabazz.

While these incitements may be protected by the First Amendment, they may also demonstrate unfitness to practice law, especially when considered against the background of the other unprofessional conduct of which Shabazz has been found guilty.

One thing is clear: no decent person should have anything to do with this anti-Semitic hatemonger, and every legitimate organization concerned about police abuse should disassociate themselves from him and from his organization.

Yet Cornel West, a professor of Philosophy and Christian Practice at Union Theological Seminary and Professor Emeritus at Princeton University, recently introduced this despicable bigot at a "March of the Oppressed" rally in Cleveland. West praised Shabazz as "my dear brother," someone whom he has known for 20 years and who "is still on the battlefield."

He compared this rancid anti-Semite to the great Martin Luther King. He asked the crowd to applaud for Shabazz, which they did. He then hugged him.

You can view West's speech at #MASSIVE rally and March in #LE #BlackLivesMatter on YouTube.

West's endorsement of Shabazz is comparable to a white professor introducing the Grand Wizard of the Ku Klux Klan with such effusive praise.

Despite West's close association with and support for this advocate of genocide against Jewish babies, West was appointed to the Democratic Party Platform Committee by Bernie Sanders.

For shame!

August 16, 2016
Black Lives Matter Targets Israel

It is a real tragedy that Black Lives Matter—which has done so much good in raising awareness of police abuses—has now moved away from its central mission and has declared war against the nation state of the Jewish people. In a recently issued "platform," more than 60 groups that form the core of the Black Lives Matter movement went out of their way to single out one foreign nation to accuse of genocide and apartheid.

No, it wasn't the Syrian government, which has killed tens of thousands of innocent people with barrel bombs, chemicals, and gas. Nor was it Saudi Arabia, which openly practices gender and religious apartheid. It wasn't Iran, which hangs gays and murders dissidents. It wasn't China, which has occupied Tibet for more than half a century. And it wasn't Turkey, which has imprisoned journalists, judges, and academics.

Finally, it wasn't any of the many countries, such as Venezuela or Mexico, where police abuses against innocent people run rampant and largely unchecked.

Nor was it the Hamas-controlled Gaza Strip, where the police are a law unto themselves who act as judge, jury, and executioner of those whose politics or religious practices they disapprove.

It was only Israel, the nation state of the Jewish people and the only democracy in the Middle East. The platform accuses the U.S. of being "complicit in the genocide taking place against the Palestinian people" by providing aid to "an apartheid state."

To be sure, Black Lives Matter is not a monolithic organization. It is a movement comprising numerous groups. Many of its supporters have no idea what the platform says. They cannot be faulted for supporting the movement or its basic mission.

But the platform is the closest thing to a formal declaration of principles by Black Lives Matter. The genocide paragraph may well have been injected by radicals who are not representative of the mainstream.

But now that it has officially been published, all decent supporters of Black Lives Matter—and there are many—must demand its removal.

Criticizing Israel is not anti-Semitic. Like other democracies, including our own, it has faults. Criticizing Israel's settlement and occupation policies is fair game. But singling Israel out and falsely accusing it of "genocide" can be explained in no other way than blatant hatred of Jews and their state.

In defending its citizens against terrorism since before its establishment as a state in 1948, Israel has killed fewer Palestinians than did Jordan and Syria in two much shorter wars.

The relatively low number of civilian deaths caused by Israeli self-defense measures over the past 68 years compares favorably to the number of civilian deaths in other conflicts.

This is because, as Colonel Richard Kemp, former commander of British Forces in Afghanistan, put it: There has been "no time in the history of warfare when an Army has made more efforts to reduce civilian casualties...than [the Israel Defense Forces]."

Though Kemp was specifically referring to the wars in the Gaza Strip—which are also the apparent focus of the Black Lives Matter Platform—his conclusion is applicable to all wars Israel has fought.

Genocide means the deliberate extermination of a race, such as done by Nazi Germany to Jews and Sinti and Roma or by the Hutu against the Tutsi in Rwanda. It has no application to deaths caused by self-defense measures taken to protect citizens against terrorism. To falsely accuse Israel of "genocide"—the worst crime of all, and the crime whose very name was coined to describe the systematic murder of 6 million Jews—is anti-Semitic.

Until and unless Black Lives Matter removes this blood libel from its platform and renounces it, no decent person—black, white, or of any other racial or ethnic background—should have anything to do with it.

We should continue to fight against police abuses by supporting other organizations or forming new ones. But we must not become complicit in the promotion of anti-Semitism just because we agree with the rest of the Black Lives Matter program.

To support an organization or movement that promotes anti-Semitism because it also supports good causes is the beginning of the road to accepting racism. Many racist groups have also promoted causes that deserve support. The Black Panthers had breakfast programs for inner-city children while advocating violence against whites. And the Ku Klux Klan organized summer camps for working-class families while advocating violence against blacks.

There must be zero tolerance for anti-Semitism, regardless of the race, religion, gender, or sexual orientation of the bigots who promote, practice, or are complicit with it. Being on the right side of one racial issue does not give one a license to be on the wrong side of the oldest—bigotry.

To give Black Lives Matter a pass on its anti-Jewish bigotry would be to engage in racism.

Black anti-Semitism is as inexcusable as white anti-Semitism or white racism. There can be no double standard when it comes to bigotry.

I write this column both in sorrow and in anger. In sorrow because I support the goals of the Black Lives Matter movement—I have long been involved in efforts to expose and prevent police abuses—and worry that this obnoxious and divisionary platform plank may destroy its credibility with regard to police abuse in America by promoting deliberate lies about Israel. It is also alienating Jewish and other supporters who could help them achieve their goals here at home—as many such individuals have historically done in actively supporting all aspects of the civil rights movement.

I write it in anger because there is never an excuse for bigotry and for promoting blood libels against the Jewish people and their state. It must stop. And those who engage in it must be called out for condemnation.

Black Lives Matter should rescind the portions of the platform that falsely accuse Israel of genocide and apartheid. If it does not, it risks ending in the dustbin of history, along with other discredited bigoted groups.

It would be sad if the good work done by Black Lives Matter were now to be sidetracked by the mendacious and irrelevant accusation of "genocide" and "apartheid" against one foreign democracy—Israel.

August 24, 2016
Are Jews Who Refuse to Renounce Israel Being Excluded from "Progressive" Groups?

Hard left activists are trying to exclude Jews who do not renounce Israel from "progressive" organizations.

Last year, Rabbi Susan Talve, a longtime activist on race issues in the St. Louis area, was told that her advocacy for Israel was incompatible with the objectives of Black Lives Matter: "Solidarity from Ferguson to Palestine has become a central tenet of the movement" she was informed, because "Israeli and U.S. state oppression are deeply interconnected." Similarly, a student who attended a Black Lives Matter rally at Northwestern University last year was told "you support Israel, so you cannot also support us."

Recently, that seems to be the response of many of the hard left activists who dominate so-called "progressive" social justice movements.

Over the past several years, progressive Jews and progressive supporters of Israel have had to come to terms with the reality that those who do not reject Israel and accept Boycott Divestment Sanctions (BDS) and its unique brand of bigotry are no longer welcome in some progressive circles. And while both Democratic and Republican parties have embraced the importance of the U.S. alliance with Israel, that dynamic is under threat more so than at any point in my lifetime.

The self-described "progressive wing" of the Democratic Party—represented by radical and often repressive organizations such as MoveOn, CodePink, Occupy Wall Street, and Black Lives Matter—has become openly opposed to the nation state of the Jewish people. Increasingly, these organizations demand that their members and "allies" renounce support for Israel and for Zionism in order to belong. Using the pretext of intersectionality—a pseudo-academic theory that insists that all social justice movements, except those supportive of Jews or Israel, are inexorably linked—anti-Israel activists have successfully made opposition to Israel and support for BDS a litmus test, especially for Jews, to belong to "progressive" movements focused on a wide range of issues.

In 2016, supporters of the LGBTQ community in Israel learned this lesson the hard way, when BDS activists together with a local Black Lives Matter chapter broke up a gay pride event, because it featured a presentation by an Israeli group. The protestors claimed that the event organizers had engaged in "pinkwashing" the Israeli occupation by showing solidarity with the Israeli LGBTQ community.

Members of the National Women's Studies Association (NWSA) who also support Israel have been similarly excluded. Last year, that organization voted to endorse BDS, and as one pro-BDS activist explained: "What is significant about this particular resolution is the rationale; the fact that the resolution makes it explicit that BDS is a feminist issue…that one cannot call themselves a feminist…without taking a stand on what is happening in Palestine." (Apparently, one can call oneself a feminist without taking a stand on Syria, Russia, Saudi Arabia, and other nations that grossly violate human rights). [And most recently, in June 2017, Jewish participants at the Chicago 'Dyke March'—a parade geared towards that city's lesbian community—were told to leave the parade because their flag—which had a Star of David printed on top of the LGBTQ rainbow flag—"made people feel unsafe." They were also told that the march was "anti-Zionist" and "pro-Palestinian."]

This type of repressive ideological packaging has left progressive Jews and liberal supporters of Israel in an increasingly uncomfortable position. On the one hand, they care deeply about causes such as women's rights, criminal justice reform, income inequality, environmental protection, and LGBT rights. On the other, they find themselves excluded from the groups that advance those very causes, because—while they are often critical of specific Israeli policies regarding settlements and the occupation—they refuse to renounce Israel as a national liberation movement of the Jewish people.

For hard left activists, this sort of nuanced position is impossible to accept. Their hostility towards Israel does not stem from any particular Israeli actions or policies. Even if Israel were to withdraw from the West Bank, destroy the security barrier, and recognize Hamas as a legitimate political organization, it would still not be enough. For these radicals, it is not what Israel *does*; it is about what Israel *is*: the nation state of the Jewish people—or to use hard left terminology: an imperialistic, apartheid, and genocidal, colonialist enterprise. The recently released Black Lives Matter policy platform_offers a perfect example of such extreme rhetoric: it states that U.S. military and economic support for Israel makes American citizens complicit in "the genocide taking place against the Palestinian people."

The fact that the BLM platform reads like it was lifted from a BDS screed is hardly coincidence: the two groups enjoy a longstanding relationship, and a prominent BDS activist apparently helped draft elements of the BLM declaration. But BLM is far from the only hard left organization that has been infected by BDS vitriol. In fact, BDS has pressured a wide range of progressive organizations into assuming an anti-Israel posture. The American Green Party, for example—which has become a haven for disaffected progressive activists this election cycle—recently came out in support of BDS and called for the US to end its support for "the Israeli apartheid regime."

This trend has been particularly pronounced on college campuses, where a host of academic groups—most absurdly the Native American Scholars Association and the Americans Studies Association—have passed resolutions in favor of BDS. Many of these organizations have also endorsed the Palestinian Academic and Cultural Boycott (PACBI), which encourages participants to engage in McCarthyite blacklisting of Israeli academic institutions, as well as groups and individuals who promote "Brand Israel." This category apparently includes artists like Matisyahu, and academics like me, as I found out last year when a prominent BDS advocate refused to debate me at the Oxford Student Union.

The PACBI also explicitly denounces "normalization projects"—programs or events aimed at Israeli-Palestinian reconciliation that do not sufficiently emphasize the colonialist nature of the state of Israel. These are exactly the types of initiatives widely supported and promoted by progressives who are critical of settlements, but remain supportive of Israel and of a two-state solution. It is no coincidence that BDS has singled them out for special treatment. BDS campaigners want to force any supporters of Israel—no matter their stances on other political issues—outside of the progressive tent.

This effort has proved alarmingly successful thus far, but despite the pressure from the hard left, liberals and progressives who support Israel must continue to carve out a political space for themselves. In doing so, they can follow the example of the Jewish Community Relations Council, which dissociated itself "from the Black Lives Matter platform and those BLM organizations that embrace[d] it" but committed itself "unequivocally to the pursuit of justice for all Americans, and to working together with our friends and neighbors in the African-American community, whose experience of the criminal justice system is, far too often, determined by race." Such efforts are critical to ensure that it is not supporters of Israel but rather those repressive bigots who falsely claim the mantle of progressivism and who subscribe to the identity politics practiced by BDS that are delegitimated by mainstream progressives and liberals.

September 28, 2016
Shimon Peres—A Leader for All Seasons

Shimon Peres has passed away, and with him, the last embodiment of Israel's great founding generation. When Peres and his family immigrated to British Mandate Palestine in 1934, Hitler was consolidating his power in Germany, and Europe was about to begin the most shameful chapter of its history. Peres lost many family members, including his grandparents, in the Holocaust. His life's work—over six decades of public service to the nation state of the Jewish people—was dedicated to ensuring that such a tragedy could never be repeated.

Perhaps more than anyone else, Peres is responsible for ensuring Israel's security by shaping a powerful and effective defense apparatus that allowed Israel to stand up to its more powerful and populous neighbors. In 1947, when he joined the Haganah—the predecessor to the Israeli Defense Forces—Israel was surrounded by hostile armies intent on its destruction. Jerusalem was under siege by the Arab "Holy War Army," and Jewish kibbutzim were being attacked across Galilee and Samaria.

During those early days, when the very survival of the Jewish state seemed improbable, David Ben-Gurion appointed Peres to secure weapons for Israel from the United States and Europe. He was so successful in this task that, after the War of Independence, he was delegated to the naval services, where his primary task was again to ensure that the Israeli army would be properly equipped if the conflict with its Arab neighbors were to resume. His tireless negotiations with American, French, and British officials led to the signing of several major arms deals and cemented Israel's status as the foremost military power in the Middle East. At age 29, Peres became director general of the Ministry of Defense. He used that position to develop Israel's nuclear arsenal, its navy, and its military industrial capacity.

But Peres also understood the Biblical verse "to everything there is a season." Much as he zealously sought to ensure Israel's security, he was also uncompromising in his quest for peace with its neighbors. When Israel became strong enough to defend itself, Peres saw a change in the seasons, and he became one of the leading voices for reconciliation with Israel's erstwhile regional enemies. As defense minister, he oversaw the Israeli disengagement from Sinai that paved the way for the peace settlement with Egypt. As foreign minister, he was one of the primary visionaries behind the Israeli-Jordanian Peace Treaty of 1993.

He was also the first prominent Israeli politician to recognize the reality that a demilitarized Palestinian state would not only be just for the Palestinians, but would also be good for the Israelis. His work alongside his great political rival, Yitzhak Rabin, to achieve a lasting solution to the Israeli-Palestinian conflict, at the 1993 Oslo accords, won him a Nobel Peace Prize, and it remains an enduring, if unfinished, chapter of his legacy.

Peres was both a man of principle and of pragmatism. He understood that morality, without the strength to defend it, might cause a repetition of the disaster the Jewish people faced during the 1930s and 1940s, when they lacked the strength to defend themselves against powerful forces intent on their destruction. As prime minister, he did not hesitate to airlift thousands of Ethiopian Jews to Israel when they were threatened with annihilation by the rise of a nationalistic military dictatorship. He showed similar resolve when arguing powerfully for the military raid on Entebbe, Uganda, that rescued over 80 hostages taken by Palestinian terrorists.

But he also understood that strength alone was not enough. For him, Israel's founding vision was a "country living in peace and security in its homeland and among its neighbors." As he said in a speech he delivered on his 90th birthday: "We long for peace with our neighbors. The yesterday between us and the Palestinians is full of sadness. I believe that the Israel of tomorrow and the Palestine of tomorrow can offer our children a ray of hope. The advancement of peace will complete the march of Israel towards the fulfillment of its founding vision." And while his dream of a two-state solution was never closer than at Oslo in 1993, his tireless work toward that end speaks volumes of the man.

I knew him for 46 years, ever since I interviewed him in Israel for PBS in 1970, and I visited him on almost every trip to Israel. Our last time together in the United States was at a state dinner at the White House for his 90th birthday. He was at the top of his game. As President Obama observed when he awarded Peres the Medal of Freedom in 2012: "In him, we see the essence of Israel itself—an indomitable spirit that will not be denied."

November 1, 2016
Obama: Don't Destroy the Peace Process by Turning It Over to the UN

The Obama administration is sending strong signals that once the election is over it may make a major push to resolve the Israeli-Palestinian conflict at the United Nations. Despite repeated invitations by Israeli Prime Minister Benjamin Netanyahu to Palestinian Authority President Abbas to meet without preconditions, the stalemate persists. Some blame it on Palestinian unwillingness to recognize Israel as the nation state of the Jewish people and to compromise to the so-called "right of return." Others—including the current U.S. administration—lay the blame largely at the feet of the Netanyahu government for continuing to build in the West Bank, most recently approval of between 98 and 300 new homes in Shiloh. Whatever the reasons—and they are complex and multifaceted—President Obama should resist any temptation during his final weeks in office to change longstanding American policy—that only direct negotiations between the parties will achieve a lasting peace.

In particular, Obama should veto an expected French resolution in the Security Council establishing an international peace conference under the auspices of the UN. The general parameters of the French resolution would likely call for:

"Borders based on the 1967 Lines with agreed equivalent land swaps; security arrangements preserving the sovereignty of the Palestinian State and guaranteeing the security of Israel; a fair, equitable, and negotiated solution to the refugee problem; an arrangement making Jerusalem the capital of both states."

These guidelines may sound reasonable. Indeed, they are strikingly similar to the offers made to and reject by the Palestinian leadership in 2000–2001 from former Israeli Prime Minister Ehud Barak and former U.S. President Bill Clinton, and in 2008 by former Israeli Prime Minister Ehud Olmert. The UN, however, has disqualified itself from playing any constructive role in the peace process. Recent attempts by the UN to intervene in the Israeli-Palestinian conflict have produced unmitigated disasters. The so-called Goldstone Report, which sought to investigate allegations of war crimes committed during the 2009 Israeli intervention in Gaza, was so blatantly biased against Israel that Richard Goldstone himself had to retract some of its key findings in 2011.

Since then, the UN has done nothing to reassure Israel that it is capable of offering an unbiased forum for negotiations. In the past year alone, the UN has singled out Israel for special criticism on issues like health rights, and most laughably, women's rights, while failing even to mention regimes whose record on these issues is truly abominable. In 2015 alone, at least twenty separate resolutions were adopted by the UN General Assembly, which singled out Israel for special criticism. Most recently UNESCO attempted to erase millennia of Jewish history with regard to the Temple Mount in Jerusalem. [And UNESCO has since attempted to deny and undermine the Jewish connection to the city of Hebron and its holy sites.] In light of such behavior, the U.S. should not trust that Israel would receive a fair hearing at any UN sponsored peace conference.

As Netanyahu said in his most recent speech to the UN General Assembly, "The road to peace runs through Jerusalem and Ramallah, not through New York." In other words, the only way forward for the Israeli-Palestinian peace process is bilateral negotiations between the two parties. Netanyahu and Abbas must sit down and agree to necessary but painful compromises aimed at establishing a Palestinian state, while addressing Israel's security concerns, and the realities on the ground. Resolutions such as the proposed French resolution undermine such efforts by encouraging the Palestinians to believe that direct negotiations—and the mutual sacrifices they would entail—are unnecessary, and that a Palestinian state can be achieved on the basis of UN resolutions alone. It would also make it more difficult, if not impossible, for the Palestinian Authority to accept anything less than that already given them by the UN—which would in turn guarantee the failure of any realistic negotiations.

It is for these and other reasons that American policy has long been to veto or otherwise derail UN attempts to interfere with the Israeli-Palestinian peace process even when it is stalled. As President Obama said in 2013:

> *"We seek an independent, viable and contiguous Palestinian state as the homeland of the Palestinian people. The only way to achieve that goal is through direct negotiations between Israelis and Palestinians themselves."*

Hillary Clinton, too, has stated in the past that she supports bilateral negotiations between the Israelis and Palestinians, and her campaign has said that she "believes that a solution to this conflict cannot be imposed from without." So, too, has Donald Trump.

Recently, however, several past and present Obama officials have apparently advised the president to support, or at least not veto the French resolution, as well as a one-sided Palestinian push to have the UN declare Israeli settlements illegal. It would be wrong—and undemocratic—for Obama to unilaterally reverse decades of U.S. foreign policy during the lame duck period. After all, in 2011 his administration vetoed an almost identical Palestinian proposal that called for Israel to "immediately and completely cease all settlement activities in occupied Palestinian territory, including East Jerusalem." Similarly, until now, Obama has repeatedly pressured the French and other European nations not to put forward any proposal related to the Israeli-Palestinian conflict, on the grounds that such initiatives discourage bilateral negotiations. This is surely the view of the majority of the Senate, which has its own constitutional authority to participate in foreign policy decisions. In fact, 88 senators signed an open letter to Obama in which they called on the president to veto any Security Council resolutions regarding the Israeli-Palestinian conflict.

The period between the election and the inauguration is the only time a president can act without the checks and balances of American democracy. He should not take action that would tie the hands of his successor.

Obama must realize that no lasting peace can be achieved in the remaining months of his presidency: there are a multitude of complex and contentious issues—most notably the status of Jerusalem, the rights of so-called Palestinian refugees, and the situation in Gaza—that must be thoroughly addressed in order to achieve a lasting peace. Our next president will undoubtedly have to wade into the Israeli-Palestinian peace process again. The new administration—with the agreement of the Senate—should have full latitude to do what it deems most appropriate. It should not be stuck with parameters bequeathed to it by a president desperate to secure a short-term foreign policy "victory" that in the long term will make a resolution of the conflict more difficult to achieve.

If Obama feels that he must intrude in an effort to break the logjam before he leaves office, he should suggest that the current Israeli government offer proposals similar to those offered in 2000–2001 and 2008 and that this time the Palestinian leadership should accept them in face-to face negotiations. But he should take no action (or inaction) that invites UN involvement in the peace process—involvement that would guarantee failure for any future president's efforts to encourage a negotiated peace.

We should hear the views of both candidates on whether the U.S. should support or veto a Security Council resolution that would tie their hands were they to be elected president. It is not too late to stop President Obama from destroying any realistic prospects for peace.

November 17, 2016
How to Assess the Bannon Appointment

President Elect Trump's appointment of Steve Bannon as his chief strategist has been criticized on the ground that Bannon is an anti-Semite. There are many reasons for opposing the appointment of Bannon, but anti-Semitism is not one of them. I do not support the Bannon appointment. But neither do I support accusing Bannon of being an anti-Semite, based on the evidence I have seen.

With regard to anti-Semitism, there are three distinct but overlapping issues: (1) Is Bannon personally an anti-Semite? (2) Does his publication, *Breitbart*, promote anti-Semitic views? (3) Do *Breitbart* and Bannon have followers who are anti-Semitic?

From what I can tell, the evidence cited in support of the accusation that personally Bannon is an anti-Semite falls into two categories: first, that his wife testified at a hotly contested divorce proceeding that he did not want his children to go to school with "whiney Jews"; and second, that he ran an article describing Bill Kristol as a "renegade Jew."

Let us consider these items of evidence in order. Senator Harry Reid tried to strengthen the first accusation against Bannon by saying that it appeared in a court document, thus suggesting that it had the imprimatur of a judge. But that is not the case. The claim was simply made by his former wife in a judicial proceeding, thus giving it no special weight. Bannon has rigorously denied making the statement and said that he and his wife were fighting over whether his children should attend Catholic school, rather than a secular school.

On the other side of the ledger is the testimony of Jewish individuals who have worked closely with him for years. These include my former research assistant, Joel Pollak, an orthodox Jew who wears a kippah and takes off all the Jewish holidays. He is married to a black woman from South Africa who converted to Judaism. Joel assures me that he never heard a single anti-Semitic utterance or saw an anti-Semitic action in the four years they worked together. The same is true of numerous other Jewish individuals who work with him, some of whom thoroughly disapprove of Bannon's politics and the way he ran *Breitbart*, but none of whom have reported any events of anti-Semitism.

The second alleged item of evidence is the following headline that appeared on *Breitbart*: "Bill Kristol: Republican Spoiler, Renegade Jew." I am advised, however, that this article and the headline were written not by Bannon but rather by David Horowitz, a right-wing Jew who was upset with Kristol for his refusal to support Trump. Horowitz deemed that a betrayal of the Jewish people. While I fundamentally disagree with that appraisal and also of the article, I find it hard to characterize Bannon as an anti-Semite because *Breitbart* ran it. *Breitbart* has also personally attacked me, but that doesn't change my views.

I keep an open mind waiting for more evidence, if there is any, but on the basis of what I have read, I think it is wrong to accuse Bannon of one of the most serious forms of bigotry. So I will not join the chorus of condemnation that employs this radioactive term against Bannon without compelling evidence. The Anti-Defamation League has now commendably acknowledged that there is no evidence of anti-Semitism by Bannon: "We are not aware of any anti-Semitic statements from Bannon."

As to whether Bannon promotes the alt-right, and whether the alt-right includes anti-Semites, I think the answer to that is yes. Both Bannon and *Breitbart* have made bigoted statements about Muslims, women, and others, which I do not condone. That is why I do not support Bannon, even though I do not think he's an anti-Semite. Bigotry against any group should be disqualifying for high office. But let's put this criticism of Bannon and *Breitbart* into context. *Haaretz* certainly serves as a platform for the alt-left in Israel. Though it features a wide range of commentary, primarily from the center-left, it also features hard left writers such as Gideon Levy, who supports academic, cultural, and economic boycotts against Israel and its "criminal" regime, as well as Amira Hass, who encourages Palestinians to throw stones and engage in "violent resistance" against Israel. These writers have certainly been accused, and with some justification, of promoting hatred not only against the current Israel government, but against the very nature of Israel and Zionism. Their hateful writings are often quoted gleefully by anti-Zionist and anti-Semites.

This is not to compare *Breitbart* with *Haaretz*, but it is to suggest caution in holding a publication responsible for all the views expressed by its writers. To be sure, *Haaretz*'s general orientation tends to be center-left, whereas *Breitbart* is hard-right, but both serve as platforms for extremes on either side. The same can be said of J Street, which is a center-left organization which serves as a platform for, and includes among its active members and contributors, BDS supporters, anti-Zionists, and opponents of Israel's existence as the Nation State of the Jewish people.

Or consider Black Lives Matter, an organization with a commendable goal that has promoted anti-Semitism by singling out one country for condemnation in its "platform": calling the Nation State of the Jewish People an "apartheid" and "genocidal" regime. In an article in *Above the Law*, Joe Patrice attacks me for my critique of Black Lives Matter, claiming that "it's certainly possible someone in the movement also has sympathy for Palestinians." But there is an enormous difference between "sympathy for Palestinians" (which I share) and accusing the entire nation state of the Jewish people of "genocide" (which I believe is anti-Semitic).

Anti-Semitism and anti-Zionism are prevalent both on the hard right and on the hard left. The Trump election has brought hard right anti-Semitism into public view, but the bigotry of the hard left is far more prevalent and influential on many university campuses, both in the United States and in Europe. A single standard of criticism must be directed at each. We must judge individuals on the basis of their own statements and actions, and we should be cautious in judging publications and organizations on the basis of who they publish, who their audience is and who supports them.

People of good will, Jews and non-Jews, must condemn with equal vigor all manifestations of bigotry whether they emanate from the hard alt-right or hard alt-left. That is why I cannot support Bannon's appointment, even though he is strongly pro-Israel. But that is also why I can't support those on the hard left who advocate good causes, while at the same time promoting anti-Semitism and the de-legitimization of Israel.

December 1, 2016
Ellison, Wrong Man at Wrong Time for DNC

What should a political party that has just lost its white working-class blue-collar base to a "make America great again" nationalist do to try to regain these voters? Why not appoint as the new head of the party a radical left-wing ideologue who has a long history of supporting an anti-American, anti-white, anti-Semitic, Nation of Islam racist?

Such an appointment will surely bring back Rust Belt voters who have lost their jobs to globalization and free trade! Is this really the thinking of those Democratic leaders who are pushing for Keith Ellison to head the Democratic National Committee?

Keith Ellison is, by all accounts, a decent guy, who is well liked by his congressional colleagues. But it is hard to imagine a worse candidate to take over the DNC at this time.

Ellison represents the extreme left wing of the Democratic Party, just when the party—if it is to win again—must move to the center in order to bring back the voters it lost to Trump.

The Democrats didn't lose because their candidates weren't left enough. They won the votes of liberals. The radical voters they lost to Jill Stein were small in number and are not likely to be influenced by the appointment of Ellison.

The centrist voters they lost to Trump will only be further alienated by the appointment of a left-wing ideologue who seems to care more about global issues than jobs in Indiana, Wisconsin, and Michigan. Ellison's selection certainly wouldn't help among Jewish voters in Florida, Ohio, and Pennsylvania or pro-Israel Christian voters around the country.

Ellison's sordid past associations with Louis Farrakhan—the longtime leader of the Nation of Islam—will hurt him in Middle America, which has little appetite for Farrakhan's anti-American ravings. Recently, Farrakhan made headlines for visiting Iran on the 35th anniversary of the Islamic Revolution where he berated the U.S., while refusing to criticize Iran's human rights violations.

Farrakhan also appeared as a special guest speaker of the Iranian president at a rally, which featured the unveiling of a float reenacting Iran's detention of 10 U.S. Navy sailors in the Persian Gulf. In addition to embracing American enemies abroad, Farrakhan has exhibited a penchant for lacing his sermons with anti-Semitic hate speech. Around the time that Ellison was working with the Nation of Islam, for example, Farrakhan was delivering speeches attacking "the synagogue as Satan." He described Jews as "wicked deceivers of the American people" that have "wrapped [their] tentacles around the U.S. government" and are "deceiving and sending this nation to hell."

Long after Jesse Jackson disavowed Farrakhan in 1984 as "reprehensible and morally indefensible" for describing Judaism as a "gutter religion,"—(Fay S. Joyce, "Jackson Criticizes Remarks Made by Farrakhan as 'Reprehensible," *The New York Times*, June 29, 1984)—Ellison was defending Farrakhan and the Nation of Islam in 1995 as a role model for African-Americans, calling him "a tireless public servant of Black people, who constantly teaches self-reliance and self-examination to the Black community."

Ellison has struggled to explain his association with Farrakhan and the Nation of Islam. He has acknowledged working with the Nation of Islam for about 18 months to organize the Minnesota delegation to Farrakhan's 1995 Million Man March in Washington

However, Ellison insists that he never joined the Nation of Islam and more recently, he has held himself out as a friend of the Jewish people and of Israel. This late conversion coincided with Ellison's decision to pursue elected office in Minnesota, and an apparent realization that his association with the Nation of Islam might hurt his political fortunes.

In 2006, he wrote a letter to the Jewish Community Relations Council in Minneapolis, in which he apologized for failing to "adequately scrutinize the positions" of Farrakhan and other Nation of Islam leaders. "They were and are anti-Semitic, and I should have come to that conclusion earlier than I did."

In his recently released memoir *My Country, 'Tis of Thee: My Faith, My Family, Our Future*, Ellison writes of Farrakhan, "He could only wax eloquent while scapegoating other groups" and of the Nation of Islam "if you're not angry in opposition to some group of people (whites, Jews, so-called 'sell out' blacks), you don't have religion."

Ellison's voting record also does not support his claim that he has become a "friend" of Israel. He was one of only eight congressmen who voted against funding the Iron Dome program, developed jointly by the U.S. and Israel, which helps protect Israeli civilians from Hamas rockets.

In 2009, Ellison was one of only two dozen congressmen to vote "present" rather than vote for a non-binding resolution "recognizing Israel's right to defend itself against attacks from, reaffirming the United States' strong support for Israel, and supporting the Israeli-Palestinian peace process."

And in 2010, Ellison co-authored a letter to President Obama, calling on him to pressure Israel into opening the border with Gaza. The letter describes the blockade of the Hamas controlled Gaza strip as "de facto collective punishment of the Palestinian residents."

Even beyond Ellison's past associations with anti-American and anti-Semitic bigotry and his troubling current voting record with regard to Israel, his appointment as head of the DNC would be a self-inflicted wound on the Democratic Party at this critical time in its history.

It would move the party in the direction of left-wing extremism at a time when centrist stability is required. The world at large is experiencing a movement toward extremes, both right and left. The Democratic Party must buck that dangerous trend and move back to the center where the votes are, and where America should be.

December 23, 2016
Trump Rightly Tried to Stop Obama From Tying His Hands on Israel

The Egyptian decision to withdraw the one-sided anti-Israel Security Council resolution should not mask the sad reality that it is the Obama administration that has been pushing for the resolution to be enacted. The United States was trying to hide its active 'behind the scenes' roll by preparing to abstain rather than voting for the resolution. But in the context of the Security Council, where only an American veto can prevent anti-Israel resolutions from automatically passing, an abstention is a vote for the resolution. And because of this automatic majority, an anti-Israel resolution like this one cannot be reversed by a future American president. A veto not cast cannot be cast retroactively

The effect, therefore, of the Obama decision to push for, and abstain from, a vote on this resolution is to deliberately tie the hands of President Obama's successors, most particularly President-elect Trump. That is why Trump did the right thing in reaction to Obama's provocation. Had the lame duck president not tried to tie the incoming president's hands, Trump would not have intervened at this time. But if he had not urged the Egyptians to withdraw the resolution, he would have made it far more difficult for himself to try to bring about a negotiated resolution to the Israeli-Palestinian conflict.

The reason for this is that a Security Council resolution declaring the 1967 border to be sacrosanct and any building behind those boarders to be illegal would make it impossible for Palestinian leaders to accept less in a negotiation. Moreover, the passage of such a resolution would disincentivize the Palestinians from accepting Israel Prime Minister Netanyahu's invitation to sit down and negotiate with no preconditions. Any such negotiations would require painful sacrifices on both sides if a resolution were to be reached. And a Security Council resolution siding with the Palestinians would give the Palestinians the false hope that they could get a state through the United Nations without having to make painful sacrifices.

President Obama's lame duck attempt to tie the hands of his successor is both counterproductive to peace and undemocratic in nature. The lame duck period of an outgoing president is a time when our system of checks and balances is effectively suspended. The outgoing president does not have to listen to Congress or the people. He can selfishly try to burnish his personal legacy at the expense of our national and international interests. He can try to even personal scores and act on pique. That is what seems to be happening here. Congress does not support this resolution; the American people do not support this resolution; no Israeli leader—from the left, to the center, to the right—supports this resolution. Even some members of Obama's own administration do not support this resolution. But Obama is determined—after 8 years of frustration and failure in bringing together the Israelis and Palestinians—to leave his mark on the Mideast peace process. But if he manages to push this resolution through, his mark may well be the end of any realistic prospect for a negotiated peace.

One would think that Obama would have learned from his past mistakes in the Mideast. He has alienated the Saudis, the Egyptians, the Jordanians, the Emirates, and other allies by his actions and inactions with regard to Iran, Syria, Egypt, and Iraq. Everything he has touched has turned to sand.

Now, in his waning days, he wants to make trouble for his successor. He should be stopped in the name of peace, democracy, and basic decency.

But it now appears that Obama will not be stopped. Four temporary Security Council members have decided to push the resolution to a vote now. It is difficult to believe that they would have done so without the implicit support of the United States. Stay tuned.

[Addendum: As predicted, the United States allowed the anti-Israel resolution to be approved by the United Nations Security Council. Votes in favor were cast by Russia, which has occupied Kornengsberg since 1945, after capturing that ancient German city, ethnically cleansing its population and bringing in hundreds of thousands of Russian settlers; China, which has occupied Tibet and brought in thousands of Chinese settlers; France, which occupied and settled Algeria for many years; Great Britain, which has occupied and colonized a significant portion of the globe; and assorted other countries, several of which have horrendous human rights records.

Israel on the other hand, offered to end the occupation and settlements in 2000–2001 and again in 2008 only to be rebuffed by the Palestinian leadership. But Israel is the only country to have been condemned by the Security Council for an occupation and settlement. This hypocrisy is typical of the United Nations as even our representative acknowledged when she explained why the United States abstained.

Now peace will be more difficult to achieve, as the Palestinians become further convinced that they do not have to accept Netanyahu's offer to negotiate without preconditions.

Thank you, President Obama, for completing your 8 years of failed foreign policy with a final blow against, peace, stability, and decency.

Congress can ameliorate the impact of this destructive resolution by enacting a statute declaring that the resolution does not represent the United States' policy, which is that peace will not come through the United Nations but only by direct negations between the parties. The law should also prohibit any United States funds to be spent directly or indirectly in support of this Security Council resolution. I suspect that the incoming president will be willing to sign such a law.]

December 27, 2016
The Consequences of Not Vetoing the Israel Resolution

Amid the continuing controversy over the Obama administration's refusal to veto the Security Council's resolution regarding Israeli "settlements," it is important to understand why Israeli leaders across the political spectrum as well as American supporters of Israel—including many who oppose settlement expansion and favor a two-state solution—feel so negatively about this resolution.

Its text states that "any changes to the 4 June 1967 lines, including with regard to Jerusalem" have "no legal validity and [constitute] a flagrant violation under international law." This resolution is not, therefore, limited to settlements in the West Bank. It applies equally to the very heart of Israel.

Before June 4, 1967, Jews were forbidden from praying at the Western Wall, Judaism's holiest site. They were forbidden to attend classes at the Hebrew University at Mt. Scopus, which had been opened in 1925 and was supported by Albert Einstein. Jews could not seek medical care at the Hadassah Hospital on Mt. Scopus, which had treated Jews and Arabs alike since 1918. Jews could not live in the Jewish Quarter of Jerusalem, where their forebears had built homes and synagogues for thousands of years. These Judenrein prohibitions were enacted by Jordan, which had captured by military force these Jewish areas during Israel's War of Independence, in 1948, and had illegally occupied the entire West Bank, which the United Nations had set aside for an Arab state.

When the Jordanian government occupied these historic Jewish sites, they destroyed all the remnants of Judaism, including synagogues, schools, and cemeteries, whose headstones they used for urinals. Between 1948 and 1967 the UN did not offer a single resolution condemning this Jordanian occupation and cultural devastation.

When Israel retook these areas in a defensive war that Jordan started by shelling civilian homes in West Jerusalem and opened them up as places where Jews could pray, study, receive medical treatment, and live, the United States took the official position that it would not recognize Israel's legitimate claims to Jewish Jerusalem. That is why it refused to move the American embassy from Tel Aviv to Jerusalem. It stated that the status of Jerusalem, including these newly liberated areas, would be left open to final negotiations and that the status quo would remain in place. That is the official rationale for why the United States refuses to recognize any part of Jerusalem, including West Jerusalem, as part of Israel. That is why the United States refuses to allow an American citizen born in any part of Jerusalem to put the words "Jerusalem, Israel" on his or her passport as their place of birth.

But that has now changed with the adoption of the Security Council Resolution. The UN has now determined that, subject to any further negotiations and agreements, the Jewish areas of Jerusalem recaptured from Jordan in 1967 are not part of Israel. Instead, according to the resolution, they are territories being illegally occupied by Israel, and any building in these areas—including places for prayer at the Western Wall, access roads to Mt. Scopus, and synagogues in the historic Jewish Quarter—"constitutes a flagrant violation under international law." If that indeed is the status quo, absent "changes...agreed by the parties through negotiations," then what incentives do the Palestinians have to enter negotiations? And if they were to do so, they could use these Jewish areas to extort unreasonable concessions from Israel, for which these now "illegally occupied" areas are sacred and nonnegotiable.

This is what President Obama has wrought in his ill-advised refusal to do what American presidents have done for decades: exercise their veto in preventing biased, destructive, and one-sided resolutions from being enacted against Israel by the automatic anti-Israel majority that exists in every institution of the UN.

The bad news is that no future president, including President-elect Trump, can undo this pernicious agreement, since a veto not cast can never be retroactively cast. And a resolution once enacted cannot be rescinded unless there is a majority vote against it, with no veto by any of its permanent members, which include Russia and China, who would be sure to veto any attempt to undo this resolution. Obama's failure to veto this resolution was thus a deliberate ploy to tie the hands of his successors, the consequence of which will be to make it far more difficult for his successors to encourage the Palestinians to accept Israel's offer to negotiate with no preconditions.

The good news is that Trump can ameliorate the effects of this resolution immediately upon assuming office. He can do so by officially recognizing Jerusalem as Israel's capital and moving its embassy there. This would dramatically demonstrate that the United States does not accept the Judenrein effects of this bigoted resolution on historic Jewish areas of Jerusalem, which are now forbidden to Jews. The prior refusal of the United States to recognize Jerusalem as Israel's capital and to move its embassy there was based explicitly on the notion that nothing should be done to change the status quo of that city, holy to three religions. But this resolution does exactly that: It changes the status quo by declaring Israel's de facto presence on these Jewish holy sites to be a "flagrant violation under international law" that "the UN will not recognize."

Since virtually everyone in the international community acknowledges that any reasonable peace would recognize Israel's legitimate claims to these and other areas in Jerusalem (and indeed, to settlement blocks in close proximity to Jerusalem), there is no reason for allowing the UN resolution to make criminals out of every Jew or Israeli who sets foot on these historically Jewish areas.

Before the enactment of this resolution, I was not in favor of Trump immediately moving the U.S. embassy to Jerusalem. I advocated that such a move should take place in stages, over time, and with consultation among America's Muslim allies in the region. But now that the UN has made it a continuing international crime for there to be any Israeli presence in disputed areas of Jerusalem, including areas whose Jewish provenance is beyond dispute, there is a need for immediate action by Trump, upon taking office, to untie his hands and to undo the damage wrought by his predecessor. Congress will surely approve such a move, since the overwhelming majority of its members disapproved of the American decision not to veto the resolution, and since, in 1995, Congress enacted a statute, signed by President Clinton, declaring that the "United States maintains it embassy in the functioning capital of every country except in the case of our democratic friend and strategic ally, the State of Israel" and urged "the United States [to] conduct official meetings and other business in the city of Jerusalem in de facto recognition of its status as the capital of Israel."

Obama's ill-advised, lame duck, and undemocratic effort to tie his successor's hands must not be allowed to destroy the prospects for a negotiated peace between Israel and the Palestinians.

[Addendum: On June 1, President Trump signed a waiver deferring the moving of the U.S. Embassy to Jerusalem for another six months—an act which the Trump administration conveyed was necessary to better lay the groundwork for fruitful negotiations.

President Trump will have the opportunity to reassess his campaign promise when the waiver is up for reevaluation in December, see page 294.]

December 31, 2016
Britain and Australia More Supportive of Israel than Obama and Kerry

When the British Prime Minster and the Australian Foreign Minister both criticize the Obama administration for being unfair to Israel, you can be sure that something is very wrong with what President Obama and Secretary Kerry have been doing. This is what Theresa May said:

"We do not believe that it is appropriate to attack the composition of the democratically elected government of an ally. [W]e are also clear that the settlements are far from the only problem in this conflict. In particular, the people of Israel deserve to live free from the threat of terrorism, with which they have had to cope for too long."

This is what Julie Bishop, the Foreign Minister of Australia, said in explaining why Australia would not have voted for the UN Security Council resolution:

"In voting at the UN, the [Australian] Coalition government has consistently not supported one-sided resolutions targeting Israel."

And these are only the *public* criticisms. In *private* several other countries have expressed dismay at the problems caused by the last-minute moves of the lame duck Obama administration.

Initially, *The New York Times* failed to report these important international developments, presumably because they disagree with them. Only after other media featured the British and Australian criticism did they decide to cover it. They *did* immediately report that the Jewish community—both in the United States and Israel—is divided between right wing Jews who oppose the Obama administration's moves and liberal Jews who support them. This is simply fake news: Israel is *not* divided over the Security Council's resolution and the Kerry speech. All Israeli leaders and the vast majority of its citizens opposed these developments. This is true even of the Israeli leftists and centrists who are critical of Israel's settlement policies. The same is true with regard to American Jews, despite *The New York Times* reporting to the contrary. Many liberal Jews and non-Jews, including Senators Schumer, Blumenthal, Gillibrand, and Wyden, have been vocally critical. So have numerous liberal congressmen and pundits. I certainly count myself as a liberal Democrat who opposes Israel's settlement policies, but who is strongly critical of the Obama/Kerry moves. Only J Street—which carries Obama's water—has expressed support, along with a few handfuls of hard left reform rabbis and professional Israel bashers, who the *Times* reporter quoted as if they were representative of the larger Jewish community.

In contrast to the relative uniformity of the Israel's leaders and citizens in opposition to the Obama/Kerry initiatives, the Obama administration itself and the Democratic Party are divided.

Most who have expressed views have been critical, but we have not yet heard from several leading Democrats, especially Keith Ellison who is seeking the chairmanship of the DNC. This is an issue on which silence is not a virtue. It is important for all Democrats to stand up and be counted.

There *is* actually some good news growing out of the Kerry speech. Arab leaders have expressed support for his proposal, which would require the Palestinian Authority to recognize Israel as a Jewish state (or as I prefer to put it "the nation state of the Jewish people"). Despite this implicit support for such recognition from Arab leaders, the Palestinian Authority adamantly persists in refusing to recognize Israel's Jewish character.

This is the phony excuse Hanan Ashwari, the official spokesperson for the Palestinian Authority, gave for why it would be "against our principles" to recognize Israel as the nation state of the Jewish people:

If you want to give religion to states, then this is against our principles. I don't recognize Islamic states. I don't recognize Christian states. I don't recognize Jewish states. A state is a state for all its citizens. It has to be democratic, inclusive, tolerant, and has to be genuinely representative of all its people. You cannot give added value to any people because of their religion or ethnicity."

This statement may win the award for Ashwari as hypocrite of the year. The Palestinian Authority, which she officially represents, has the following in its Constitution:

"Islam is the official religion in Palestine....The principles of Islamic Shari'a shall be the main source of legislation."

Moreover, the Palestinian Authority recognizes Iran, Saudi Arabia, Egypt, and Jordan, which are all countries that define Islam as their state religion and discriminate against non-believers in their particular brand of Islam.

Is Ashwari really saying that the principles of the Palestinian Authority require it to renounce their own Constitution and to withdraw recognition from all their Muslim allies? What about from Great Britain, which has an official state religion? If so, I challenge her to say that explicitly!

Israel is the only state in the Middle East that grants religious equality to all its citizens as a matter of law. Israeli Arabs enjoy more rights than do Arabs (let alone Jews) of any Arab state. They serve in all branches of government, including the Knesset and the Supreme Court. They have their own religious authorities recognized by the state.

Contrast this to the Palestinian leadership that has vowed that "not a single" Israeli Jew will be able to reside in the future Palestinian state. Furthermore, Israeli Jews are banned from Palestinian universities and other institutions.

So let's have three cheers for Great Britain and Australia, a cheer and a half for Arab leaders, and a big raspberry for the hypocrisy of Hanan Ashwari and her Palestinian Authority.

January 15, 2017
Obama's Mideast Legacy Is One of Tragic Failure

The Middle East is a more dangerous place after eight years of the Obama presidency than it was before. The eight disastrous Obama years follow eight disastrous George W. Bush years, during which that part of the world became more dangerous as well. So have many other international hotspots.

In sum, the past sixteen years have seen major foreign policy blunders all over the world, and most especially in the area between Libya and Iran—that includes Israel, Egypt, Syria, Iraq, Lebanon, Turkey, and the Gulf.

With regard to the conflict between Israel and the Palestinians, the Obama policies have made the prospects for a compromise peace more difficult to achieve. When Israel felt that America had its back—under both Presidents Clinton and George W. Bush—they offered generous proposals to end settlements and occupation in nearly all of the West Bank.

Tragically the Palestinian leadership—first under Yasser Arafat and then under Mahmoud Abbas—did not accept either offers from Israel Prime Minister Ehud Barak and Clinton in 2000–2001, nor Prime Minister Ehud Olmert's offer in 2008. Now they are ignoring current Prime Minister Benjamin Netanyahu's open offer to negotiate with no preconditions.

In his brilliant book chronicling American-Israeli relationship, *Doomed to Succeed*, Dennis Ross proves conclusively that whenever the Israeli government has confidence in America's backing, it has been more willing to make generous compromise offers than when it has reason to doubt American support.

Obama did not understand this crucial reality. Instead of having Israel's back, he repeatedly stabbed Israel in the back, beginning with his one-sided Cairo speech near the beginning of his tenure, continuing with his failure to enforce the red line on chemical weapons use by Syria, then allowing a sunset provision to be included in the Iran deal, and culminating in his refusal to veto the one-sided UN Security Council resolution, which placed the lion's share of blame on the Israelis for the current stalemate.

These ill-advised actions—especially the Security Council resolution—have disincentivized the Palestinian leadership from accepting Netanyahu's offer to sit down and negotiation a compromise peace. They have been falsely led to believe that they can achieve statehood through the United Nations, or by other means that do not require compromise.

The Iran deal, while it delayed Iran's acquisition of nuclear weapons, virtually guaranteed that it would be allowed to develop a nuclear arsenal as soon as the major restrictions on the deal expire in the next decade. Israel will never allow a regime sworn to the destruction of the nation state of the Jewish people to secure such a weapon.

So the likelihood of an eventual dangerous military confrontation has been increased, rather than decreased, by the poorly negotiated Iran deal.

Obama's failure to carry out his red-line threat against the Syrian regime's use of chemical weapons has weakened American credibility among its allies and adversaries alike. It has created a power vacuum that Russia was quick to fill. Turkey, too, has flexed its bullying muscles, as its irascible and egomaniacal leader has used the excuse of the Islamic State in Iraq and Syria (ISIS) to go after another American ally, the Kurds, who have at least as strong a claim to statehood as the Palestinians.

America's traditional allies in the Middle East—Israel, Egypt, Saudi Arabia, the United Arab Emirates, and Jordan—have all been weakened by Obama's policies, most especially the Iran deal. America's traditional enemies—Iran, Syria, and Hezbollah—have been strengthened, along with Turkey.

Terrorism has increased and moved northward to Europe partly as a result of the Syrian crisis. ISIS, al Qaeda, the Taliban, and other terrorist offshoots, though weakened, remain a serious threat to regional stability and to civilians.

A destabilized Middle East poses increasing dangers to American allies and to peace. The blame for this instability is shared by Presidents George W. Bush and Obama. The invasion of Iraq and the overthrow of Saddam Hussein divided that country, rendering it ungovernable, and invited Iran to play a major role in its current destabilized condition.

The toppling of Moammar Gadhafi left Libya open to increasing terrorist influences. The attempt to replace Bashar Assad has turned Syria into a nightmare.

The forced resignation of Hosni Mubarak initially placed Egypt under the control of the Muslim Brotherhood, and strengthened Hamas in the Gaza Strip. Only a coup, opposed by the Obama administration, restored some semblance of stability to Egypt.

Lebanon has become a wholly owned subsidiary of Hezbollah, a terrorist group under the influence of Iran that has 100,000 missiles aimed at Israel's population centers. The "Shiite arc" now runs from Iran through parts of Iraq and Syria and into Lebanon.

This is the tragic legacy of the Obama administration's failed efforts to undo the harms caused by the George W. Bush administration. Radical Islamic terrorists have replaced authoritarian secular tyrants.

Both are bad, but tyrants at least produce a degree of stability and predictability. They also tend to keep their tyranny domestic, whereas terrorists tend to export their evil tactics.

We should have learned the lesson from the replacement of the tyrannical Shah of Iran by the far more tyrannical and dangerous ayatollahs. But we did not. We insisted on supporting the "democracy" of the Arab spring, which resulted in the replacement of undemocratic domestic tyrants by undemocratic international terrorists.

History will look kindly on Obama's domestic successes, but it will judge his Mideast policy harshly.

February 13, 2017
Trump Welcomes Netanyahu

I know them both—Netanyahu better than Trump—and I believe they will get along well. They are both no-nonsense pragmatists who understand the relationship between economic development and political progress. We all know of Trump's business background and focus on jobs and trade. Less well-known is Netanyahu's business background. Like Trump, Netanyahu went to business school and began his career as a businessman, working for Boston Consulting Group. When he entered politics, he helped transform Israel from an agrarian-based economy into "start-up nation," which has become a technological superpower with a strong economy. He is the Alexander Hamilton of Israel to David Ben Gurion's Jefferson. Trump has to admire that.

Trump will also admire Netanyahu's strong nationalism and love of country. He has made Israel great, militarily, technologically, and economically. He may soon become Israel's longest-serving Prime Minister, surpassing the legendary Ben Gurion.

Each leader would like to be the one who succeeds in bringing a peaceful resolution to the Israeli-Palestinian conflict. So many others—people of goodwill and considerable effort—have been unable to achieve this goal. There is no certainty that Trump and Netanyahu can succeed when so many others have come close but have never been able to close the deal. Both are respected for their deal-making capabilities—Trump in business, Netanyahu in domestic politics.

But there are considerable barriers to achieving a peaceful resolution. Netanyahu and his Palestinian counterpart, Mahmoud Abbas, each have domestic constituencies that would oppose the compromise necessary to achieve a two-state solution. Some of Netanyahu's right-wing coalition partners oppose a two-state solution in which Israel would turn over most of the West Bank to establish a Palestinian state. And many West Bank Palestinians—not to mention Hamas in Gaza—oppose recognizing the legitimacy of Israel as the nation state of the Jewish people. They also demand the "return" of millions of Palestinian refugees to Israel, despite the reality that there are probably only a hundred thousand or so actual refugees who themselves left Israel in 1948–1949, many voluntarily.

It must be remembered that Israel has twice in recent times offered the Palestinians a state on 95 percent of the West Bank. In 2000–2001, then Prime Minister Ehud Barak and then President Bill Clinton made a generous offer. Yasser Arafat, who was being advised by Jimmy Carter, rejected it and started a violent *intifada*, in which more than 4,000 people were killed. Then in 2008, Prime Minister Ehud Olmert made an even more generous offer, to which Mahmoud Abbas did not respond. And in 2005, Prime Minister Ariel Sharon unilaterally ended the military occupation and settlements in the Gaza Strip, only to be greeted with thousands of rocket attacks and terror tunnels from Hamas.

Much has changed since these Israeli offers and actions. The current Israeli government is not likely to offer more than what was rejected by the Palestinians. So the pressure must now be placed on the Palestinian leadership to make good faith counteroffers. That pressure can only come from the United States. This is so because the rest of the international community—the United Nations, the

European Union, the courts in The Hague, the BDS campaign—all disincentivize the Palestinians from making compromises, by falsely telling them they can get a state without negotiating with Israel.

President Trump must make it crystal clear that unless the Palestinians negotiate a reasonable solution with Israel, they will *never* have a state. President Obama did not send that message with clarity, especially when he ordered his United Nations Representative to allow a one-sided anti-Israel resolution to be passed by the Security Council.

President Trump must reassure Prime Minister Netanyahu that he will apply pressure—perhaps through our Sunni allies—on the Palestinian Authority, and not only on Israel, as the Obama administration did. History shows that American administrations that really have Israel's back—not to stab, but to support—are more likely to persuade Israel to offer compromises.

So, I hope that Benjamin Netanyahu will emerge from the White House meeting with the confidence in American support to stand up to those in his cabinet who oppose the two-state solution and who want to expand settlement activity. And I hope the Palestinian leadership will understand that they have no option other than to accept the Netanyahu offer to negotiate anywhere, anytime, and with no preconditions. Perhaps then we will finally see a reasonable resolution to the age-old conflict.

February 20, 2017
Trump: Palestinians Must Earn a Two-State Solution

President Trump raised eyebrows when he mentioned the possibility of a one-state solution.

The context was ambiguous and no one can know for sure what message he was intending to convey. One possibility is that he was telling the Palestinian leadership that if they want a two-state solution, they have to do something. They have to come to the negotiating table with the Israelis and make the kinds of painful sacrifices that will be required from both sides for a peaceful resolution to be achieved. Put most directly, the Palestinians must earn the right to a state. They are not simply entitled to statehood, especially since their leaders missed so many opportunities over the years to secure a state. As Abba Eben once put it: "The Palestinians never miss an opportunity to miss an opportunity."

It began back in the 1930s, when Great Britain established the Peel Commission which was tasked to recommend a solution to the conflict between Arabs and Jews in Mandatory Palestine. It recommended a two-state solution with a tiny noncontiguous Jewish state alongside a large Arab state. The Jewish leadership reluctantly accepted this sliver of a state; the Palestinian leadership rejected the deal, saying they wanted there to be no Jewish state more than they wanted a state of their own.

In 1947, the United Nations partitioned Mandatory Palestine into two areas: one for a Jewish state; the other for an Arab state. The Jews declared statehood on 1948; all the surrounding Arab countries joined the local Arab population in attacking the new state of Israel and killing one percent of its citizens, but Israel survived.

In 1967, Egypt and Syria were planning to attack and destroy Israel, but Israel preempted and won a decisive victory, capturing the West Bank, Gaza Strip, and Sinai. Israel offered to return captured areas in exchange for peace, but the Arabs met with Palestinian leaders in Khartoum and issued their three infamous "nos": no peace, no recognition, and no negotiation.

In 2000–2001 and again in 2008, Israel made generous peace offers that would have established a demilitarized Palestinian state, but these offers were not accepted. And for the past several years, the current Israeli government has offered to sit down and negotiate a two-state solution with no pre-conditions—not even advanced recognition of Israel as the nation state of the Jewish people. The Palestinian leadership has refused to negotiate.

President Trump may be telling them that if they want a state they have to show up at the negotiating table and bargain for it. No one is going to hand it to them on a silver platter in the way that former Israeli Prime Minister Ariel Sharon handed over the Gaza Strip in 2005, only to see it turned into a launching pad for terror rockets and terror tunnels. Israel must get something in return: namely real peace and a permanent end to the conflict.

The Palestinian leadership's unwillingness to come to the negotiating table reminds me of my mother's favorite Jewish joke about Sam, a 79-year-old man who prayed every day for God to let him win the New York lottery before he turns 80. On the eve of his 80th birthday, he rails against God: "All these years I've prayed to you every day asking to win the lottery. You couldn't give me that one little thing!" God responded: "Sam, you have to help me out here—buy a ticket!" The Palestinians haven't bought a ticket. They haven't negotiated in good faith. They haven't accepted generous offers. They haven't made realistic counter-proposals. They haven't offered sacrifices to match those offered by the Israelis.

Now President Trump is telling them that they have to "buy a ticket." They are not going to get a state by going to the United Nations, the European Union, or the international criminal court. They aren't going to get a state as a result of the BDS or other anti-Israel tactics. They will only get a state if they sit down and negotiate in good faith with the Israelis.

The Obama administration applied pressure only to the Israeli side, not to the Palestinians. The time has come—indeed it is long past—for the United States to tell the Palestinians in no uncertain terms that they must negotiate with Israel if they want a Palestinian state, and they must agree to end the conflict, permanently and unequivocally. Otherwise, the status quo will continue, and there will be only one state, and that state will be Israel.

The Palestinians are not going to win the lottery without buying a ticket.

February 22, 2017
Israel Does Not Cause Anti-Semitism

In a recent letter to *The New York Times*, the current Earl of Balfour, Roderick Balfour, argued that it is Israel's fault that there is "growing anti-Semitism around the world." Balfour, who is a descendant of Arthur Balfour, the British Foreign Secretary who wrote the Balfour Declaration a hundred years ago, wrote the following: "The increasing inability of Israel to address [the condition of Palestinians], coupled with the expansion into Arab territory of the Jewish settlements, are major factors in growing anti-Semitism around the world." He argued further that Prime Minister Benjamin Netanyahu "owes it to the millions of Jews around the world" who suffer anti-Semitism, to resolve the Israel-Palestine conflict.

This well-intentioned but benighted view is particularly ironic in light of the fact that the Balfour Declaration had, as one of its purposes, to end anti-Semitism around the world by creating a homeland for the Jewish people. But now the scion of Lord Balfour is arguing that it is Israel that is causing anti-Semitism.

Roderick Balfour's views are simply wrong both as a matter of fact and as a matter of morality. Anyone who hates Jews "around the world" because they disagree with the policy of Israel would be ready to hate Jews on the basis of any pretext. Modern-day anti-Semites, unlike their forebears, need to find excuses for their hatred, and anti-Zionism has become the excuse de jure.

To prove the point, let us consider other countries: has there been growing anti-Chinese feelings around the world as the result of China's occupation of Tibet? Is there growing hatred of Americans of Turkish background because of Turkey's unwillingness to end the conflict in Cypress? Do Europeans of Russian background suffer bigotry because of Russia's invasion of Crimea? The answer to all these questions is a resounding no. If Jews are the only group that suffers because of controversial policies by Israel, then the onus lies on the anti-Semites rather than on the nation state of the Jewish people.

Moreover, Benjamin Netanyahu's responsibility is to the safety and security of Israelis. Even if it were true that anti-Semitism is increasing as the result of Israeli policies, no Israeli policy should ever be decided based on the reaction of bigots around the world. Anti-Semitism, the oldest of bigotries, will persist as long as it is seen to be justified by apologists like Roderick Balfour. Though Balfour does not explicitly justify anti-Semitism, the entire thrust of his letter is that Jew hatred is at least understandable in light of Israel's policies.

Balfour doesn't say a word about the unwillingness of the Palestinian leadership to accept Israel's repeated offers of statehood to the Palestinians. From 1938 through 2008, the Palestinians have been offered and repeatedly rejected agreements that would have given them statehood. Even today, the Palestinian leadership refuses to accept Netanyahu's offer to sit down and negotiate a final status agreement without any pre-conditions. Nor does Balfour mention Hamas, Hezbollah, and other terrorist groups that constantly threaten Israel, along with Iran's publicly declared determination to destroy the state that Lord Balfour helped to create. It's all Israel's fault, according to Balfour, and the resulting increase in anti-Semitism is Israel's fault as well.

Roderick Balfour ends his letter by essentially joining the boycott campaign against Israel. He has declared his unwillingness to participate in the Centenary Celebration of the Balfour Declaration, until and unless Israel takes unilateral action to end the conflict. So be it. I am confident that the author of the Balfour Declaration would have willingly participated in this celebration, recognizing that no country in history has ever contributed more to the world—in terms of medical, technological, environmental, and other innovations—in so short a period of time (69 years) than has Israel. Nor has any country, faced with comparable threats, ever been more generous in its offers of peace, more committed to the Rule of Law, or more protective of civilians who are used as human shields by those who attack its civilians.

So let the Celebration of the Balfour Declaration go forward without the participation of Roderick Balfour. Let Israel continue to offer a peaceful resolution to its conflict with the Palestinians. And let the Palestinians finally come to the bargaining table, and recognize Israel as the nation state of the Jewish people in the way that the Balfour Declaration intended.

February 24, 2017
I Will Leave Dems if Ellison Elected Chair

Tomorrow the Democratic National Committee (DNC) will have to choose the direction of the Democratic Party, as well as its likely composition. It will be among the most important choices the DNC has ever had to make.

There has been powerful push from the hard left of the Democrats, led by Senator Bernie Sanders, to elect Keith Ellison chairman.

If he is elected, I will quit the party after 60 years of loyal association and voting.

I will become an independent, continuing to vote for the best candidates, most of whom, I assume, will still be Democrats. But I will not contribute to the DNC or support it as an institution. My loyalty to my country and my principles and my heritage exceeds any loyalty to my party.

I will urge other like-minded people—centrist liberals—to follow my lead and quit the Democratic Party if Ellison is elected chairman.

We will not be leaving the Democratic Party we have long supported. The Democratic Party will be leaving us!

Let me explain the reasons for this difficult decision on my part.

Ellison has a long history of sordid association with anti-Semitism. He worked closely and supported one of a handful of the most notorious and public anti-Semites in our country, the Rev. Louis Farrakhan. And he worked with Farrakhan at the very time this anti-Semite was publicly describing Judaism as a "gutter religion," insisting that the Jews were a primary force in the African slave trade.

Ellison has publicly stated that he was unaware of Farrakhan's anti-Semitism.

That is not a credible statement. Everyone was aware of Farrakhan's anti-Semitism.

Farrakhan did not try to hide it. Indeed, he proclaimed it on every occasion.

Ellison is either lying or he willfully blinded himself to what was obvious to everyone else.

Neither of these qualities makes him suitable to be the next Chairman of the DNC. Moreover, Ellison himself has made anti-Semitic statements.

A prominent lawyer with significant credibility told me that while he was a law student, Ellison approached her and said he could not respect her, because she was a Jew and because she was a woman who should not be at a law school.

This woman immediately disclosed that anti-Semitic and anti-feminist statement to her husband and friends. I believe she is telling the truth.

Ellison's anti-Semitism is confirmed by his support for another anti-Semite, Stokely Carmichael. When there were protests about Carmichael's speaking at the University of Minnesota, Ellison responded that "Political Zionism is off-limits no matter what dubious circumstances Israel was founded under; no matter what the Zionists do to the Palestinians; and no matter what wicked regimes Israel allies itself with—like South Africa. This position is untenable."

At a fundraiser for his re-election in 2010, hosted by Esam Omeish who had told Palestinians that "Jihad way is the way to liberate your land," he complained that Jews had too much influence in American politics.

With regard to Israel, Ellison was one of only a small number of congresspeople who recently voted against funding the Iron Dome, a missile system used by Israel to protect its civilians against rocket attacks by Hamas and Hezbollah. His voting record with regard to the nation state of the Jewish people is among the very worst in Congress.

Ellison is now on an apology tour, but his apologies and renunciations of his past association with anti-Semitism have been tactical and timed to his political aspirations.

He first claimed to realize that Farrakhan was an anti-Semite was when he ran for office seeking Jewish support. His claim to be a supporter of Israel was timed to coincide with his run for the chairmanship of DNC. I do not trust him. I do not believe him. And neither should centrist liberal supporters of Israel and opponents of anti-Semitism.

The DNC has a momentous choice this weekend. It can move the party in the direction of Jeremy Corbyn's Labor party in England, in the hope of attracting Jill Stein Green Party voters and millennials who stayed home. In doing so they would be giving up on any attempt to recapture the working class and Rust Belt voters in the Midwestern states that turned the Electoral College over to Donald Trump.

I do not want to see the Democratic Party relegated to permanent minority status as a hard left fringe. Remember what happened when the Democrats moved left by nominating George McGovern, Walter Mondale, and Michael Dukakis—all good men.

The total combined electoral votes for these candidates would not have won a single election. There is no reason to think the country has moved so far to the left since those days that the Democrats can win by pushing even further in the direction of the hard left.

The self-destructive election of Keith Ellison will be hard to undue for many years.

So tomorrow, the Democrats must choose between electing Ellison or keeping centrist liberals, who support Israel, like me and many others in their party.

I hope they choose wisely. But if they do not, I have made my choice.

February 27, 2017
Keith Ellison Defeated by His Own Actions, Not Any Smear

The close vote by the Democratic National Committee to reject Keith Ellison as its chairperson was a victory for basic decency and a defeat for the kind of bigotry represented by Ellison's past associations with Louis Farrakhan and his current voting record against Israel's Iron Dome. Ellison's loss is not attributable to any "smear campaign," as some of his supporters have falsely alleged, but rather to his own actions, both past and present. Would anyone call it a smear if a candidate's history of sexism, racism, or homophobia had been exposed? Why, then, is it a smear to have raised questions based on Ellison's past associations with anti-Semitism and his current anti-Israel voting record? Nor was it a smear to question Ellison's credibility when he said that he was not aware that Farrakhan was an anti-Semite, when Farrakhan himself was publicly boasting about his Jew hatred.

The smear charge itself reflects the kind of double standard within elements of the Democratic Party that worry centrist pro-

Israel voters. Both Democrats and Republicans alike must have the same zero tolerance for anti-Semitism as they do for sexism, racism, and homophobia.

The growing influence of intolerant hard left extremists endangers both our country and the Democratic Party. Democrats must recognize the reality that the United States is not a hard-left country. Unlike some European countries, we have never had significant Communist or socialist parties. Nor are we a hard-right country, with a history of fascist parties. We govern from the center, alternating centrist liberals, such as Obama and Clinton, with centrist conservatives like the Bushes and Reagan.

When the Democrats tried to move leftward, even with such moderate leftists as McGovern, Mondale, and Dukakis, they have been overwhelmingly defeated. The combined electoral votes of these three leftish candidates would not have been enough to win a single election. The Republicans experienced similar rejection when they went to the far right of their party and nominated Barry Goldwater.

Had Sanders won the Democratic nomination, he would have won no more than a handful of states. It is far easier for the hard-left fringe of the Democrats to win primaries and conduct loud demonstrations than to win national or state wide elections. If the Democratic Party fails to understand this reality they will emulate the British Labor Party, which rejected the kind of moderate liberal leadership represented by Tony Blair in favor of the extreme leftist Jeremy Corbyn. The Corbyn-led Labor Party is popular among left wing extremists, but was not able to win the national election. Nor would the Democrats be competitive if they allow themselves to be taken over by the Sanders fringe.

Great Britain has a far greater proportion of hard left voters than the United States. Yet even there, the radical Corbyn left cannot attract enough voters to be competitive—even in the post-Brexit environment. It would be worse—much worse—for the Democrats if they become the party of the extreme left.

Those who believe that Democrats can win by attracting the kind of hard left radicals who voted for Green Party candidates such as Jill Stein or Ralph Nader are blinking reality. The Democrats could never nominate a winning candidate far left enough for those hard-left ideologues to abandon their extremist candidates. Extremists like Susan Sarandon seem to believe that a vote for Trump will hasten the revolution. This is how she put it: "Some people feel that Donald Trump will bring the revolution immediately if he gets in, things will really explode."

Nor can the Democrats win by emulating the tactics of the Republican Party. The Tea Party did move the Republicans to the right by their uncompromising and obstructionist approach. But the United States has more tolerance—unfortunately in my view—for rightward movement (as long as it's not too extreme) than the Democrats gave for leftward movement.

The current leadership of the Democratic Party is reacting short-term to a long-term problem. They are responding to the loudest, shrillest, and most demanding voices—voices that are hardly representative of the tens of millions of voters they will need to remain competitive in upcoming races.

The Democrats can win only by regaining their traditional base among working class Rust Belt voters they lost to Trump. These voters will never support the kind of radical left-wing candidates promoted by the Keith Ellison wing of the party.

Ellison's appointment as the deputy to Tom Perez the man who defeated him, elevated unity over principle. His past history and current voting record should have disqualified him for any office within the Democratic Party. But despite that unfortunate appointment, I will remain in the Democratic Party and work from within to move it back to its vibrant liberal center and away from its radical fringe. I will also work to maintain bipartisan support for Israel and against efforts by the hard left to abandon the only democracy in the Middle East.

It will be a daunting task but it is worth the effort. We won the fight against Ellison, though it was close. We must continue to win if the Democratic Party is to remain competitive.

March 15, 2017
Why Must Women Choose Between Feminism and Zionism, but Not Other "Isms"?

On March 8, women abstained from work as part of the International Women's Strike (IWS)—a grassroots feminist movement aimed at bringing attention "to the current social, legal, political, moral and verbal violence experienced by contemporary women at various latitudes." But these positive goals were distorted by the inclusion of anti-Israel rhetoric in the platform of the IWS.

There are many countries and movements throughout the world that treat women as second-class citizens: Israel is not among them. Yet this platform singles out for condemnation only Israel, the nation state of the Jewish people. There is a word for applying a double standard to Jews. That word is anti-Semitism.

It is a tragedy that this women's movement—which has done so much good in refocusing attention on important women's issues in the United States—from gender violence, to reproductive rights and equal pay—has now moved away from its central mission and gone out of its way to single out one foreign nation by calling for the "decolonization of Palestine." Not of Tibet. Not of Kurdistan. Not of Ukraine. Not of Cyprus. Only Palestine.

The platform, which is published on IWS's website under the headline "Antiracist and Anti-imperialist Feminism" also says: "we want to dismantle all walls, from prison walls to border walls, from Mexico to Palestine." No mention is made of the walls that imprison gays in Iran, dissidents in China, feminists in Gaza, or Kurds in Turkey. Only the walls erected by Israel.

Criticizing Israel's settlement and occupation policies is fair game. But singling out Israel for "decolonization" when it has repeatedly offered to end the occupation and to create a Palestinian state on the West Bank and Gaza; and when other countries continue to colonize, can be explained in no other way than applying a double standard to Jews and their state.

Linda Sarsour, a Palestinian-American who helped organize the Women's March on Washington in January, responded to criticism of the anti-Israel plank appearing in a feminist platform. In an interview with *The Nation* Sarsour said the following:

> *"When you talk about feminism you're talking about the rights of all women and their families to live in dignity, peace, and security. It's about giving women access to health care and other basic rights. And Israel is a country that continues to occupy territories in Palestine, has people under siege at checkpoints—we have women who have babies on checkpoints because they're not able to get to hospitals [in time]. It just doesn't make any sense for someone to say, 'Is there room for people who support the state of Israel and do not criticize it in the movement?' There can't be in feminism. You either stand up for the rights of all women, including Palestinians, or none. There's just no way around it."*

Sarsour was responding directly to an op-ed published by Emily Shire, the politics editor of the online newsite *Bustle*. In her piece published in *The New York Times*, Shire asked why, increasingly, women have to choose between their Zionism and feminism. Shire wrote:

> *"My prime concern is not that people hold this view of Israel. Rather, I find it troubling that embracing such a view is considered an essential part of an event that is supposed to unite feminists. I am happy to debate Middle East politics or listen to critiques of Israeli policies. But why should criticism of Israel be key to feminism in 2017?"*

Israel, like every country including our own, is far from perfect—and I and other supporters of Israel have been critical of its flaws—but its commitment to gender equality can be traced back to its Declaration of Independence, which states that Israel "will ensure complete equality of social and political rights to all its inhabitants irrespective of religion, race or sex." As the only democracy in the Middle East Israel's legal guarantee of rights has meant that women play crucial roles in all aspects of Israeli society. It elected the first woman head of government in history—Golda Meir—who was not related to a male political leader. There is no legitimate reason for singling Israel out for condemnation, as the platform does, based on a denial of "basic rights" to women.

Sarsour presents a Catch-22. Under her own all-or-nothing criteria, she herself cannot be pro-Palestinian and a feminist because the Palestinian Authority and Hamas treat women and gays far worse than Israel does. If Sarsour was concerned with addressing structural causes of all female oppression, she would mention the status of women in the PA-controlled West Bank where just a few months ago the names and photos of female candidates for the municipal elections were omitted, referring to the women instead as "wife of" or "sister of." Sarsour would also call out the Hamas-controlled Gaza Strip, where the police are a law unto themselves who act as judge, jury, and executioner of those who speak out against their oppression and misogyny. She would condemn the tolerance, if not acceptance, by so many Muslim countries of the "honor killings" and genital mutilation of women. Instead the IWS platform exploits the feminist cause in order to de-legitimize and demonize only one nation: that of the Jewish people.

Nor does Sarsour address the fact that one of the organizers of the strike, Rasmea Odeh, was a member of the Popular Front for the Liberation of Palestine (PFLP), who was convicted and sentenced to life in prison by an Israeli military court for her role in a 1969 terror attack that killed two university students and injured nine others, including several women, at a supermarket in Jerusalem. Odeh was later freed in a prisoner exchange and moved to the United States, but she is being deported for perjuriously failing to disclose her murder conviction.

This double standard is reflective of a broader trend in hard left politics. Increasingly, groups such as Black Lives Matter, MoveOn, Code Pink, and Occupy Wall Street have embraced intersectionality—a radical academic theory, which holds that all forms of social oppression are inexorably linked—as an underpinning to their anti-Israel activism. This type of selective ideological packaging has left liberal supporters of Israel in an increasingly uncomfortable position. On the one hand, they care deeply about causes such as women's rights, criminal justice reform, income inequality, environmental protection, and LGBT rights. On the other, they find themselves excluded from the groups that advance those very causes unless they agree to de-legitimize Israel and denounce Zionism as the national liberation movement of the Jewish people.

Addressing the structural causes of sexism in the United States will take more than reproaching Israel—it will require far-reaching legislative and grassroots action. By morphing the discussion about women's rights into a polemic against Israel, the IWS makes progress of the feminist cause even more difficult. All decent people should continue to fight for the absolute equal status of women in society. But we must not be forced to become complicit in the promotion of anti-Israel bigotry as a pre-condition for supporting the broader feminist movement.

The real choice to be made now by all those who care about the feminist cause is whether to allow Sarsour and her radical anti-Israel allies to hijack the movement in support of their own bigoted views. The alternative is to maintain feminism's focus on key issues that pertain to women and to call out countries and movements according to how seriously they violate women's rights, rather than singling out the one Jewish democracy—Israel.

March 17, 2017
A Supporter of Israel Must Have a "Bias" on Trump Travel Ban: The Newest Bigotry!

A recent panel discussion regarding the Trump travel ban was infected by the bigotry of one of the participants. The host, Don Lemon, called on former prosecutor, John Flannery, to express his views on the decision of a federal judge to stay the order. This was Flannery's response:

"...Here's Trump saying that we have to write rules. What have they been doing? They've been sitting on their hands doing nothing this entire time. And our dear colleague, Alan Dershowitz, I think, hopes that this may secure Israel and thinks that this is a bogus argument..."

I asked him what he was talking about, since in my dozens of TV appearances discussing the travel ban, I have never once mentioned Israel, and certainly never made the argument that the ban—which I oppose as a matter of policy—would "secure Israel."

He replied: "I think that's what you believe."

I shot back: "I never said a word about Israel. You know when you focus everything I say on Israel it really raises questions about your own bigotry and bias."

I then asked him directly "What does this have to do with Israel? Why...do you have to bring in Israel to attack me and criticize me? Is it because I'm Jewish? You know your bigotry is showing?"

He then said it has "everything" to do with Israel. He insisted that Israel is the "reason you're taking the position you are. Because of your own bias."

The "position" to which he was referring is my view that although the travel ban is bad policy, it is probably not unconstitutional. Instead of responding to my "position" on the merits, he again—quite irrelevantly—repeated that he doesn't think the ban "will help Israel."

Having heard variations on this argument many times in my debates about a wide range of issues—that my loyalty to Israel clouds my judgement and disqualifies me as an objective critic—I really tore into him: "You can't believe anything I say because I'm a Jew and a Zionist? For shame on you sir." I then announced that I don't want to be on panels with him in the future.

At the end of the segment Don Lemon asked if anyone wanted to "apologize" or explain if they feel they "were taken out of context."

Flannery chimed in: "I have trouble understanding you, Alan, in connection with this argument about the appeal...we have an honest disagreement about that."

I responded: "My only criticism of you was that you raised the issue of Israel and somehow questioned my motives because yes, I'm a Jew who supports Israel."

There was no legitimate reason for Flannery to bring Israel into the discussion. At no point during my analysis of Trump's revised travel ban—and I have spoken on this issue broadly both on TV and in print—did I suggest that this executive order relates to Israel, let alone would "secure" her. In suggesting that the reason for my position on the travel ban is "because of [my] own bias" toward Israel—and by doubling down on this position throughout the segment—Flannery engaged in an old trope: that one's dual loyalty undercuts their objectivity when it comes to analysis of domestic political issues here in the United States. By morphing the discussion about the constitutionality of U.S. immigration policy into a polemic against me, and my pro-Israel "bias," Flannery displayed his own bias.

I'm glad I called Flannery out on this issue. I don't know generally what his views are about Israel. But his willingness to argue to an international TV audience that I am biased on the travel ban issue because I see every issue through the lens of my pro-Israel views, is dangerous if unrebutted. The reality is that the U.S. travel ban has little or nothing to do with Israel, but in Flannery's distorted mind has "everything" to do with Israel if expressed by a Jewish supporter of Israel.

There is an old joke about a European student who was obsessed with Jews. Every time the professor gave an assignment the student would find a way to bring in the Jews. Finally, in exasperation, he assigned the students to write an essay on the pachyderm. The obsessed student handed in his essay, with the title: "The Elephant and the Jewish Question."

March 29, 2017
The Bigotry of "Intersectionality"

What do the terrorist group Hamas and the anti-violence group Black Lives Matter have in common? What does the democracy of Israel have in common with the anti-Semitic Ku Klux Klan? What does the Islamic Republic of Iran, which throws gays off rooftops, have in common with gay right activists? What do feminists have in common with radical Islamic sexists who support the honor killing and genital mutilation of women? Nothing, of course. Unless you subscribe to the pseudo-academic concept of intersectionality.

Intersectionality—the radical academic theory, which holds that all forms of social oppression are inexorably linked—has become a code word for anti-American, anti-Western, anti-Israel, and anti-Semitic bigotry. Nowhere has adoption of this radical paradigm been more pronounced then on college campuses where in the name of "identity politics" and "solidarity," intersectionality has forced artificial coalitions between causes that have nothing to do with each other except a hatred for their fellow students who are "privileged" because they are white, heterosexual, male, and especially Jewish.

Students at the University of Illinois (UIC) recently took to social media to express their distress after flyers were plastered around campus calling for the "end of Jewish privilege." The flyer stated in bold letters that: "ending white privilege starts with ending Jewish privilege." The posters had outlines of silhouettes with Stars of David printed on their chests and an arrow pointing to them with the accompanying caption "the 1%." Although some of the posters identified Black Lives Matter as sponsors, it isn't clear whether they were distributed by extreme right wing groups using hard left anti-Semitic tropes or by hard left anti-Semites. In some respects, it doesn't really matter because many on the hard right and hard left share a disdain for Jews, their nation state, and so called "Jewish privilege."

The very concept of "privilege"—the idea that white people benefit from certain privileges in Western society, compared to non-whites living in the same social, political, and economic environment—has a long and complex history in the United States. The subjugation of black Americans and other non-whites is an endemic problem that requires far-reaching legislative and grassroots action. By attributing this domestic social problem to so called "Jewish privilege," radicals are engaging in traditional economic anti-Semitism, attributing far-reaching societal problems to Jewish status, occupation, or economic performance.

This practice resembles the vile anti-Semitic propaganda splashed across *Der Sturmer* in the 1930s, which blamed Jews—and so called disproportionate Jewish wealth—for Germany losing WWI and its subsequent economic downturn. Canards about Jews' controlling world finances—first promulgated by the Tzarist forgery, the Protocols of the Elders of Zion—was anti-Semitic back then and it is still anti-Semitic today, whether espoused by the extreme left or right. There is no more evidence that Jews are responsible for economic or social inequality in contemporary America than there was that Jews were responsible for any of the other crimes that formed the basis for traditional blood libels. Indeed, Jews disproportionately support racial equality and other liberal causes. Most successful Jews, like most successful people of other religions and ethnicities, earned this success by hard work, not special privilege. I certainly didn't begin life with any privilege—indeed despite finishing first in my class at Yale Law School, I was rejected by all 32 of the law firms to which I applied.

The linking of unrelated "victimizations," despite their tenuous connections, is reflective of a broader trend in hard left politics, whereby increasingly radical activists demand that the demonization of "Zionists"—often used as a euphemism for Jews—be included, indeed featured, in the package of causes that must be embraced by anyone claiming the label of "progressive." Lumping seemingly disparate groups under the "umbrella of oppression" leads to the forming of alliances between causes that at best, have nothing to do with each other, and at worst, are averse to one another's stated mission. Their only common feature is that in order to join, they must demonize the nation state of the Jewish people.

Some intersectional feminists involved with the recent Women's March on Washington, for example, purport to be natural allies with anti-Israel Muslim groups that tolerate, if not accept, the "honor killings" and genital mutilation of women. Similarly, Jewish Voices for Peace (JVP)—an organization that calls for "an end to violence against civilians; and peace and justice for all peoples of the Middle East"—invited Rasmieh Odeh, a member of the Popular Front for the Liberation of Palestine (PFLP) and convicted terrorist, to appear as a speaker at their national conference later this month. The idea of Odeh—a terrorist who quite literally has blood on her hands—speaking for a Jewish organization that claims to propagate peace flies in the face of logic. Fortunately, Odeh is being deported for perjuriously failing to disclose her murder conviction. I guess the peace-loving members of JVP will have to applaud her on Skype.

The following are among many examples of radical leftists conflating unrelated grievances. Consider, the linking of our government's handling of the Flint water crisis to the "severe" water crisis in Gaza. Black Lives Matter activists have visited Gaza to express solidarity with the terrorist group Hamas, and with Palestinians oppressed by so-called racist Israeli self-defense measures. While Black Lives Matter claims to disavow violence in securing its political objectives, many of its most prominent members are far more eager to criticize the "Israeli genocide of Palestinians" than to criticize Hamas for using rockets to target Israeli civilians.

During a recent interview on PBS's *Charlie Rose* program, Jonathan Haidt—social psychologist and Professor of Ethical Leadership at New York University's Stern School of Business—had this to say about the conflation of various left-wing causes under the banner of intersectionality:

"... There is a good kind of identity politics, which is, you know, if black people are being denied rights, let's fight for their rights, that's the good kind. But there is a bad kind, which is to train students, train young people to say let's divide everybody up by their race, gender, other categories. We'll assign them moral merit based on their level of privilege is bad, and victimhood is good. Okay, now let's look at everything through this lens. Israel, the Palestinians are the victims. So therefore, they are the good and the Jews or the Israelis are the bad. And then you get—and then that, so there is one totalizing perspective. All social problems get reduced to this simple framework. I think we are doing them a disservice. I think where actually making students less wise."

There is a certain irony of many feminists and gay-rights activists refusing to condemn the sexism and homophobia in the Arab world. Increasingly, they try and force other progressives to adopt a "No True Scotsman" worldview, in which they are made to feel that to be a "true progressive," one must embrace a wide variety of so-called hard left causes, regardless of how unrelated they may be—as long as they also condemn Israel.

The essence of anti-Semitism is the bigoted claim that if there is a problem, then Jews must be its cause. Hitler started by blaming Jews for Germany's economic downturn. Today, many hard left activists explicitly or implicitly blame Jews and Zionists for many of the evils of the world. All decent people must join in calling out intersectionality for what it is: a euphemism for anti-American, anti-Semitic, and anti-Israel bigotry. Exposing and condemning "intersectionality" for the bigotry that it represents is critical to ensuring that those repressive extremists who falsely claim the mantle of progressivism are not able to hijack important liberal causes in support of their own bigoted agenda.

April 19, 2017
What North Korea Should Teach Us About Iran

We failed to prevent North Korea from developing nuclear weapons. As a result, our options to stop them from developing a delivery system capable of reaching our shores are severely limited.

The hard lesson from our failure to stop North Korea before they became a nuclear power is that we MUST stop Iran from ever developing or acquiring a nuclear arsenal. A nuclear Iran would be far more dangerous to American interest than a nuclear North Korea.

Iran already has rockets capable of reaching numerous American allies. They are in the process of upgrading them and making them capable of delivering a nuclear payload to our shores. Its fundamentalist religious leaders would be willing to sacrifice millions of Iranians to destroy the big Satan (United States) or the little Satan (Israel).

The late "moderate" leader Hashemi Rafsanjani once told an American journalist that if Iran attacked Israel with nuclear weapons, they "would kill as many as five million Jews," and that if Israel retaliated, they would kill fifteen million Iranians, which would be "a small sacrifice from among the billion Muslims in the world." He concluded that "it is not irrational to contemplate such an eventuality." Recall that the Iranian mullahs were willing to sacrifice thousands of "child-soldiers" in their futile war with Iraq. There is nothing more dangerous than a "suicide regime" armed with nuclear weapons.

The deal signed by Iran in 2015 postpones Iran's quest for a nuclear arsenal, but it doesn't prevent it, despite Iran's unequivocal statement in the preamble to the agreement that "Iran reaffirms that under no circumstances will Iran ever seek, develop or acquire nuclear weapons." (Emphasis added).

Recall that North Korea provided similar assurances to the Clinton administration back in 1994, only to break them several years later—with no real consequences.

The Iranian mullahs apparently regard their reaffirmation as merely hortatory and not legally binding. The body of the agreement itself—the portion Iran believes is legally binding—does not preclude Iran from developing nuclear weapons after a certain time, variously estimated as between 10 to 15 years from the signing of the agreement. Nor does it prevent Iran from perfecting its delivery systems, including nuclear tipped intercontinental ballistic missiles capable of reaching the United States.

If we are not to make the same mistake with Iran that we made with North Korea, we must do something now—before Iran secures a weapon—to deter the mullahs from becoming a nuclear power, over which we would have little or no leverage.

Congress should now enact legislation declaring that Iran's reaffirmation that it will never "develop or acquire nuclear weapons" is an integral part of the agreement and represents the policy of the United States. It is too late to change the words of the deal, but it is not too late for Congress to insist that Iran comply fully with all of its provisions, even those in the preamble.

In order to ensure that the entirety of the agreement is carried out, including that reaffirmation, Congress should adopt the proposal made by Thomas L. Friedman on July 22, 2015, and by myself on September 5, 2013.

To quote Friedman: "Congress should pass a resolution authorizing this and future presidents to use force to prevent Iran from ever becoming a nuclear weapons state...Iran must know now that the U.S. president is authorized to destroy—without warning or negotiation—any attempt by Tehran to build a bomb." I put it similarly: Congress should authorize the president "to take military action against Iran's nuclear weapon's program if it were to cross the red lines...."

The benefits of enacting such legislation are clear: the law would underline the centrality to the deal of Iran's reaffirmation never to acquire nuclear weapons, and would provide both a deterrent against Iran violating its reaffirmation and an enforcement authorization in the event it does.

A law based on these two elements—adopting Iran's reaffirmation as the official American policy and authorizing a preventive military strike if Iran tried to obtain nuclear weapons—may be an alternative we can live with. But without such an alternative, the deal is currently interpreted by Iran will not prevent Iran from obtaining nuclear weapons.

In all probability, it would merely postpone that catastrophe for about a decade while legitimating its occurrence. This is not an outcome we can live with as evidenced by the crisis we are now confronting with North Korea.

So let us learn from our mistake and not repeat it with Iran.

May 23, 2017
Terrorism Persists Because It Works

Every time a horrendous terrorist attack victimizes innocent victims we wring our hands and promise to increase security and take other necessary preventive measures. But we fail to recognize how our friends and allies play such an important role in encouraging, incentivizing, and inciting terrorism.

If we are to have any chance of reducing terrorism, we must get to its root cause. It is not poverty, disenfranchisement, despair, or any of the other abuse excuses offered to explain, if not to justify, terrorism as an act of desperation. It is anything but. Many terrorists, such as those who participated in the 9/11 attacks, were educated, well-off, mobile, and even successful. They made a rational cost-benefit decision to murder innocent civilians for one simple reason: they believe that terrorism works.

And tragically they are right. The international community has rewarded terrorism while punishing those who try to fight it by reasonable means. It all began with a decision by Yasser Arafat and other Palestinian terrorist groups to employ the tactic of terrorism as a primary means of bringing the Palestinian issue to the forefront of world concern. Based on the merits and demerits of the Palestinian case, it does not deserve this stature. The treatment of the Tibetans by China, the Kurds by most of the Arab world, and the people of Chechen by Russia has been at least as bad. But their response to grievances has been largely ignored by the international community and the media because they mostly sought remedies within the law rather than through terrorism.

The Palestinian situation has been different. The hijacking of airplanes, the murders of Olympic athletes at Munich, the killing of Israeli children at Ma'alot, and the many other terrorist atrocities perpetrated by Palestinian terrorists has elevated their cause above all other causes in the human rights community. Although the Palestinians have not yet gotten a state—because they twice rejected generous offers of statehood—their cause still dominates the United Nations and numerous human rights groups.

Other groups with grievances have learned from the success of Palestinian terrorism and have emulated the use of that barbaric tactic. Even today, when the Palestinian Authority claims to reject terrorism, they reward the families of suicide bombers and other terrorists by large compensation packages that increase with the number of innocent victims.

If the perpetrator of the Manchester massacre had been Palestinian and if the massacre had taken place in an Israeli auditorium, the Palestinian Authority would have paid his family a small fortune for murdering so many children. There is a name for people and organizations that pay other people for killing innocent civilians: it's called accessory to murder. If the Mafia offered bounties to kill its opponents, no one would sympathize with those who made the offer. Yet the Palestinian leadership that does the same thing is welcomed and honored throughout the world.

The Palestinian Authority also glorifies terrorists by naming parks, stadiums, streets, and other public places after the mass murderers of children. Our "ally" Qatar allegedly finances Hamas, which the United States has correctly declared to be a terrorist organization.[64] Our enemy Iran also finances, facilitates, and encourages terrorism against the United States, Israel, and other Western democracies, without suffering any real consequences. The United Nations glorifies terrorism by placing countries that support terrorism in high positions of authority and honor and by welcoming with open arms the promoters of terrorism.

On the other hand, Israel, which has led the world in efforts to combat terrorism by reasonable and lawful means, gets attacked by the international community more than any other country in the world. Promoters of terrorism are treated better at the United Nations than opponents of terrorism. The boycott divestment tactic (BDS) is directed only against Israel and not against the many nations that support terrorism.

Terrorisms will continue as long as it continues to bear fruits. The fruits may be different for different causes. Sometimes it is simply publicity. Sometimes it is a recruitment tool. Sometimes it brings about concessions as it did in many European countries. Some European countries that have now been plagued by terrorism even released captured Palestinian terrorists. England, France, Italy, and Germany were among the countries that released Palestinian terrorists in the hope of preventing terrorist attacks on their soil. Their selfish and immoral tactic backfired: it only caused them to become even more inviting targets for the murderous terrorists.

But no matter how terrorism works, the reality that it does will make it difficult if not impossible to stem its malignant spread around the world. To make it not work, the entire world must unite in never rewarding terrorism and always punishing those who facilitate it.

June 6, 2017
A New Tolerance for Anti-Semitism

All over the world anti-Semites are becoming mainstreamed. It is no longer disqualifying to be outed as a Jew hater. This is especially so if the anti-Semite uses the cover of rabid hatred for the nation state of the Jewish people. These bigots succeed in becoming accepted—even praised—not because of their anti-Semitism, but despite it. Increasingly, they are given a pass on their Jew hatred because those who support them admire or share other aspects of what they represent. This implicit tolerance of anti-Semitism—as long as it comes from someone whose other views are acceptable—represents a dangerous new trend from both the right and left.

In the United States, the Trump election has brought hard-right anti-Semitism into public view, but the bigotry of the hard left is far more prevalent and influential on many university campuses. Those on the left who support left wing anti-Semites try to downplay, ignore, or deny that those they support are really anti-Semites. "They are anti-Zionist" is the excuse de jure. Those on the right do essentially the same: "they are nationalists." Neither side would accept such transparent and hollow justifications if the shoe were on the other foot. I believe that when analyzing and exposing these dangerous trends, a single standard of criticism must be directed at each.

Generally speaking, extreme right-wing anti-Semitism continues to be a problem in many parts of Europe and among a relatively small group of "alt-right" Americans. But it also exists among those who self-identify as run-of-the-mill conservatives. Consider, for example, former presidential candidate and Reagan staffer, Pat Buchanan. The list of Buchanan's anti-Jewish bigotry is exhaustive. Over the years he has consistently blamed Jews for wide-ranging societal and political problems. In his criticism of the Iraq War, for example, Buchanan infamously quipped: "There are only two groups that are beating the drums for war in the Middle East—the Israeli Defense Ministry and its amen corner in the United States." He then singled out for rebuke only Jewish political figures and commentators such as Henry Kissinger, Charles Krauthammer, and A.M. Rosenthal. He did not mention any of the vocal non-Jewish supporters of the war. Furthermore, Buchanan also said that "the Israeli lobby" would be responsible if President Obama decided to strike Iran, threatening that if it were to happen, "Netanyahu and his amen corner in Congress" would face "backlash worldwide." Buchanan's sordid flirtation with Nazi revisionism is also well documented.

Meanwhile, on university campuses the absurd concept of "intersectionality"—which has become a code word for anti-Semitism—is dominating discussions and actions by the hard left. The warm embrace of Palestinian American activist, Linda Sarsour—who recently delivered the commencement address at a City University of New York graduation—is a case in point. Since co-organizing the Women's March on Washington in January, Sarsour has become a feminist icon for so called "progressives." This is the same Linda Sarsour who has said that feminism and Zionism are incompatible, stating: "You either stand up for the rights of all women, including Palestinians, or none. There's just no way around it." And when speaking about two leading female anti-Islamists, Brigitte Gabriel and Ayaan Hirsi Ali (who is a victim of female genital mutilation) the feminist de jure Linda Sarsour, said: "I wish I could take away their vaginas."

The irony is palpable. Under her own all or nothing criteria, Sarsour—who is also a staunch BDS supporter—cannot be pro-Palestinian and a feminist because the Palestinian Authority and Hamas subjugate women and treat gays far worse than Israel does.

Indeed, Sarsour has emerged as a champion of the hard left. Both New York City Mayor Bill de Blasio and Bernie Sanders have sought her endorsement. Moreover, Deputy DNC Chair Keith Ellison—who himself has a sordid history with anti-Semitism stemming from his association with Louis Farrakhan, who publicly boasted about his own Jew hatred—has come out in support of the bigoted Sarsour. When it comes to Ellison an old idiom comes to mind: a man is known by the company he keeps.

The same trend is detectable among the hard left in Europe, particularly in Britain, which, at the time of this writing, is days away from an election. The British Labour Party has now been hijacked by radical extremists on the left, and is known for being soft on anti-Semitism. In a recent interview with a BBC reporter, Emma Barnett—who happens to be Jewish—Labour's leader, Jeremy Corbyn, fumbled when answering a question about how much his proposed childcare policy would cost. Rather than critique Corbyn, Labour supporters viciously trolled the Jewish BBC reporter. Tweets such as these abounded: "Allegations have surfaced that @Emmabarnett is a Zionist" and "Zionist Emma Barnett (family lived off brothels) attacks Jeremy Corbyn." Corbyn has also been accused of anti-Jewish bigotry himself. He has said in the past that the genocidal Hamas terrorist group should be removed from the UK's designated terror list, and has called Hezbollah and Hamas (which are both vowed to the destruction of the nation state of the Jewish people) "my friends." (I recently wrote extensively on Corbyn's association with some of Britain's most notorious Holocaust deniers and anti-Semites.)

Increasingly, anti-Semitic discourse is also seeping into the arts and academia. Consider the anti-Israel and anti-Jewish bigotry of former Pink Floyd front man Roger Waters. A staunch supporter of the BDS tactic, Waters has said about the Palestinians that "parallels with what went on in the 30s in Germany are so crushingly obvious." He also had a pig-shaped balloon with a Star of David on it at one of his concerts. And when asked about his aggressive effort to recruit people to join the BDS, Waters blamed "the Jewish lobby," which he explained is "extraordinary powerful here and particularly in the industry that I work in, the music industry." In 2013 the ADL declared that "anti-Semitic conspiracy theories" had "seeped into the totality" of Waters' views.

Likewise, the market place of ideas on college campuses and within academic institutions has seen an embrace of anti-Semitism often disguised as anti-Zionism. Several years ago, I identified the dangerous trend of academics crossing a red line between acceptable criticism of Israel and legitimizing Jew-hatred. This was in light of the disgraceful endorsement by a number of prominent academics of an anti-Semitic book written by Gilad Arzmon—a notorious Jew-hater who denies the Holocaust and attributed widespread economic troubles to a "Zio-punch."

When asked recently about the hullabaloo surrounding her CUNY address, Linda Sarsour disingenuously played the victim card: "since the Women's March on Washington, once the right-wing saw a very prominent Muslim-American woman in a hijab who was a Palestinian who was resonating with a community in a very large way, they made it their mission to do everything they can to take my platform away."

No, Ms. Sarsour. You are wrong. This is not a smear campaign by the "right-wing," but rather, a show that people of good will reject your manifestations of bigotry.

Those who tolerate anti-Semitism from those they otherwise admire would never accept other forms of bigotry, such as racism, sexism, or homophobia. It's difficult to imagine Bernie Sanders campaigning for a socialist who didn't like black people or who was against gay marriage. But he is comfortable campaigning for Jeremy Corbyn, who has made a career out of condemning Zionists by which he means Jews.

The growing tolerance for anti-Semitism by both the extreme left and right is quickly becoming mainstream. That is why it is so dangerous and must be exposed for what it is: complicity in, and encouragement of, the oldest form of bigotry. Shame on those who tolerate anti-Semitism when it comes from their side of the political spectrum.

People on both sides of the aisle must have the same zero tolerance for anti-Semitism as they do for sexism, racism and homophobia. Decent people everywhere—Jews and non-Jews—must condemn with equal vigor all manifestations of bigotry whether they emanate from the hard alt-right or hard alt-left. I will continue to judge individuals on the basis of their own statements and actions, regardless of which side of the aisle they come from.

June 12, 2017
Why Won't Abbas Accept "Two States for Two Peoples?"

There is a widespread but false belief that Mahmoud Abbas is finally prepared to accept the two-state solution proposed by the UN in November 1947 when it divided mandatory Palestine into two areas: one for the Jewish people; the other for the Arab people. The Jews of Palestine accepted the compromise division and declared a nation state for the Jewish people to be called by its historic name: Israel. The Arabs of Palestine, on the other hand, rejected the division and declared that they would never accept a state for the Jewish people and statehood for the Palestinian people. They wanted for there not to be a state for the Jewish people more than for there to be a state for their own people. Accordingly, they joined the surrounding Arab armies in trying to destroy Israel and drive its Jewish residents into the sea. They failed back then, but over the years, and to the current day, they continue to want no state for the Jewish people more than they want a state for Palestinian Arabs. That is why Abbas refuses to say that he would ever accept the UN principle of two states for two peoples. I know, because I have personally asked him on several occasions.

In a few months Israel will be celebrating the 70th anniversary of the historic UN compromise, but the leaders of the Palestinian

Authority still refuse to accept the principle of that resolution: two states for two peoples.

President Trump, for his part, has expressed an eagerness to make "the ultimate deal" between the Israelis and the Palestinians. This has propelled discussions about the dormant peace process back into the spotlight. Shortly before travelling to the Middle East—where he met with Prime Minister Netanyahu in Israel and President Abbas in Bethlehem—Trump invited the Palestinian leader to the White House. Abbas was last at the White House in March 2014 shortly before the Obama administration's shuttle diplomacy efforts—led by Secretary of State John Kerry—fell apart.

Leading up to his meeting with President Trump in Washington, Abbas said to a German publication: "We're ready to collaborate with him and meet the Israeli prime minister under his [Trump's] auspices to build peace." He then went on to voice his support for a two-state solution saying, "it's high time to work on the requirements for it." This was interpreted as a willingness on Abbas's part to accept the idea of a state for the Jewish people. Generally speaking, the international community supports the idea of resolving the Israeli-Palestinian conflict with two states for two peoples: a state for the Jewish people alongside a state for the Palestinians. Yet presenting Mahmoud Abbas as a supporter of the two states for two people formulation is to deny truth. The general idea of a two-state solution—which Abbas has nominally supported—does not specify that one state would be for the Jewish people and the other one for the Arabs. Over the years President Abbas has expressed a commitment to a two-state solution—stating that he supports an Arab state along the 1967 borders with East Jerusalem as its capital—but has so far refused to accept the legitimacy of a nation state for the Jews existing by its side.

Consider President Abbas's own words. In a 2003 interview he said: "I've said it before, and I'll say it again: I will never recognize the Jewishness of the state, or a 'Jewish state.'" When asked about Israel being the nation state of the Jewish people (in the context of Ehud Olmert's generous peace proposal in 2008) the PA leader said: "from a historical perspective, there are two states: Israel and Palestine. In Israel, there are Jews and others living there. This we

The Case Against BDS

are willing to recognize, nothing else." And in a later interview with the *Al-Quds* newspaper Abbas reiterated this refusal to recognize that Israel is the nation state of the Jewish people: "We're not talking about a Jewish state and we won't talk about one. For us, there is the state of Israel and we won't recognize Israel as a Jewish state. I told them that this is their business and that they are free to call themselves whatever they want. But [I told them] you can't expect us to accept this." The list of such pronouncements from the man at the head of the Palestinian Authority goes on and on. Not only has Abbas refused to accept the formulation "Jewish state," he adamantly refuses to accept the more descriptive formulation "nation state of the Jewish people."

Abbas is of course committed to Palestine being a Muslim state under Sharia Law, despite the reality that Christian Palestinians constitute a significant (if forcibly shrinking) percentage of Palestinian Arabs. Article 4 of the Palestinian Basic Law states that "1. Islam is the official religion in Palestine. Respect and sanctity of all other heavenly religions shall be maintained. 2. The principles of Islamic Shari'a shall be the main source of legislation."

Writing for *The New York Times* on the advent of the 50th anniversary of the Six Day War, Israel's former Ambassador to Israel, Michael Oren, said: "The conflict is not about the territory Israel captured in 1967. It is about whether a Jewish state has a right to exist in the Middle East in the first place. As Mr. Abbas has publicly stated, 'I will never accept a Jewish state.'" Oren argues that until Abbas and other Palestinian leaders can say the words "two states for two peoples," no reasonable resolution will be reached.

The Palestinian leader's conditional support for a peaceful resolution is also undermined by his own actions. For years, the Palestinian Authority—first under the leadership of Yasser Arafat and now under the 82-year-old Abbas—has perpetuated a vile policy of making payments to terrorists and their families. According to the official PA budget, in 2016 the Palestinian Authority directed $174 million of its total budget in payments to families of so-called "martyrs," and an additional $128 million for security prisoners—terrorists in Israeli prisons. Abbas claims to be a man of peace yet in reality he incentivizes, rewards, and incites terrorism.

It must also be remembered that Israel has offered to end the occupation and settlements in 2000–2001. These generous peace initiatives would have established a demilitarized Palestinian state. In 2008, Prime Minister Ehud Olmert made an even more generous proposal by offering the Palestinians 97% of the West Bank but Mahmoud Abbas did not respond. For the past several years, the current Israeli government has offered to sit down and negotiate a two-state solution with no pre-conditions—not even advanced recognition of Israel as the nation state of the Jewish people. Yet no substantive negotiations have taken place.

Some of the blame rests on the shoulders of Barack Obama. By applying pressure only to the Israeli side, not to the Palestinians, Obama consistently disincentivized Abbas from embracing the two-states for two-peoples paradigm. This came to a head in December when Obama allowed the U.S. not to veto the inane UN Resolution, under which the Western Wall and other historically Jewish sites are not recognized as part of Israel. (Recall that UN Resolution 181 mandated a "special international regime for the city of Jerusalem," and Jordan captured it illegally. Israel liberated Jerusalem in 1967, and allowed everybody to go to the Western Wall.)

It is a tragedy that the international community—headed by the U.N.—encourages the Palestinian Authority's rejectionism, rather than pushing it to make the painful compromises that will be needed from both sides in reaching a negotiated two-state outcome. Indeed, just a few days ago the UN once again demonstrated that it is a barrier to the peace-process. In his address at the UN General Assembly marking the 50th anniversary of the Six Day War and Israel's "occupation" of the West Bank, UN Secretary General, Antonio Guterres said:

> *"In 1947, on the basis of United Nations General Assembly resolution 181, the world recognized the two-state solution and called for the emergence of 'independent Arab and Jewish states.' On 14 May 1948, the State of Israel was born. Almost seven decades later, the world still awaits the birth of an independent Palestinian state."*

Guterres failed to acknowledge that "the reason the world still awaits the birth of an independent Palestinian state" is because the Arabs rejected the UN partition plan, which would have given them their own state, committing instead to seven decades of undermining Israel's legitimacy.[65]

When the Palestinian leadership and people want their own state more than they want there not to be a state for the Jewish people, the goal of the 1947 UN Resolution—two states for two peoples—will be achieved. A good beginning would be for Abbas finally to agree with the UN Resolution and say the following words: "I accept the 1947 UN Resolution that calls for two states for two peoples." It's not too much to ask from a leader seeking to establish a Palestinian Muslim state.

June 14, 2017
Oliver Stone's Response to Being Laughed at for Defending Putin: Blame the Jews

When film director Oliver Stone could not come up with a plausible response to Stephen Colbert's tough questions about why he gave a pass to Vladimir Putin for trying to influence the American presidential election, Stone resorted to an age-old bigotry: blame the Jews—or, in its current incarnation, shift the blame to the nation state of the Jewish people, Israel. Colbert was interviewing Stone about his new documentary, *The Putin Interviews*—a film comprised of conversations he had with the Russian president over the past two years. The exchange regarding Israel did not make it to air but was relayed to the *New York Post*'s "Page Six" by a source who was in the audience.

When pressed by Colbert about his apparent fondness of the Russian dictator, Stone replied: "Israel had far more involvement in the U.S. election than Russia." He then said again, "Why don't you ask me about that?" Colbert responded: "I'll ask you about that when you make a documentary about Israel!"

If Stone's absurd response were not reflective of a growing anti-Semitism by the intolerant hard left (of which Stone is a charter member) it would be laughable. Indeed, Stone resorted to the "socialism of fools" (which is what German Social Democrat August Bebel called anti-Semitism) precisely to save face because he was being mockingly laughed off stage by Colbert's audience for giving Colbert ridiculous answers. Some of Stone's bizarre pronouncements included:

"I'm amazed at his [Putin's] calmness, his courtesy...he never really said anything bad about anybody. He's been through a lot. He's been insulted and abused." Stone also expressed his "respect" for Putin's leadership. But no answer was more ridiculous than his bigoted claim that Israel did more to try to influence the election than Russia.

We know for certain that Russia (and that means Putin) desperately wanted Hillary Clinton to lose. We know that their surrogates timed leaks to cause maximum damage to her campaign. All of our intelligence agencies, in a rare show of unanimity, concluded that Russia went to great lengths to try to defeat Clinton.

What did Israel do? Stone hasn't said. He just let the blood libel hang out there for other bigots, so they could say, "See, we knew the Jews were behind this; they always are." There was an old Polish expression that said "If there is a bad outcome, the Jews must be behind it." Indeed, throughout history the last recourse of desperate bigots has been "blame the Jews." The modern version—pervasive among the hard left—is blame their nation state, Israel.

The reason Stone did not provide any proof of his anti-Semitic accusation is because there is none. It simply is not true. Israel did not try to influence this election. The Israeli government took no position and its leaders were probably divided, as were its citizens, concerning the desired outcome. Prime Minister Netanyahu, for his part, remained neutral, emphatically stating before the election that he was "happy to work with whoever gets elected."

Moreover, American Jews voted overwhelmingly in favor of Clinton. To be sure, some, such as Sheldon Adelson, contributed to Trump, but others, including many strong supporters of Israel, contributed heavily to Clinton. I would not be surprised if even in the face of Adelson's huge contributions, more money from Jewish sources was contributed to Hillary Clinton's campaign, but no one keeps track of such matters.

It is important to note that this is not an isolated incident. Stone's bigotry towards Jews and their nation state is well documented. He has said that, "Hitler did far more damage to the Russians than [to] the Jewish people."

And then argued that this fact is largely unknown because of "the Jewish domination of the media...there's a major lobby in the United States. They are hard workers. They stay on top of every comment, the most powerful lobby in Washington." He continued to say: "Israel has f***** up United States foreign policy for years."

Moreover, Stone has also stated that, "Hitler is an easy scapegoat throughout history" and expressed affection for Cuban dictator, Fidel Castro, whom he called "a great leader."

Clearly, there was no legitimate reason for Stone to bring up Israel in the context of a dialogue regarding Russia's interference in the U.S. presidential election. By ducking questions about Putin and Russia, and then bizarrely accusing Israel of wrongdoing, Stone engaged in an old trope: blaming Jews—or the nation state of the Jewish people—for far-reaching domestic political issues in foreign countries. By morphing the discussion about Putin's untoward history of suppressing the press, killing political opponents, and engaging in cyber-attacks against the U.S., into a polemic against Israel, Stone displayed his own bias.

The essence of anti-Semitism is the bigoted claim that if there is a problem, then Jews must be its cause. This is the exact canard peddled by Stone—and is extremely dangerous if unrebutted. I challenge my old friend (and co-producer of *Reversal of Fortune*, the film based on my book) to debate me on the following proposition: did Israel do more to influence the 2016 election than Russia? If he agrees, he will once again be laughed off the stage.

July 14, 2017
So Now American Zionists Want to Boycott Israel

Several prominent American Zionists—including long-time supporters of Israel—are so outraged at the Israeli government's recent decision regarding the Western Wall and non-Orthodox conversion, that they are urging American Jews to reduce or even eliminate their support for Israel. According to an article by Elliot Abrams in *Mosaic*, Ike Fisher, a prominent member of the Aipac board, threatened to "suspend" all further financial support for Israel. Daniel Gordis, a leading voice for Conservative Judaism, urged American Jews to cancel their El Al tickets and fly Delta or United. He also proposed "withholding donations to Israeli hospitals, so that 'They start running out of money' and 'begin to falter.'" This sort of emotional response is reminiscent of the temper tantrum outgoing President Barak Obama engaged in when he refused to veto the UN's recent anti-Israel resolution.

I strongly disagree both with the Israeli government's capitulation to the minority of ultra-Orthodox Jews, who wield far too much influence in Israeli politics, and with the proposals to cut back on support for Israel by some of my fellow critics of the Israeli government's recent decisions with regard to religion.

I strongly support greater separation between religion and state in Israel, as Theodor Herzl outlined in his plan for the nation state of the Jewish people in *Der Judenstaat* 120 years ago: "We shall...prevent any theocratic tendencies from coming to the fore on the part of our priesthood. We shall keep our priests [by which is meant rabbis] within the confines of their temples." It was David Ben Gurion, Israel's founding prime minister, who made the deal with the Orthodox Rabbinate that violated Herzl's mandate and knocked down the wall of separation between religion and state. He allocated to the Chief Rabbinate authority over many secular matters, such as marriage, divorce, and child custody. He also laid the groundwork for the creation of religious parties that have been a necessary part of most Israeli coalitions for many years.

So don't blame Israel's current prime minister, Benjamin Netanyahu, for the recent capitulation. His government's survival depends on his unholy alliance with allegedly holy parties that threaten to leave the coalition and bring down his government unless he capitulated. The alternative to a Netanyahu government might well be far to the right of the current government, both on religious matters and on prospects for peace. Reasonable people may disagree as to whether Netanyahu did the right thing, but I believe that given the choice between the current government and what may well replace it, PM Netanyahu acted on acceptable priorities.

This is not to say that I am happy with the end result. As a post-denominational Jew, I want to see a part of the Western Wall opened to conservative and reform prayer. I also want to see conservative and reform and modern orthodox rabbis deemed fully competent to perform rituals including marriage and divorce. I will continue to fight for these outcomes, and I think we will ultimately be successful. But in the meantime, I will also continue to fly El Al, contribute to Israeli hospitals, attend APAC events, and encourage Americans to support Israel, both politically and financially. To do otherwise is to engage in a form of BDS—the tactic currently employed by Israel's enemies to de-legitimate the nation state of the Jewish people. Supporters of BDS will point to these benign boycotts as a way of justifying their malignant ones. If BDS is an immoral tactic, as it surely is, so, too, is punishing the people of Israel for the failure of its government to be fully inclusive of Jews who do not align themselves with the ultra-Orthodox.

Tough love may be an appropriate response in family matters, but boycotting a troubled nation that has become a pariah among the hard left is not the appropriate response to the Israeli government's recent decisions regarding religion. The answer is not disengagement, but rather greater engagement with Israel on matters that involve world Jewry. I, too, am furious about the arrogant and destructive threats of the ultra-Orthodox parties in the current government. I, too, would prefer to see a coalition that excluded the ultra-Orthodox parties. I, too, would like to see a high wall of separation that kept the Rabbis out of politics. But I do not live in Israel, and Israel is a democracy. Ultimately it is up to the citizens of Israel to change the current system. The role of American Jews is limited to persuasion, not coercion. In the end, we will be successful in persuading the Israeli people to take the power of religious, coercion out of the hands of the ultra-Orthodox minority because that would not only be good for secular Israelis—who are a majority—but also for religious Israelis. History has proved that separation of state from religion is better not only for the state, but also for religion.

August 8, 2017
How Can LGBTQs Oppose Israel?

When the so-called "Dyke March" organized a protest for lesbian rights, they decided to take sides in the divisive Israel-Palestine conflict. So some Jewish lesbians were forced to leave the march because they carried a flag that had a Star of David printed on top of the LGBTQ rainbow flag. They were told that the march was "anti-Zionists" "pro-Palestinian," and that some Israel haters in the parade were "made [to] feel unsafe" by the age-old Jewish symbol.

Shortly after this fiasco, another event called "Slut Walk Chicago" tweeted that they would stand by the Dyke Marchers' "decision to remove the Zionists contingent from their events." They insisted that they "won't allow Zionists displays at ours." After some protests against their stance as anti-Semitic as well as anti-Israel, Slut Walk relented and decided that it would no longer ban "any symbols or any kind of ethnic or heritage flag," while still proclaiming that they are anti-Zionist.

These events followed an earlier one in 2016 where gay BDS activists together with a local Black Lives Matter chapter broke up an LGBTQ event in Chicago because it featured a presentation by an organization that focuses on fostering the relationship between LGBTQ communities in North America and Israel. The protestors claimed that the event organizers had engaged in "pinkwashing"—a concept that claims that Israel exploits its "gay friendly" reputation in order to distract from its occupation—by showing solidarity with the Israeli LGBTQ community.

By foolishly taking sides on the Arab-Israeli conflict, and supporting the Muslim side, these lesbians have not only sidetracked their core mission, they have also aligned themselves with some of the most repressive anti-gay countries in the world today. They have also aligned themselves against the one nation in the Middle East that is among the world's strongest supporters of gay rights. Israel has granted asylum to gay Muslims who have been threatened with death by neighboring Arab countries.

Though no country is perfect when it comes to gay rights, Israel has long been a leader in promoting equality. While the United States military still had a "don't ask don't tell" policy, the Israeli army actively recruited openly gay and lesbian soldiers into its highest ranks, both as combat and intelligence officers. Tel Aviv's Gay Pride Parade is world famous, and that city has been declared one of the most gay friendly places in the world. Even in Jerusalem—the home of many ultra-Orthodox traditionalists—gay pride parades have taken place, though not without some counter-protests.

The only "parade" of gays in the Muslim world has been when they have been lined up and paraded to prison, sometimes to be executed. There are no gay or lesbian rights in the Palestinian Authority, Jordan, Egypt, Iran, or the Gulf states. Being openly gay is an invitation to state-sanctioned violence.

Why then, would radical lesbians support a movement, which if successful in establishing a Muslim state in place of Israel, would criminalize being gay or lesbian? Let there be no mistake about what the Palestinian state would be. Just look at its proposed constitution, which requires that the state be governed by Sharia law, the Muslim code that demands the death penalty for gays and lesbians. The Quran refers to sexual relations between two men as an "abomination" and calls on the legal punishment of death for all illicit sexual relations: "And as for those who are guilty of an indecency...call to witnesses against them four (witnesses) from among you; then if they bear witness confine them to the houses until death takes them away or Allah opens some way for them." The Torah has similar prohibitions, but they are not enforced in secular Israel.

The reason for this self-destructive alliance with the forces of anti-gay expression inheres in the concept of "intersectionality," the pseudo-academic theory, which holds that all forms of social oppression are inexorably linked. Increasingly, hard-left radicals insist on a package of unrelated left-wing causes that must be embraced by anyone claiming the label of progressive—including the demonization of Jews and their nation state, Israel.

The time has come for the organizations that purport to represent lesbians and gay men to stick to their mission and to stop supporting nations, groups, and leaders who would kill them if they had the chance. If they think I'm being overdramatic, let them try to conduct a "Dyke March" or "Slut Walk" in Ramallah.

August 23, 2017
The President Has a Special Obligation to Condemn Nazis and KKK

All decent Americans have an obligation to condemn the violent bigotry of the Nazi and KKK demonstrators in Charlottesville or wherever else they spew their poisonous and threatening rhetoric. But President Donald Trump has a special obligation to single out for condemnation, and distance himself from, individuals and groups that claim—even if falsely—to speak in his name, as the racist provocateurs in Charlottesville did.

David Duke, the notorious bigot, told reporters that white nationalists were working to "fulfill the promises of Donald Trump." Richard Spencer, the founder of the *Daily Stormer* (a not-so-coded homage to the Nazi publication *Der Stürmer*,) attributed the growth of the ultra-nationalist alt-right to the Trump presidency: "Obviously the alt-right has come very far in the past two years in terms of public exposure...is Donald Trump one of the major causes of that? Of course."

Trump initially responded as follows: "We must ALL be united and condemn all that hate stands for. There is no place for this kind of violence in America." But then, following the car ramming that killed a peaceful protestor, President Trump made the following statement: "We condemn in the strongest possible terms this egregious display of hatred, bigotry, and violence on many sides—on many sides."

President Trump's inclusion of the words "violence on many sides"—which seemed improvised—suggested to some a moral equivalence between the Nazis and the KKK, on the one hand, and those protesting and resisting them, on the other hand. Trump denied that he was suggesting any such equivalence and made the following statement:

"Racism is evil. And those who cause violence in its name are criminals and thugs, including KKK, Neo-Nazis, White Supremacists, and other hate groups are repugnant to everything we hold dear as Americans. Those who spread violence in the name of bigotry strike at the very core of America."

But then a day later he seemed to double down on his attempt to be even-handed in his comments about the "many sides" of this conflict. He pointed to "very fine people on both sides," implying that Nazis and Klansmen could be "fine," because their protests were "very legal." Then he denounced "alt-left" groups that were "very, very violent." Once again, he blamed "both sides," and asked rhetorically, "what about the 'alt-left,' that as you say, came charging at the alt-right? Don't they have any semblance of guilt?"

David Duke immediately praised President Trump's condemnation of the "alt-left," thanking him "for your honesty & courage to tell the truth about #Charlottesville & condemn the leftist terrorists in BLM/Antifa."

Finally (though nothing this president ever tweets is final), President Trump praised the anti-racist "protestors in Boston who are speaking out against bigotry and hate."

It is against this background that the president's back-and-forth statements must be evaluated.

Even if it were true—and the evidence is to the contrary—that Black Lives Matter and Antifa were as blameworthy for Charlottesville as the Nazis and KKK, it would still be incumbent on President Trump to focus his condemnation especially on the violent racists on the right that claim to speak on his behalf. The hard left—which does, in part, include some violent and bigoted elements—does not purport to speak on the president's behalf and does not claim to be trying to "fulfill the promises of Donald Trump." To the contrary, they oppose everything he stands for.

This situation poses a delicate dilemma for President Trump. He has denounced the ideology of the violent racists on the alt-right who claim to be acting in his name—not quickly or forcefully enough. And he has declared his opposition to "racism" and specifically to "those who cause violence in its name," whom he has called "criminals" and "thugs." He specifically included within these categories the "KKK, Neo-Nazis [and] White Supremacists," the very groups that purport to speak in his name.

Why is that not enough? Why should he not at the same time condemn the alt-left for its violence? These are reasonable questions that require nuanced answers. Let me try to provide some.

I have long believed that it is the special responsibility of decent conservatives to expose, condemn, and marginalize hard-right extremists and bigots. William F. Buckley showed the way when he refused to defend Patrick Buchanan against charges that what he had said amounted to anti-Semitism. Other decent conservatives followed Buckley's lead, and marginalized anti-Semites and racists who expressed bigotry in the false name of conservatism.

I also believe that it is the special responsibility of decent liberals to do the same with regard to hard-left bigoted extremists. I must acknowledge, as a liberal, that we have not done as good a job as decent conservatives have done. Perhaps this is because hard-left extremists often march under banners of benevolence, whereas, hard-rights extremists tend not to hide their malevolence.

Consider, for example, Antifa, the radical hard-left group, some of whose members violently confronted the Nazis and Klansmen in Charlottesville. As reported by *The New York Times*, the organization is comprised of a "diverse collection of anarchists, communists and socialists" with its "antecedents in Germany and Italy." According to the *Times*, "Its adherents express disdain for mainstream liberal politics" and support "direct action" by which they mean "using force and violence," rather than free speech and civil disobedience. Their leaders claim that violence is necessary because "it's full on war."

Nor is this merely rhetoric. On university campuses, particularly at Berkeley, "black-clad protestors, some of whom identified themselves as Antifa, smashed windows, threw gasoline bombs and broke into campus buildings, causing $100,000 in damage." They model themselves on the "Weathermen" of the 1970s, who were responsible for numerous acts of violence and even murder.

They claim to be using "counter-violence" in defense against the violence of neo-Nazis and Klansmen, but that is not true. They also use violence to shut down speakers with whose worldviews they disagree. They include not only right-wing extremists, but also mainstream conservatives, moderate Zionists, and even some liberals. They reject dialogue in favor of intimidation and force.

As a liberal, I will not give these hard-left violent bigots a pass. It is true that the Nazis and KKK are currently more dangerous in terms of physical violence than hard-left groups. (It is also true that the most violent groups by far are radical Islamic terrorists, who are not the targets of Antifa protests.) But the violence of racists on the right (and radical jihadists) must not lead us to ignore the reality that Antifa and its radical allies pose real danger to the future of our nation, because of their increasing influence on university campuses, where our future leaders are being educated. The recent events in Charlottesville and elsewhere have made them heroes among some mainstream liberals who are willing to excuse their anti-liberal bigotry because they are on the barricades against fascism.

It's far too easy to self-righteously condemn your political enemies when they step (or leap) over the line to bigotry and violence. It's far more difficult to condemn those who share your wing, whether left or right, but who go too far. But that is what morality and decency require, as Buckley taught us.

So, President Trump must stop being even-handed in his condemnations. He should focus his condemnation on extreme right-wing bigots who speak and act in his name, and leave it to those of us on the left to focus our condemnation on left-wing extremists and bigots.

August 31, 2017
Both the Left and the Right Must Guard Against Campus Extremism

As students and faculty begin to return to university campuses, we should anticipate an uptick in confrontations between those expressing provocatively controversial views, and those seeking to prevent the expression of such views on their campuses.

The provocatively controversial speech will come largely from the hard right, both from outsiders such as Ann Coulter, Dinesh D'Souza, and Milo Yiannopoulos, as well as from students, and perhaps a few professors. The attempts to censure these views will come largely from the hard left, from some minority groups, and increasingly from outsiders, such as Antifa (the shorthand name for antifascist activists).

The expected uptick will be the result of the increasing influence and power of extremist groups on both sides of the ideological spectrum. Charlottesville emboldened both the white supremacist groups that organized the initial protest march and the radical groups such as Antifa that confronted the KKK, Nazis, and other racists. It was a win-win for violent extremists on both sides, and a loss for centrists who support both antiracism and freedom of speech, even for racist views.

There is little support for right-wing racist groups on most university campuses, but there is widespread support for hard-left groups that are intolerant of views they regard as unacceptable. And the definition of "unacceptable" now extends beyond deliberate provocations from hard-right extremists. For some campus censors, unacceptable views now include opposition to race-based affirmative action, support for Israel, opposition to global free-market capitalism, demanding due process for students accused of sexual assault, and even defending the right of racists to speak on campus.

We have seen efforts—some successful, some not—to shut down Condoleezza Rice (former Bush administration secretary of state), Suzanne Venker (a critic of feminism), Bill Maher (a TV talk show comedian), Greg Lukianoff (the president of the Foundation for Individual Rights in Education), Nicholas and Erika Christakis (Yale faculty members), Michael Oren (former Israeli ambassador to the United States), Nir Barkat (mayor of Jerusalem), and other moderate speakers who do not fit the hard left's definition of politically correct.

These and other efforts to prevent speakers from being heard took place at Rutgers, Williams, Berkeley, Yale, the University of California and at other elite universities. At Berkeley, "Antifa"[66] led a violent protest that resulted in $100,000 in property damage. At Middlebury College, there were physical injuries and threats. There were efforts to prevent me from advocating a two-state solution to the Israeli-Palestinian conflict at three universities.

There is no way of knowing precisely how widespread among students and faculty is this intolerance for "unacceptable"—which generally translates into "conservative"—views. What we do know is that even a relatively small number of vocal students can shut down speakers and even threaten to shut down universities. University administrators cannot ignore these censorial voices, especially if they claim to represent racial or gender minorities pitted against "white privilege." There may even be a "silent majority" on many campuses, who oppose censorship, but those students are pressured into silence by fear of being labeled racist, sexist, homophobic, or Islamophobic.

The vocal opposition to this movement away from intellectual and ideological diversity comes primarily from outside the current student body and faculty—from alumni, from board members, from contributors, and from legislators. Some of this opposition is based on principled support for academic freedom, but some comes from conservatives who dislike the fact that it is their conservative views that are being censored. During the McCarthy era, it was precisely these groups that supported censorship of left-wing views.

There are far too many people—both on campus and off—who support "free speech for me and not for thee." For them, freedom of speech is a self-serving tactic, not a neutral principle. Universities must resist such unprincipled partisanship. More importantly, resistance to the current left-wing intolerance must come primarily from liberals. It is too easy (and too self-serving) for conservatives to rail against censorship of conservative ideas, just as it is too easy (and too self-serving) for liberals to rail against racist provocateurs. All reasonable people should condemn both hard-right racism and hard-left censorship, but it is the special obligation of the centrist left to condemn hard-left censorship, just as it is the special obligation of the centrist right to condemn hard-right bigotry.

William F. Buckley showed the way in 1991 when he refused to defend fellow right-winger Pat Buchanan against the accusation that what he had said "amounted to anti-Semitism." Buckley's courageous statement led the conservative movement to distance itself from anti-Semites who claimed to be speaking in the name of conservatism.

Now we need equally courageous academics from the left to call out the intolerance of the censorial hard left that sometimes morphs into bigotry.

September 10, 2017
The Hard Right and Hard Left Pose Different Dangers

The extreme right—neo-Nazis, the Ku Klux Klan, and other assorted racists and anti-Semites—and the extreme left—anti-American and anti-Israel zealots, intolerant censors, violent anarchists such as Antifa, and other assorted radicals—both pose a danger in the U.S. and abroad.

Which group poses a greater threat? The question resists a quantitative answer, because much may depend on time and place. It may also be in the eye of the beholder: For many on the center left, the greater danger is posed by the hard right, and vice versa. Yet the most important reason for this lack of a definitive quantitative answer is that they pose qualitatively different dangers.

History has set limits on how far to the extremes of the hard right reasonable right-wingers are prepared to go. Following the horrors of the Holocaust and Southern lynchings, no one claiming the mantle of conservative is willing to be associated with Nazi anti-Semitism or the KKK. Neo-Nazi and Klan speakers are not invited to university campuses.

The hard left lacks comparable limits. Despite what Stalin, Mao, the Castros, Pol Pot, Hugo Chavez, and North Korea's Kims have done in the name of communism, there are still those on the left—including some university professors and students—who do not shrink from declaring themselves communists, or even Stalinists or Maoists. Their numbers are not high, but the mere fact that it is acceptable on campuses, even if not praiseworthy, to be identified with hard-left mass murderers, but not hard-right mass murderers, is telling.

The ultimate goals of the hard right are different, and far less commendable, than those of the hard left. The hard-right utopia might be a fascist society modeled on the Italy or Germany of the 1930s, or the segregationist post-Reconstruction American South.

The hard-left utopia would be a socialist or communist state-regulated economy aiming for economic and racial equality. The means for achieving these important goals might be similar to those of the hard right. Hitler, Stalin, and Mao all killed millions of innocent people in an effort to achieve their goals.

For the vast majority of reasonable people, including centrist conservatives, the hard-right utopia would be a dystopia to be avoided at all costs. The hard-left utopia would be somewhat more acceptable to many on the center left, so long as it was achieved nonviolently.

The danger posed by the extreme left is directly related to its more benign goals, which seduce some people, including university students and faculty. Believing that noble ends justify ignoble means, they are willing to accept the antidemocratic, intolerant, and sometimes violent censorship policies and actions of Antifa and its radical cohorts.

For that reason, the most extreme left zealots are welcomed today on many campuses to express their radical views. That is not true of the most extreme neo-Nazi or KKK zealots, such as David Duke and Richard Spencer. Former White House aide Steve Bannon recently told *60 Minutes* that "the neo-Nazis and neo-Confederates and the Klan, who by the way are absolutely awful—there's no room in American politics for that." In contrast, prominent American leftists, such as Noam Chomsky and even Bernie Sanders, supported the candidacy of British hard-left extremist Jeremy Corbyn, despite his flirtation with anti-Semitism.

The hard right is dangerous largely for what it has done in the past. For those who believe that past is prologue, the danger persists. It also persists for those who look to Europe for hints of what may be in store for us: Neofascism is on the rise in Hungary, Slovakia, Austria, Greece, Lithuania, and even France. Some of this rise may be attributable to regional issues, such as the mass migration of Muslims from Syria and other parts of the Middle East. But some may also be a function of growing nationalism and nostalgia for the "glory" days of Europe—or, as evidenced in our last election, of America.

The danger posed by the extreme hard left is more about the future. Leaders of tomorrow are being educated today on campus. The tolerance for censorship and even violence to suppress dissenting voices may be a foretaste of things to come. The growing influence of "intersectionality"—which creates alliances among "oppressed" groups—has led to a strange acceptance by much of the extreme left of the far-from-progressive goals and violent means of radical Islamic terrorist groups that are sexist, homophobic, anti-Semitic, and anti-Western. This combination of hard-left secular views and extreme Islamic theological views is toxic.

We must recognize the different dangers posed by different extremist groups that preach and practice violence, if we are to combat them effectively in the marketplace of ideas, and perhaps more importantly, on the campuses and streets.

September 14, 2017
Berkeley Must Defend Ben Shapiro's Right to Speak

I vividly recall the famous "free speech" movement at Berkeley several decades ago. The hard left demanded the right to express radical, often obnoxious, views on campus. Some on the hard right sought to ban these hard left expressions. Free speech prevailed.

Now it is the hard right that is demanding the right to make provocative speeches on campus and it is elements of the hard left that are trying to censor them.

But there is no symmetry in the means used to silence opponents. Today's hard left, led by Antifa and other radical and anarchistic gangs, do not shrink from the threat or use of violence to silence speakers with whom they disagree. These unlawful tactics have prevailed and several right-wing speakers were forced to cancel their scheduled appearances on the Berkeley campus. This time free speech is losing.

Now there is a test case: Ben Shapiro, a thoughtful conservative with whose views I often personally disagree, is not merely a provocateur, as some other extreme right speakers are. These provocateurs come to campuses not so much to educate as to provoke responses. Although deliberately provocative speech is as constitutionally protected as other kinds of offensive expression, it is easy to understand why some administrators, faculty, and students object to being used as part of what they regard as staged political theater deliberately designed to create conflict.

Ben Shapiro is different. He has something substantively important to share with the Berkeley academic community. If I were on that campus, I would want to listen to what he has to say, despite my disagreement with many of his views.

Yet there are those on the hard left who would stop me and others from hearing him. They cannot be allowed to do that.

Berkeley, as a state university, is bound by the First Amendment. It has a constitutional obligation to protect the speaker and allow him to address his audience. It also has an obligation to protect those who seek to protest Shapiro's presence on campus and the content of his speech. But the protests may not interfere with the right of the speaker to communicate his ideas to the audience. Protesters must not be allowed to block access to the speech, to threaten violence against the speaker or his audience, to shout down the speaker, or to take any other action that prevents the speaker from completing his talk.

Protesters may show disagreement with specific ideas by briefly booing or even shouting words of disapproval, but these disruptions must be brief and not continuous. They must not have the intent or effect of stopping the speaker from delivering his or her message.

These lines are difficult to draw in practice, but disagreements must be resolved in favor of the speaker, not the disrupters. And the university must have the same rules for the right as for the left. It may not take ideological sides when it comes to freedom of expression. It must remain scrupulously neutral, even if its constituents favor the left over the right.

Berkeley, as expected, is in the eye of the storm. It passed the test when the hard left demanded free speech. It must now pass the test when the hard right is demanding equal protection.

Ben Shapiro must not be prevented from speaking. His talk must not be cancelled, as others were. Berkeley must do whatever it takes to protect Shapiro and those who follow him from the intolerant mobs that don't want anyone to hear his conservative message.

What is at stake is more than Shapiro's personal freedom of speech, important as that is. What is at stake is the right of every American to participate in the open marketplace of ideas. If a great university shuts down that marketplace, the rights of all Americans are endangered.

September 22, 2017
Plame Knew What She Was Tweeting

Valerie Plame had to know what she was tweeting. Plame retweeted a virulently anti-Semitic article by a well-known bigot, which she characterized as "thoughtful." Now she's trying to make excuses, but they don't wash.

The article by Phillip Giraldi itself contains the usual anti-Semitic tropes: Jews are guilty of dual loyalty; they control politicians, the media, and entertainment; they want the U.S. to fight wars for the country to which they have real allegiance—Israel; they are dangerous to America. Giraldi has been pushing this garbage for years and Plame is one of his fans.

But this particular article goes much further in its neo-Nazi imagery. It advocates that "The media should be required to label [Jews like Bill Kristol] at the bottom of the television screen whenever they pop up...That would be kind of like a warning label on a bottle of rat poison—translating roughly as ingest even the tiniest little dosage of the nonsense spewed by Bill Kristol at your own peril."

In other words, Jewish supporters of Israel, like Kristol and me, should have to wear the modern-day equivalent of a yellow star before we are allowed to appear on TV and poison real Americans. Nice stuff that Plame was retweeting and characterizing as thoughtful.

This was not the first time Plame retweeted Giraldi's garbage. In 2014, she retweeted one of his screeds with the following notation: "Well put." And after tweeting the current anti-Semitic article she described it as: "Yes, very provocative, but thoughtful. Many neocon hawks ARE Jewish." Nor is this the only time that Plame has re-tweeted other nonsense from the bigoted platform this piece came from—a platform of which she has pleaded ignorance. According to journalist Yashar Ali, Plame has tweeted at least eight other articles from the same website since 2014. Sounds like she is into some strange websites.

I actually read the Philip Giraldi article before I was aware of the Plame tweet. I read it on a neo-Nazi website, where Giraldi's articles are frequently featured. That's where Giraldi's articles belong—on overtly anti-Semitic and neo-Nazi websites. For Plame, a former CIA operative, to claim that she was unaware of the anti-Semitic content of Giraldi's article is to blink reality. Plame had to know what she was doing, since she was aware of Giraldi's bigotry. Her apologies ring hollow. Her true feelings were revealed in what she said before she realized that she would be widely condemned for her original re-tweet. She must now do more than apologize. She must explain how she came upon the article? Who sent it to her? Does she regularly read bigoted website? Why is she reading and re-tweeting a known anti-Semite? What are her own personal views regarding the content of the Giraldi's article?

The Plame incident reflects a broader problem about which I have written. There is a growing tolerance for anti-Semitism. Even when some people themselves do not harbor these feelings, they are willing to support those who do, as long as the anti-Semites are on their side of the political spectrum. This is an unacceptable approach, especially in the post-Holocaust era. Unfortunately, Valerie Plame is the poster child for this growing tolerance. She must be called out on it, as must others who follow the same path of bigotry.

The problem exists both on the hard right and the hard left. Both extremist groups see the world in racial, ethnic, and religious terms. Both engage in identity politics: the hard left gives more weight to the views of certain minorities; while the hard right gives less weight to the views of these same minorities. Both are equally guilty of reductionism and stereotyping. Neither group is prepared to judge individuals on their individual merits and demerits. Both insist on judging entire groups and of stereotyping.

American Jews—like other Americans—are deeply divided on important issues, such as the Iran deal, the current prospects for peace between the Israelis and Palestinians, and the Trump administration's foreign policies. To generalize about "Jews" is both factually and morally wrong.

What the hard right and hard left share in common is special bigotry toward Jews: the neo-Nazi right hates the Jewish people, and the hard left hates the nation state of the Jewish people and those Jews who support it. Both views are bigoted and must not become acceptable among centrist liberals and conservatives.

September 26, 2017
Listen or Censor?
Columbia's Free Speech Test

On Wednesday evening, I am scheduled to engage in a public conversation at Columbia University about the prospects for peace in the Middle East. The question—a critical one at a time when far too many campuses are hostile to ideas that challenge existing dogma—is whether I'll be heard or shouted down.

I am a centrist liberal who voted for Hillary Clinton. I support a two-state solution. I have long opposed Israel's settlement policies. I am not one of those hard-right provocateurs who come to campus in order to stoke the flames of controversy (though they, too, have First Amendment rights). I am a retired professor who wants to contribute to the education of students with regard to a complex, divisive issue.

Yet according to reports in the media, radical students plan to disrupt my speech in an effort to prevent me from sharing my moderate ideas with Columbia students. The protesters are apparently afraid that I may actually persuade some open-minded students that the issues surrounding the Israel-Palestine conflict are nuanced and that Israel alone is not to blame for the current stalemate.

The students who would prevent me from speaking would also prevent other centrist moderates from expressing views on other hot-button issues with which they disagree. They see no reason for conversation, since they believe they know the truth. And they are certain that the truth is a matter of black and white, with no greys.

Though young—and enrolled in an institution of higher learning that's supposed to be opening their minds and challenging their beliefs—they are enemies of ideas, complexity, and thinking for oneself. They believe that the university should not be a place for open-minded students to hear diverse views and make up their own minds, but rather an institution where professors propagandize captive students to one particular point of view.

In too many classes at Columbia and elsewhere, that has been the norm for too long.

This closeminded approach to the role of universities is particularly evident when it comes to the Israeli-Palestinian conflict, but it transcends that conflict as well. It applies to virtually all issues on which the hard left has a singular point of view.

I expect that my speech will be protested not only by anti-Israel and anti-Semitic students and outsiders, but also by some radical feminists, gay rights activists, Black Lives Matter supporters, and others who, under the false banner of "intersectionality," believe they must stand together against their common oppressors.

These days, their supposed common oppressors include the United States, Israel, Christianity, and other personifications of Western culture. These "intersectionalists" will try to censor me despite my lifelong devotion to feminism, gay rights, civil rights, and other liberal causes.

They believe that you can't be both a Zionist and a feminist, a Zionist and supporter of gay rights, or a Zionist and a supporter of equality for African Americans. Under their narrow and exclusionary way of thinking, support for Israel—even critical support for its very existence as the nation state of the Jewish people—disqualifies one from supporting other liberal causes. Indeed, it disqualifies one from expressing views at a university.

I will challenge that censorious worldview at Columbia on Wednesday night. I will do it politely but firmly, and I expect Columbia to assure not only my physical safety and the physical safety of those students who come to listen to me, but also my ability to communicate my views to open-minded students.

In commencement remarks earlier this year, the school's president, Lee Bollinger, said "being able to listen to and then effectively rebut those with whom we disagree—particularly those who themselves peddle intolerance—is one of the greatest skills our education can bestow."

I will defend the right of protesters to hold signs, distribute literature and communicate their disagreement with my views by brief boos or other manifestations of displeasure. But I will not be shouted down, silenced or frightened away. I will insist on my right, and that of my audience, to hear what I have to say from beginning to end. I will invite those who disagree with me to pose challenging questions, which I will try to answer. Indeed, I will prioritize critical questions over favorable ones. Everyone will have an opportunity to contribute to the marketplace of ideas.

That is what universities should be about.

October 2, 2017
The Case for Kurdish Independence

Over 90% of Iraq's Kurdish population have now voted for independence from Iraq. While the referendum is not binding, it reflects the will of a minority group that has a long history of persecution and statelessness.

The independence referendum is an important step toward remedying a historic injustice inflicted on the Kurdish population in the aftermath of WWI. Yet while millions took to the streets to celebrate, it is clear that the challenges of moving forward towards establishing an independent Kurdistan are only just beginning. Already, Iraqi Prime Minister Haider al-Abadi has said: "We will impose the rule of Iraq in all of the areas of the KRG, with the strength of the constitution." Meanwhile, other Iraqi lawmakers have called for the prosecution of Kurdish representatives who organized the referendum—singling out Kurdish Regional Government President (KRG) Marsouni Barzani specifically.

While Israel immediately supported the Kurdish bid for independence, Turkish leader Recep Tayyip Erdogan tried to extort Israel to withdraw its support, threatening to end the process of normalization unless it does so. It is worth noting that Turkey strongly supports statehood for the Palestinians but not for their own Kurdish population. The Palestinian leadership, which is seeking statehood for its people, also opposes statehood for the Kurds. Hypocrisy abounds in the international community, but that should surprise no one.

The case for Palestinian statehood is at least as compelling as the case for Kurdish statehood, but you wouldn't know that by the way so many countries support the former but not the latter. The reason for this disparity has little to do with the merits of their respective cases and much to do with the countries from which they seek independence. The reason then for this double standard is that few countries want to oppose Turkey, Iraq, Iran, and Syria; many of these same countries are perfectly willing to demonize the nation state of the Jewish people. Here is the comparative case for the Kurds and the Palestinians.

First, some historical context. In the aftermath of WWI the allied forces signed a treaty to reshape the Middle East from the remnants of the fallen Ottoman Empire. The 1920 Treaty of Sevres set out parameters for a unified Kurdish state, albeit under British control. However, the Kurdish state was never implemented owing to Turkish opposition and its victory in the Turkish War of Independence, whereby swaths of land intended for the Kurds became part of the modern Turkish state. As a result, the Kurdish region was split between Turkey, Syria, and Iran and the Kurds became dispersed around northern Iraq, southeast Turkey, and parts of Iran and Syria. Though today no one knows its exact population size, it is estimated that there are around 30 million Kurds living in these areas.

In contrast to the Palestinian people who adhere to the same traditions and practices as their Arab neighbors and speak the same language, Kurds have their own language (although different groups speak different dialects) and subscribe to their own culture, dress code, and holidays. While the history and genealogy of Palestinians is intertwined with that of their Arab neighbors (Jordan's population is approximately 50% Palestinian), the Kurds have largely kept separate from their host-states, constantly aspiring for political and national autonomy.

Over the years there have been countless protests and uprisings by Kurdish populations against their host-states. Some Arab rulers have used brutal force to crackdown on dissent. Consider Turkey, for example, where the "Kurdish issue" influences domestic and foreign policy more than any other matter. Suffering from what some historians refer to as "the Sevres Syndrome"—paranoia stemming from the allies' attempt to carve up parts of the former Ottoman Empire for a Kurdish state—President Erdogan has subjected the country's Kurdish population to terror and tyranny, and arrested Kurds who are caught speaking their native language.

But perhaps no group has had it worse than the Kurds of Iraq, who now total 5 million—approximately 10–15% of Iraq's total population. Under the Baathist regime in the 1970s, the Kurds were subject to "ethnic cleansing." Under the rule of Saddam Hussein they were sent to concentration camps, exposed to chemical weapons, and many were summarily executed. It is estimated that approximately 100,000 Kurds were killed at the hands of the Baath regime. So "restitution" is an entirely appropriate factor to consider—though certainly not the only one—in supporting the establishment of an independent Kurdistan in northern Iraq.

In contrast, the Palestinians have suffered far fewer deaths at the hands of Israel (and Jordan) yet many within the international community cite Palestinian deaths as a justification for Palestinian statehood. Why the double standard?

There are many other compelling reasons for why the Kurds should have their own state. First, the Iraqi Kurds have their own identity, practices, language, and culture. They are a coherent nation with profound historical ties to their territory. They have their own national institutions that separate them from their neighbors, their own army (the Pashmerga), and their own oil and energy strategy. Moreover, international law stipulated in Article 1 of the Montevideo Convention on the Rights and Duties of States, lays the foundation for the recognition of state sovereignty. The edict states: "the state as a person of international law should possess the following qualifications: (a) a permanent population; (b) a defined territory; (c) government; and (d) capacity to enter into relations with the other states. The KRG meets these criteria, as least as well as do the Palestinians.

Moreover, the autonomous Kurdish region in northern Iraq—the closest it has come to having its own state—has thrived and maintained relative peace and order against the backdrop of a weak, ineffectual Iraqi government and a brutal civil war. As such, it represents a semblance of stability in a region comprised of bloody violence, destruction and failed states.

Why then did the United States—along with Russia, the EU, China, and the UN—come out against independence for one of the largest ethnic groups without a state, when they push so hard for Palestinian statehood? The U.S. State Department said it was "deeply disappointed" with the action taken, while the White House issued a statement calling it "provocative and destabilizing."

Essentially, the international community cites the following two factors for its broad rejectionism: 1. That it will cause a destabilizing effect in an already fragile Iraq that may reverberate in neighboring states with Kurdish populations; 2. That the bid for independence will distract from the broader effort to defeat ISIS—which is being fought largely by Kurdish Pashmerga forces.

These arguments are not compelling. Iraq is a failed state that has been plagued by civil war for the last 14 years, and the Kurdish population in its north represent the only real stability in that country, while also assuming the largest military role in combatting ISIS' occupation of Iraqi territory. There is also nothing to suggest that an independent Kurdistan would cease its cooperation with the anti-ISIS coalition. If anything, the stakes in maintaining its newfound sovereignty would be higher. Additionally, Iraqi Kurds were a key partner for the U.S. coalition that toppled Saddam Hussein's regime and has staved off further sectarian tensions in that country. One thing is clear: if the United States continues to neglect its "friends" and allies in the region—those on the front line in the fight against ISIS—the damage to its credibility will only increase.

Israel is the only Western democracy to come out in support of Kurdish independence in northern Iraq. One would expect that the state-seeking Palestinian Authority—which has cynically used international forums to push for Palestinian self-determination—would back Kurdish efforts for independence. However, while seeking recognition for its own right to nationhood, the PA instead subscribed to the Arab League's opposing position. This is what Hasan Khreisheh of the Palestinian Legislative Council said about the referendum: "The Kurds are a nation, same as Arabs, French, and English. But this referendum is not an innocent step. The only country behind them is Israel. Once Israel is behind them, then from my point of view, we have to be careful." Clearly, there are no limits to the Palestinian Authority's hypocrisy.

Nor are there any limits to the hypocrisy of those university students and faculty who demonstrate so loudly for Palestinian statehood, but ignore or oppose the Kurds. When is the last time you read about a demonstration in favor of the Kurds on a university campus? The answer is never. No one who supports statehood for the Palestinians can morally oppose Kurdish independence. But they do, because double-standard hypocrisy, and not morality, frames the debate over the Israeli-Palestinian conflict.

October 8, 2017
Trump's "Calm Before the Storm" Is a Message to North Korea and Iran

Reporters continue scratching their heads about what President Trump meant when he spoke of the "calm before the storm" Thursday as he was hosting a dinner for military commanders and their spouses. It seems clear to me that he was sending a powerful message to North Korea and Iran: Change your behavior now, or prepare to face new but unspecified painful consequences.

North Korea and Iran are taking the measure of President Trump to see how far they can push him and how much they can get away with. The North Koreans continue testing nuclear weapons and long-range missiles and threaten to launch a nuclear attack on America and our allies that could kills millions. Iran is likely engaging in activities that could contribute to the design and development of its own nuclear explosive device.

If these worrisome actions by the two rogue nations persist, there will be a storm. And as candidate Trump said during his campaign for the White House, he will not tell our enemies what kind of storm to expect—only that he will not allow current trends that endanger our national security and that of our allies to continue unabated.

The president must make some difficult decisions: whether to continue to rely on economic sanctions that don't appear to be working against North Korea; and whether to refuse to certify Iranian compliance with the bad nuclear deal and demand that additional constraints be placed on the Islamic Republic's dangerous and provocative activities.

President Trump faces an October 15 deadline to decide whether to certify Iranian compliance with the nuclear agreement, which is designed to keep it from developing nuclear weapons for the next few years. News reports say he is expected to refuse to make that certification.

U.S. policy toward both Iran and North Korea is closely related, because we must prevent Iran from joining the nuclear club and becoming another, even more dangerous version of North Korea.

The sad reality is that even if Iran were to comply with the letter of the nuclear agreement, it will still be able to develop the capability to build up a vast nuclear arsenal within a relatively short time. This is the fundamental flaw of the agreement.

And Iran claims that the nuclear deal permits it to refuse to allow the International Atomic Energy Agency (IAEA) to inspect military facilities. This has led the IAEA to conclude that it cannot assure the world that Iran is not even now designing and developing a nuclear arsenal with missiles capable of delivering them to American allies in the Mideast and Europe, and soon the U.S. itself.

All the Iranians need to do to become a nuclear power is to resume spinning centrifuges. The nuclear agreement, which was reached with the Obama administration in 2015, will allow them to do that in a few years.

So whether we like it or not, a storm is coming. Whether that storm will be diplomatic, economic, or military depends on the leaders of North Korea and Iran. If they choose to negotiate constraints on their increasingly dangerous activities, they can avoid the other more painful options.

Our military options are and should always be a last resort. They are the worst possible options—other than Iran developing a nuclear arsenal and North Korea developing a nuclear delivery system that can reach our population centers and wipe out major American cities.

With fanatical dictators like those in control of North Korea and Iran, we cannot rely on containment and deterrence as acceptable policies to prevent them from using nuclear weapons, as we have done for years with the Soviet Union (and now Russia) and China.

So President Trump cannot afford to wait and do nothing as Iran and North Korea grow ever stronger, ever more menacing and become greater and greater threats. He must do something—now. The nature of what is done, and what kind of storm it may be, is up to our enemies. I hope they choose wisely.

October 15, 2017
President Trump Did the Right Thing by Walking Away from UNESCO—for Now

The State Department announced on Thursday that the United States would be withdrawing from the UN agency UNESCO, citing financial reasons, the need for reform, and the body's "continuing anti-Israel bias." President Trump's decision to leave UNESCO—the United Nations Educational, Scientific and Cultural Organization—as of December 31, 2018, was an appropriate foreign policy decision that will hopefully prompt a much-needed rethink of the United Nations, its purpose, and practices. It will also send a strong message to the Palestinians that statehood cannot be achieved on the basis of UN resolutions alone, and that the only way forward is to engage in direct negotiations with Israel where mutual sacrifices will be required.

In the aftermath of WWII, the intended goal of the Paris-based UN body was a noble one: to promote basic freedoms and security through international collaboration on education, science and cultural projects. UNESCO-sponsored projects focused on literacy, vocational training, equal access to basic education and preservation of human rights and historical sites are indeed praiseworthy. However, in practice, the 195-member body—with its automatic anti-Israel majority that exists in every institution of the UN—has become a springboard for Jew hatred and the rewriting of history.

To be sure, UNESCO is far from the only UN agency to regularly single out Israel for reproach. Yet, its anti-Israel adoptions have been abhorrent even by the low standards established by the broader multilateral institution. Consider a resolution introduced in May, which denied Israel—and the Jewish people's—legal and historic ties to the city of Jerusalem, including its holiest sites. It called the Cave of the Patriarchs in Hebron—considered the resting place of the Jewish Patriarchs and Matriarchs—and Rachel's Tomb near Bethlehem, "Palestinian sites." Shamefully, this vote was deliberately held on Israel's Independence Day. Only two months later, the cultural body convened in Krakow, Poland—a city soaked in Jewish blood—and declared the city of Hebron, holy to Jews, an endangered Palestinian heritage site.

Even for some of the harshest critics of Israel, this historical ignorance is sometimes too much to swallow. In October 2016, for example, when UNESCO passed a resolution denying Israel's connection to the Temple Mount and the Western Wall—referring to them only by their Muslin names—UNESCO chief Irina Bokov (whose intentions and motivations are themselves often curious) questioned the text of the Arab-sponsored resolution on Jerusalem.

This egregious distortion of history is not particularly surprising when considering the anti-Semitic political culture that has come to underpin UNESCO, particularly since 2011, when it became the first UN agency to admit the Palestinians as a full member. Hillel Neur of the watchdog organization, UN Watch, noted that between 2009–2014 the cultural body has adopted 46 resolutions against Israel, yet only one on Syria and none on Iran, Sudan, North Korea, or any of the other known violators of human rights around the world. In fact, a representative of the regime of Syrian dictator and mass murderer Bashar al-Assad sits on a UNESCO human rights committee.

Neur further highlights this double standard: "UNESCO paid tribute to mass murderer Che Guevara, elected Syria to its human rights committee, and created prizes named after the dictators of Bahrain and Equatorial Guinea, whose ruler Obiang says God empowered him to kill whomever he wants. UNESCO has a noble founding mission, but that has been completely hijacked by the world's worst tyrannies and supporters of terror."

This is not the first time that the United States has pulled out of the hypocritical UN cultural body. Under President Reagan in 1984, the United States walked away from UNESCO owing to financial mismanagement and "hostility toward the basic institutions of a free society." It was only in 2002 that President G.W. Bush rejoined the body stating that the United States wanted to "participate fully in its mission to advance human rights, tolerance and learning." But this vision was upturned when President Obama halted funding to the UN body in 2011 (U.S. funding at the time accounted for one-fifth of UNESCO's budget) when Palestine was accepted as a full member. This original level of financial support has not been restored and the cultural body has since missed out on close to $600 million of American funding.

The United States is also the greatest contributor to the overall United Nation budget. It pays 25 percent of the regular operating budget and 28 percent of the separate peacekeeping budget. As such, by withdrawing from UNESCO—again—President Trump is sending a powerful message to the international community: The United States holds the purse strings and we will no longer tolerate international organizations that serve as forums for Jew-bashing. This important message was encapsulated in a powerful statement made by U.S. Ambassador to the United Nations, Nikki Haley: "The purpose of UNESCO is a good one. Unfortunately, its extreme politicization has become a chronic embarrassment... US taxpayers should no longer be on the hook to pay for policies that are hostile to our values and make a mockery of justice and common sense."

The political thinker Charles de Montesquieu famously said: "There is no crueler tyranny than that which is perpetuated under the shield of law and in the name of justice." It is precisely because UNESCO purports to be a cultural and educational body that its false credibility masks its pervasive bigotry.

On Friday afternoon it was announced that former French Culture Minister Audrey Azoulay—a Jewish woman—was elected as UNESCO Chief. Azoulay said that "UNESCO is going through a profound crisis" but that she hopes to fix it from within. I hope she succeeds in this mission. I hope she can turn UNESCO from an organization that promotes bigotry in the false name of culture, into one that opposes all forms of bigotry. Given the nature of its voting membership, this will not be easy, but with pressure from the U.S., it may have a chance of succeeding. Perhaps then the U.S. will maintain its membership in and financial support for UNESCO.

October 19, 2017
Why Are So Many Claiming that Iran Is Complying with the Deal, When Evidence Shows They Aren't?

The evidence is mounting that Iran is not only violating the spirit of the no-nukes deal, but that it is also violating its letter. The prologue to the deal explicitly states: "Iran reaffirms that under no circumstances will Iran ever seek, develop or acquire any nuclear weapons." This reaffirmation has no sunset provision: it is supposed to be forever.

Yet German officials have concluded that Iran has not given up on its goal to produce nuclear weapons that can be mounted on rockets. According to *Der Tagesspiegel*, a Berlin newspaper; "Despite the nuclear agreement [reached with world powers in July 2015], Iran has not given up its illegal activities in Germany. The mullah regime also made efforts this year to obtain material from [German] firms for its nuclear program and the construction of missiles, said security sources." Frank Jansen, a prominent journalist, has reported that the "Revolutionary Guards want to continue the nuclear program at all costs."

The International Atomic Energy Agency (IAEA) recently stated that it could not verify that Iran was "fully implementing the agreement" by not engaging in activities that would allow it to make a nuclear explosive device. Yukiya Amano of the IAEA told Reuters that when it comes to inspections—which are stipulated in section T of the agreement—"our tools are limited." Amano continued to say: "In other sections, for example, Iran has committed to submit declarations, place their activities under safeguards or ensure access by us. But in Section T I don't see any (such commitment)."

It is well established that Tehran has consistently denied IAEA inspectors' access to military sites and other research locations. This is in direct contravention to the Joint Comprehensive Plan of Action (JCPOA) and bipartisan legislation set out by Congress, which compels the president to verify that "Iran is transparently, verifiably, and fully implementing the agreement." Yet, according to the Institute for Science and International Security, as of the last quarterly report released in August, the IAEA had not visited any military site in Iran since implementation day.

For its part, the IAEA has been complicit in allowing Tehran to circumvent the agreement and act as a law unto itself. Consider that after the deal was negotiated with the P5+1 nations, it was revealed that Tehran and the IAEA had entered into a secret agreement which allowed the Iranian regime to carry out its own nuclear trace testing at the Parchin complex—a site long suspected of being a nuclear testing ground—and would report back to the IAEA with "selective" videos and photos. This arrangement—which went behind the back of Congress—is especially suspect when considered in light of the Iranian regime's history of duplicity.

To be sure, revelations about Iran testing the boundaries of the JCPOA—and crossing the line into violation—are not new. While many of these violations have not been disclosed by the previous U.S. administration, or by the IAEA, there is a myriad of information and analysis suggesting that Iran has previously failed to comply with several provisions of the JCPOA. It has twice been revealed that Iran exceeded the cap on heavy water mandated by the agreement, and has also refused to allow testing of its carbon fiber acquired before the deal was implemented. Moreover, it has also been reported that Tehran has found new ways to conduct additional mechanical testing of centrifuges, in clear violation of the JCPOA.

These violations are not surprising when considering Iran's belligerent posture in the Middle East. Iran continues to exploit the instability in the region to prop up and fund terror groups such as Hamas, Hezbollah, and the Houthis, whose chants of "Death to Israel" are now also accompanied by vows of "Death to America." For its part, the Iranian-funded Hezbollah has an estimated 100,000 missiles aimed directly at Israel. As such, it is clear that rather than combatting Iran's threatening posture, the influx of money thrust into the Iranian economy, coupled with ambiguities in the text of the agreement, have had the reverse effect of emboldening the Iranian regime and fortifying its hegemonic ambitions. Iran also continues to test its vast ballistic missile program and deny its own people fundamental human rights.

Yet, even if Iran were to comply with the letter of the nuclear agreement, it would still be able to build up a vast nuclear arsenal within a relatively short timeframe. The approach adopted by the Trump administration—articulated in a statement delivered by the president several days ago—is justified by the realities on the ground. By announcing that he is decertifying Iran's compliance with the nuclear agreement, President Trump is giving Congress 60 days to act. Not only is President Trump giving the United States back some of its leverage, but he is also sending a powerful message to the rogue leaders in Iran and North Korea—who are believed to have cooperated on missile technology—that the era of containment and deterrence policies is over. The United States is returning to its original mission of prevention.

Interestingly, in the aftermath of President Trump's address, the Saudi Press Agency reported that King Salman called the U.S. president to offer his support for America's more "firm strategy" on Iran and commitment to fighting "Iranian aggression." Israel's Prime Minister, Benjamin Netanyahu, offered similar praise for the new U.S. posture, saying in a statement that President Trump "has created an opportunity to fix this bad deal, to roll back Iran's aggression and to confront its criminal support of terrorism." It is no secret that these two previously discordant states are now cooperating in unprecedented ways as they try to counter the threat posed by a nuclear Iran. When Israel and the Gulf States are on the same page, the world should listen.

There are those that argue that by decertifying, President Trump has undercut American credibility and sent a message to the world that it can't count on one American president following through on deals made by his predecessor. But the fault for that lies squarely with President Obama who refused not only to make his deal a binding treaty, but also to seek any congressional approval—both of which would have assured greater continuity. He knew when he signed the deal that it could be undone by any future president. The goal, of course, is not to undo the deal but rather to undo its sunset provision and to make Iran keep the commitment it made in the prologue: never to obtain "any nuclear weapons."

The available evidence now strongly supports the conclusion that Iran is not keeping that commitment: that it is determined to develop a nuclear arsenal capable of being mounted on intercontinental ballistic missiles. If the current deal is not changed, it is likely that Iran will become the new North Korea—or worse—before very long.

October 26, 2017
An Anti-Semitic Caricature of Me Generates No Criticism from Berkeley Hard Left

I was recently invited to present the liberal case for Israel at Berkeley. In my remarks, I advocated the establishment of a Palestinian state and a negotiated end of the conflict. I encouraged hostile questions from protestors and answered all of them. The audience responded positively to the dialogue.

Then immediately after my address, a poster was plastered outside Berkeley Law School with a swastika drawn on my face.

The Dean of Berkeley Law School, Erwin Cherwinsky, sent a letter condemning the swastika: "Several of our students expressed their disagreement with him [Dershowitz] and did so in a completely appropriate way that led to discussion and dialogue. I was pleased to hear of how this went, but then shocked to learn of the swastika drawn on a flyer that someone had posted about him."

Shortly after, *The Daily Californian*—Berkeley's student newspaper—published an anti-Semitic cartoon, depicting an ugly caricature of me sticking my head through a cardboard cutout. Behind the cardboard I am portrayed stomping on a Palestinian child with my foot, while holding in my hand an Israeli soldier who is shooting an unarmed Palestinian youth. Above the cardboard cutout the title of my speech—The Liberal Case for Israel—is scrawled in capital letters.

In a letter to the editor, the university's chancellor, Carol Christ, wrote the following:

> *"Your recent editorial cartoon targeting Alan Dershowitz was offensive, appalling and deeply disappointing. I condemn its publication. Are you aware that its anti-Semitic imagery connects directly to the centuries-old "blood libel" that falsely ac-*

> cused Jews of engaging in ritual murder? I cannot recall anything similar in the Daily Cal, and I call on the paper's editors to reflect on whether they would sanction a similar assault on other ethnic or religious groups. We cannot build a campus community where everyone feels safe, respected and welcome if hatred and the perpetuation of harmful stereotypes become an acceptable part of our discourse."

It is shocking that this vile caricature—which would fit comfortably in a Nazi publication—was published in "the official paper of record of the City of Berkeley" (according to the editor.) The cartoon resembles the grotesque anti-Semitic blood libel propaganda splashed across *Der Stürmer* in the 1930s, which depicted Jews drinking the blood of Gentile children. Canards about Jews as predators—prominently promulgated by the Tzarist forgery, the Protocols of the Elders of Zion—were anti-Semitic back then and are still anti-Semitic today, whether espoused by the extreme left or the extreme right.

This sequence of events—by hard-left students who originally protested my right to speak at Berkeley—confirmed what I've long believed: that there is very little difference between the Nazis of the hard right and the anti-Semites of the hard left. There is little doubt that this abhorrent caricature was a hard-left Neo-Nazi expression.

These anti-Semitic displays against me were in reaction to a speech in which I advocated a Palestinian state, an end to the occupation, and opposition to Israeli settlement policies. Many on the hard left refuse to acknowledge this sort of nuanced positioning. That is because their hostility towards Israel does not stem from any particular Israeli actions or policies. Even if Israel were to withdraw from the West Bank, destroy the security barrier, and recognize Hamas as a legitimate political organization, it would still not be enough. For these radicals, it is not about what Israel *does*; it is about what Israel *is*: the nation state of the Jewish people. To many on the hard left, Israel is an imperialistic, apartheid, genocidal, and colonialist enterprise that must be destroyed.

Nonetheless, just as I defended the rights of Nazis to march in Skokie, I defend the right of hard-left bigots to produce this sort of anti-Semitic material, despite it being hate speech. Those who condemn hate speech when it comes from the right should also speak up when hate speech comes from the left. The silence from those on the left is steeped in hypocrisy. It reflects the old adage: free speech for me but not for thee.

To be sure, the students had the right to publish this cartoon, but they also had the right <u>not</u> to publish it. I am confident that if the shoe were on the other foot—if a cartoon of comparable hate directed against women, gays, blacks, or Muslims were proposed—they would not have published it. There is one word for this double standard. It's called bigotry.

The best response to bigotry is the opposite of censorship: it is exposure and shaming in the court of public opinion. The offensive cartoon should not be removed, as some have suggested. It should be widely circulated along with the names prominently displayed of the anti-Semite who drew it and the bigoted editors who decided to publish it. Every potential employer or admissions officer should ask them to justify their bigotry.

Joel Mayorga is the anti-Semitic cartoonist. Karim Doumar (editor in chief and president), Alexandra Yoon-Hendricks (managing editor) and Suhauna Hussain (opinion editor) head the editorial board that oversaw the decision to publish it. They must be held accountable for their reprehensible actions. I challenge them to justify their bigotry. It will not be enough to hide behind the shield of freedom of speech, because that freedom also entails the right <u>not</u> to publish anti-Semitic expression, if they would refuse to publish other bigoted expression.

After I submitted my op-ed, the *Daily Cal* tried to censor my piece in a self-serving way by omitting my characterization of the cartoonist as an anti-Semite. As far as I know they did not edit the offending cartoon. Also, the editor claimed that the intent of the cartoon was to expose the "hypocrisy" of my talk. Yet, the newspaper never even reported on the content of my talk and I don't know whether the cartoonist was even at my talk. The cartoon was clearly based on a stereotype not on the content of my talk.

October 31, 2017
Forward Defends Anti-Semitic Cartoon

When the official newspaper of Berkeley published a color caricature of me as a spiderlike creature with one leg stomping on a Palestinian child and another holding an IDF soldier spilling the blood of an unarmed Palestinian, there was universal condemnation of what was widely seen as a throwback to the anti-Semitic imagery of the Nazi era. The chancellor condemned the cartoon, stating that, "its anti-Semitic imagery connects directly to the centuries-old 'blood libel' that falsely accused Jews of engaging in ritual murder."

Writing in the *Daily Cal*, students from a pro-Israel organization at Berkeley debunked the claim that the cartoonist and the student paper editors at the *Daily Cal* could not have known that this cartoon was steeped in traditional anti-Semitic stereotyping, when considering its deep roots in European, and even American, publications.

> *"In the cartoon, Dershowitz is depicted with a hooked nose and a body of a large amorphous black sphere. His exaggerated head and contorted legs and hands evoke images of a spider. The rhetoric of Jews as 'invasive' insects in society, trying to take over resources and power, has long been used to justify violence, persecution and murder. The two elements of the cartoon, with Dershowitz's face in the front and the black body in the back, plays into the anti-Semitic trope of Jews as shape-shifting, sub-human entities using deception and trickery in order to advance their own agendas. This rhetoric is nowhere more common than in Nazi propaganda, and can be traced far beyond WWII in European and American media."*

The students also wrote about the "pain" the anti-Semitic cartoon had caused them:

> *"To a Jewish student on this campus, seeing this cartoon in the Daily Cal is a reminder that we are not always welcome in the spaces we call home…*

Telling Jews that we can or cannot define what is offensive to us, because of our status as privileged minority in the United States, is anti-Semitic."

Some students also pointed to the swastika that had defaced my picture on a poster outside Berkeley Law School, as evidence of a pervasive anti-Semitism disguised as anti-Zionism on that campus.

Not surprisingly, it was only an op-ed writer for *The Forward* who not only denied that the imagery was anti-Semitic, but actually justified it:

"The mere appearance of blood near a Jew is not a blood libel. The State of Israel has an army, and that army sometimes kills Palestinians, including women and children. When you prick those people, I am told, they bleed. It is perverse to demand of artists that they represent actual, real Israeli violence without blood, just because European Christians invented a fake accusation."

But how then does the writer justify my depiction as a hulky black spider with an overbearing shape and twisted spiderlike hands—imagery traditionally used to depict Jews as offensive, venomous insects. The Forward also did not show readers the color cartoon. Instead they showed them a black and white version that makes it harder to see the spider like imagery.

Echoing the editor of *The Daily Cal*, the op-ed writer published by *The Forward* also argued that the cartoon was a legitimate criticism of my talk. But the cartoonist has now admitted that he didn't hear my talk. Nor did *The Daily Cal* report on it. Had they listened, they would have heard a pro-peace, pro two-state, pro compromise proposal.

Would *The Forward* publish an op-ed that justified comparable images of women, blacks, or gays? The baseball player, Yuri Gurriel, who made a slanted-eye gesture was also reflecting the "truth" about facial differences, but no one would suggest that it wasn't a racist stereotype.

By publishing an op-ed that defends bigoted caricatures only of a Jewish supporter of Israel—when no college newspaper would ever peddle stereotypes of other ethnic, religious or social groups—*The Forward*, too, engages in an unacceptable double standard.

November 6, 2017
Taylor Crosses His Own Line Into Bigotry

[On November 3, *The Daily Californian* published an op-ed by Matthew Taylor, explicitly accusing me of having "blood on his [my] hands" and being "culpable for the perpetuation of...[Israeli] atrocities." The article was worse than the cartoon itself. But when I tried to write a factual response to his false accusations, *The Daily Californian* categorically refused to publish it, thus demonstrating their obvious bias. I have attached my response here so it can be widely read.]

A recent op-ed by Matthew Taylor in *The Daily Californian* condemns the cartoonist for caricaturing me as a predatory spider. He argues, however, that it was "fair criticism" to portray me with "blood on [my] hands" and "crushing a Palestinian with one foot and holding up an IDF soldier who assassinates a Palestinian civilian." In support of this conclusion he proclaims—without citing any evidence—that Israel is "in fact an egregious human rights abuser," murders unarmed and innocent civilians, including "underage Palestinians," commits "intentional...atrocities" and engages in "pinkwashing." He calls me a "privileged professor who is culpable for the perpetuation of Israel's atrocities," despite my long record of advocating a peaceful two-state outcome.

I would not usually reply to such ignorance and oversimplified ad hominems. But because these false accusations have become a staple of hard left attacks singling out only the nation state of the Jewish people for such defamation, I will disprove each of them in turn.

Let me begin with "pinkwashing." The accusation that Israel is "pinkwashing" its bad treatment of Palestinians by its good treatment of gays is a new variation on a discredited old theme. The core characteristic of anti-Semitism is the assertion that everything the Jews do is wrong, and everything that is wrong is done by the Jews. That is the bigoted thesis of the anti-Israel campaign whose supporters absurdly claim that Israel is engaging in "pinkwashing." Bigots such as Taylor would apparently prefer to see Israel treat gays the way Israel's enemies do, because they hate Israel more than they care about gay rights. Well, to the unthinking anti-Semite, it doesn't matter how the Jewish manipulation works. The anti-Semite just knows that there must be something sinister at work if Jews do anything positive. The same is now true for the unthinking anti-Israel bigot. The fact is that the very Israelis who are most supportive of gay rights are also the most supportive of Palestinian rights. Pinkwashing is an anti-Semitic canard.

Moreover, Taylor argues that Israel commits "intentional" atrocities against innocent Palestinians including children. The reality is that the Israeli military's efforts to stop Hamas from indiscriminately killing Israeli citizens with rockets and through terror tunnels has been the opposite of indiscriminate, as Colonel Richard Kemp and other military experts have attested. Colonel Kemp has argued that no other country in history has gone to such great lengths as Israel, to distinguish between military and civilian targets, even in the face of an enemy that regularly uses its own population as human shields, and that hides military equipment in schools and hospitals. Israel's efforts to protect its citizens compare favorably to the U.S.- and NATO-led military bombing campaigns in Iraq, Syria, and other areas, in which civilians have also been used as human shields. Israel goes to enormous lengths to reduce the number of civilian casualties—even to the point of foregoing legitimate targets that are too close to civilians. Yes, Israel has defended its citizens against terrorist attacks by underage Palestinians because Palestinian terrorist leaders deliberately recruit underage Palestinians. When I engaged in a debate on BDS at the Oxford Union I issued the following challenge to the audience and to my opponent: name a single country in the history of the world, faced with threats comparable to those faced by Israel, that has a better record of human rights, compliance with the rule of law or seeking to minimize civilian casualties. The room was completely silent.

The author also refers to the security barrier erected by the Israeli government—in response to a spate of deadly suicide attacks where the bombers had infiltrated from Palestinian villages in the

West Bank—as "the apartheid" wall. In doing so, he reveals his own ignorance of the realities on the ground, and wrongly exploits the apartheid analogy and devalues the antiapartheid struggle itself. It is well known that Israel recognizes fully the rights of Christians and Muslims and prohibits any discrimination based on religion. Muslim and Christian citizens of Israel (of which there are more than a million) have the right to vote and have elected members of the Knesset, some of whom even oppose Israel's right to exist. There is complete freedom of dissent in Israel and Muslims, Christians and Jews alike practice it vigorously. That cannot be said of any Arab or Muslim state, nor of the Palestinian Authority.

Taylor reveals his own bigotry when he says that "Israel's apologists intimidated *The Daily Californian* into retracting the entire cartoon." But as he himself acknowledges, the most significant criticism came from the university's Chancellor, Carol Christ, who is not an "Israel apologist." He also mendaciously fails to mention that I adamantly opposed withdrawing or censoring the anti-Semitic cartoon, because I want the world to see it and hold accountable those responsible for it. Likewise, I would oppose censoring Taylor's anti-Semitic op-ed. Yes, anti-Semitic. Let me explain why. I agree that there is a vast difference between "actual anti-Semitism" and "legitimate criticism of Israel." But Taylor is not merely criticizing Israel. He is deliberately lying about its actions and policies in order to de-legitimize its very existence. He is singling out only the nation state of the Jewish people for such defamatory de-legitmization, and he is invoking the crassly anti-Semitic libel of "pinkwashing." Finally, he uses code words—such as "privileged" and "Israel's apologists"—to suggest a conspiracy of Jewish power that censors anti-Israel expression.

So yes, Taylor's op-ed falls on the anti-Semitic side of the very line he proposes: "actual anti-Semitism" versus "legitimate criticism of Israel." In that respect, his op-ed is even more bigoted than the spider cartoon he condemns as "crossing the line into anti-Semitism." The spider cartoon crossed the line with historic images. Taylor crossed the line with current lies.

December 28, 2017
Why Trump Is Right in Recognizing Jerusalem as Israel's Capital

President Trump's decision to recognize Jerusalem as Israel's capital is a perfect response to President Obama's benighted decision to change American policy by engineering the United Nations Security Council resolution declaring Judaism's holiest places in Jerusalem to be occupied territory and a "flagrant violation under international law." It was President Obama who changed the status quo and made peace more difficult by handing the Palestinians enormous leverage in future negotiations and disincentivizing them from making a compromised peace.

It had long been American foreign policy to veto any one-sided Security Council resolutions that declared Judaism's holiest places to be illegally occupied. Obama's decision to change that policy was not based on American interests or in the interests of peace. It was done out of personal revenge against Prime Minister Netanyahu and as an act of pique by the outgoing president. It was also designed improperly to tie the hands of president-elect Trump. President Trump is doing the right thing by telling the United Nations that the United States now rejects the one-sided Security Council resolution.

So if there is any change to the status quo, let the blame lie where it should be: at the hands of President Obama for his cowardly decision to wait until he was a lame-duck president to get even with Prime Minister Netanyahu. President Trump deserves praise for restoring balance in negotiations with Israel and the Palestinians. It was President Obama who made peace more difficult. It was President Trump who made it more feasible again.

The outrageously one-sided Security Council resolution declared that "any changes to the 4 June 1967 lines, including with regard to Jerusalem, have "no legal validity and constitutes a flagrant violation under international law." This means, among other things, that Israel's decision to build a plaza for prayer at the Western Wall—Judaism's holiest site—constitutes a "flagrant violation of international law." This resolution was, therefore, not limited to settlements in the West Bank, as the Obama administration later claimed in a bait-and-switch. The resolution applied equally to the very heart of Israel.

Before June 4, 1967, Jews were forbidden from praying at the Western Wall, Judaism's holiest site. They were forbidden to attend classes at the Hebrew University at Mt. Scopus, which had been opened in 1925 and was supported by Albert Einstein. Jews could not seek medical care at the Hadassah Hospital on Mt. Scopus, which had treated Jews and Arabs alike since 1918. Jews could not live in the Jewish Quarter of Jerusalem, where their forbearers had built homes and synagogues for thousands of years.

These Judenrein prohibitions were enacted by Jordan, which had captured by military force these Jewish areas during Israel's War of Independence, in 1948, and had illegally occupied the entire West Bank, which the United Nations had set aside for an Arab state. When the Jordanian government occupied these historic Jewish sites, they destroyed all the remnants of Judaism, including synagogues, schools, and cemeteries, whose headstones they used for urinals. Between 1948 to 1967, the United Nations did not offer a single resolution condemning this Jordanian occupation and cultural devastation.

When Israel retook these areas in a defensive war that Jordan started by shelling civilian homes in West Jerusalem, and opened them up as places where Jews could pray, study, receive medical treatment, and live, the United States took the official position that it would not recognize Israel's legitimate claims to Jewish Jerusalem.

It stated that the status of Jerusalem, including these newly liberated areas, would be left open to final negotiations and that the status quo would remain in place. That is the official rationale why the United States refused to recognize any part of Jerusalem, including West Jerusalem, as part of Israel. That is why the United States refused to allow an American citizen born in any part of Jerusalem to put the words "Jerusalem, Israel" on his or her passport as their place of birth.

But even that historic status quo was changed with President Obama's unjustified decision not to veto the Security Council Resolution from last December. The United Nations, all of the sudden, determined that, subject to any further negotiations and agreements, the Jewish areas of Jerusalem recaptured from Jordan in 1967 are not part of Israel. Instead, they are territories being illegally occupied by Israel, and any building in these areas—including places for prayer at the Western Wall, access roads to Mt. Scopus, and synagogues in the historic Jewish Quarter—"constitutes a flagrant violation under international law." If that indeed is the new status quo, then what incentives do the Palestinians have to enter negotiations? And if they were to do so, they could use these Jewish areas to extort unreasonable concessions from Israel, for which these now "illegally occupied" areas are sacred and nonnegotiable.

President Obama's refusal to veto this one-sided resolution was a deliberate ploy to tie the hands of his successor, the consequence of which was to make it far more difficult for his successor to encourage the Palestinians to accept Israel's offer to negotiate with no preconditions. No future president can undo this pernicious agreement, since a veto not cast can never be retroactively cast. And a resolution once enacted cannot be rescinded unless there is a majority vote against it, with no veto by any of its permanent members, which include Russia and China, who would be sure to veto any attempt to undo this resolution.

President Trump's decision to officially recognize Jerusalem as Israel's capital helps restore the appropriate balance. It demonstrates that the United States does not accept the Judenrein effects of this bigoted resolution on historic Jewish areas of Jerusalem, which were forbidden to Jews. The prior refusal of the United States to recognize Jerusalem as Israel's capital was based explicitly on the notion that nothing should be done to change the status quo of that city, holy to three religions. But the Security Council resolution did exactly that. It changed the status quo by declaring Israel's de facto presence on these Jewish holy sites to be a "flagrant violation under international law" that "the U.N. will not recognize."

Since virtually everyone in the international community acknowledges that any reasonable peace would recognize Israel's legitimate claims to these and other areas in Jerusalem, there is no reason for allowing the U.N. resolution to make criminals out of every Jew or Israeli who sets foot on these historically Jewish areas. (Ironically, President Obama prayed at what he regarded as the illegally occupied Western Wall.)

After the United Nations, at the urging of President Obama, made it a continuing international crime for there to be any Israeli presence in disputed areas of Jerusalem, including areas whose Jewish provenance is beyond dispute, President Trump was right to untie his own hands and to undo the damage wrought by his predecessor.

Some have argued that the United States should not recognize Jerusalem because it will stimulate violence by Arab terrorists. No American decision should ever be influenced by the threat of violence. Terrorists should not have a veto over American policy. If the United States were to give in to threat of violence, it would only incentivize others to threaten violence in response to any peace plan. So let's praise President Trump for doing the right thing by undoing the wrong thing President Obama did at the end of his presidency.

December 28, 2017
Debating BDS with Cornel West

I recently debated Professor Cornel West of Harvard about the boycott movement against Israel. The topic was resolved: "The boycott, divesture and sanctions (BDS) movement will help bring about the resolution of the Israeli-Palestinian conflict."

West argued that Israel is a "colonialist-settler" state and that apartheid in the West Bank was "worse" than it was in white-ruled South Africa and, should be subject to the same kind of economic and cultural isolation that helped bring about the fall of that regime.

I replied that the Jews who emigrated to Israel—a land in which Jews have lived continuously for thousands of years—were escaping from the countries that persecuted them, not acting as colonial settlers for those countries. Indeed, Israel fought against British colonial rule. Zionism was the national liberation movement of the Jewish people, not a colonial enterprise. Nor is Israel in any way like South Africa, where a minority of whites ruled over a majority of blacks who were denied the most fundamental human rights. Jews were, and are, a majority in Israel, although the Arab population has increased considerably since 1948. In Israel, Arabs, Druze, and Christians have equal rights and serve in high positions in government, business, the arts, and academia. Even the situation on the West Bank—where Palestinians have the right to vote for their leaders and criticize Israel—and in cities like Ramallah there is no Israeli military or police presence. The situation is no way comparable to apartheid South Africa.

West then argued that BDS was a nonviolent movement that was the best way to protest Israel's occupation and settlement policies.

I responded that BDS is not a "movement"; a movement requires universality, like the feminist, gay rights, and civil rights movements. BDS is an anti-Semitic tactic directed only against Jewish citizens and supporters of Israel. The boycott against Israel and its Jewish supporters began before any occupation or settlements and picked up steam just as Israel offered to end the occupation and settlements as part of a two-state solution that the Palestinians rejected. BDS was not a protest against Israel's policies. It was a protest against Israel's very existence.

West argued that BDS would help the Palestinians. I argued that it has hurt them by causing unemployment among Palestinian workers in companies such as SodaStream, which was pressured to move out of the West Bank, where it had paid high wages to Palestinian men and women who worked side by side with Israeli men and women. I explained that the leadership of the Palestinian Authority is opposed to broad boycotts of Israeli products, artists, and academics.

West argued that BDS would encourage Israel to make peace with the Palestinians. I replied that Israel would never be blackmailed into compromising its security, and that the Palestinians are disincentivised into making compromises by the fantasy that they will get a state through economic and cultural extortion. The Palestinians will get a state only by sitting down and negotiating directly with Israel. I told my mother's favorite joke about Sam, an Orthodox Jew, who prayed every day to win the N.Y. Lottery before he turned 80. On his 80th birthday, he complains to God that he hasn't won. God replies, "Sam, help me out a little—buy a ticket." I argued that the Palestinians expect to "win" a state without "buying a ticket" by sitting down to negotiate a compromise solution.

The debate in its entirety—which was conducted in front of an audience of business people in Dallas, Texas, as part of the "Old Parkland Debate Series"—continued with broad arguments about the Israeli-Palestinian conflict, the refugee situation, the peace process, terrorism, and other familiar issues. It can be seen in full on C-SPAN. I think it is worth watching.

The audience voted twice, once before the debate and once after. The final tally was 129 opposed to BDS and 16 in favor. The vote before the debate was 93 opposed and 14 in favor. I swayed 36 votes; West swayed 2. The anti-BDS position won overwhelmingly, not because I'm a better debater than West—he's quite articulate and everyone watching the C-SPAN clip can judge for themselves who is the better debater—but because the facts, the morality, and the practicalities are against BDS.

The important point is never to give up on making the case against unjust tactics being employed against Israel. In some forums—at the United Nations, at numerous American university campuses, in some parts of Western Europe—it is an uphill battle. But it is a battle that can be won among open-minded people of all backgrounds. BDS lost in Dallas. BDS lost in a debate between me and an articulate human rights activist at the Oxford Union. BDS is losing in legislative chambers. And if the case is effectively and honestly presented, it will lose in the court of public opinion.

Conclusion

BDS is an anti-Semitic tactic that is supported by some well-meaning people who are not themselves anti-Semites. This is because the leaders of BDS willfully hide from their followers the history, purpose, and reach of their bigoted tactic. Former Harvard president Lawrence Summers called BDS: "Anti-Semitic in effect if not in intent." I would put it a bit differently: for many, including most of its leaders, BDS is anti-Semitic both in effect and intent, but for some followers, it is not anti-Semitic in intent, because they are unaware of its true intent. *The New York Times* columnist Thomas L. Friedman, who is often quite critical of Israel's policies, got it right when he sent this message to those who support BDS:

> *"[The] campaign for divesture from Israel is deeply dishonest and hypocritical, and any university that goes along with it does not deserve the title of institution of higher learning.*
>
> *You are dishonest because to single out Israel as the only party to blame for the current impasse is to perpetuate a lie.*
>
> *Criticizing Israel is not anti-Semitic, and saying so is vile. But singling out Israel for opprobrium and international sanction—out of all proportion to any other party in the Middle East—is anti-Semitic, and not saying so is dishonest. Just because there are anti-Semites who blame Israel for everything that is wrong does not mean that whatever Israel does is right, or in its self-interest, or just."*

Criticism of Israel is not only not anti-Semitic, it is healthy, as long as it doesn't violate my friend Natan Sharansky's "three Ds":

> *"I believe that we can apply a simple test—I call it the '3D's' test—to help us distinguish legitimate criticism of Israel from*

anti-Semitism. The first 'D' is the test of demonization. When the Jewish state is being demonized; when Israel's actions are blown out of all sensible proportion; when comparisons are made between Israelis and Nazis and between Palestinian refugee camps and Auschwitz—this is anti-Semitism, not legitimate criticism of Israel.

The second 'D' is the test of double standards. When criticism of Israel is applied selectively; when Israel is singled out by the United Nations for human rights abuses while the behavior of known and major abusers, such as China, Iran, Cuba, and Syria, is ignored; when Israel's Magen David Adom, along among the world's ambulance services, is denied admission to the International Red Cross—this is anti-Semitism.

The third 'D' is the test of delegitimization: when Israel's fundamental right to exist is denied—alone among all peoples in the world—this too is anti-Semitism."

In this book, I have demonstrated that BDS violates each of the three Ds. I also believe BDS violates several other important D's as well:
- It <u>distorts</u> history and is based on a narrative that is <u>demonstrably</u> false.
- It <u>disincentivizes</u> Palestinian leadership from offering compromises.
- It <u>destroys</u> the prospects for peace.
- It <u>demeans</u> the fundamental principle of human rights: the Worst First.
- It <u>denies</u> scientists, artists, and academics the ability to work with each other.
- It refuses to <u>debate</u> or dialogue with its opponents.
- It has become the <u>darling</u> of neo-Nazi's and other Jew haters, on both the alt-right and extreme left.
- It is <u>directed</u> at the wrong people.
- It <u>distorts</u> morality.
- It does not deserve the support of <u>decent</u> people.

- It <u>defies</u> logic.
- It will be <u>defeated</u> in the marketplace of ideas.

The only reason BDS continues to receive support among many hard left and some alt-right extremists is that it is directed exclusively against the only nation state of the Jewish people. It would already be in the wastebasket of history if it were directed against the many real abusers of human rights throughout the world. But the double standard practiced by the hard left and neo-Nazi alt-right against Israel can only be understood by looking at that nation's Jewish character. No rational person can honestly believe that Israel's Jewish character plays no role in garnering support for the immoral tactic of BDS. This reality should dissuade all decent people from joining the indecent people who are at the center of the bigoted tactic of singling out Israel for economic, cultural, academic and political capital punishment. Shame on anyone who supports BDS.

ANALYTICAL INDEX

	Name	Publication / Organization	Date	Page number
	History			
1	Alan Dershowitz Address at AIPAC Policy Conference	AIPAC	March 20, 2010	40
2	Are Israeli Settlements the Barrier to Peace?	Prager University	January 12, 2015	129
3	Israel's Legal Founding	Prager University	February 23, 2015	139
4	A Visit to the Old and New Hells of Europe Provides a Reminder of Israel's Importance	FOX/ Gatestone Institute	March 17, 2016	166
5	The Holocaust: Many Villains, Few Heroes	Gatestone Institute/ The Jerusalem Post	May 2, 2016	174
6	The Mixed Legacy of Nuremberg	Gatestone Institute/ The Jerusalem Post	May 4, 2016	176
7	A Tribute to Humanity's Teacher	The Boston Globe	July 6, 2016	184
8	Shimon Peres – A Leader for All Seasons	The Boston Globe	September 28, 2016	197
9	Why Won't Abbas Accept "Two States for Two Peoples?"	Gatestone Institute	June 12, 2017	249
10	The Case for Kurdish Independence	Gatestone Institute/ FOX	October 2, 2017	274

	Academic Boycotts and Efforts to De-legitimize Israel on College Campuses			
11	Let's Have a Real Apartheid Education Week	Huffington Post/ Gatestone Institute	March 4, 2010	37
12	Alan Dershowitz Speech at Tel Aviv University Upon Accepting Honorary Doctorate	Haaretz	May 12, 2010	47
13	Civil Libertarians and Academics Who Support Censors	Huffington Post/ Gatestone Institute	May 13, 2011	69
14	Yale's Distressing Decision To Shut Down Its "Initiative for the Interdisciplinary Study of Anti-Semitism"	Huffington Post	June 14, 2011	72
15	Why Are John Mearsheimer and Richard Falk Endorsing a Blatantly Anti-Semitic Book?	The New Republic	November 4, 2011	78
16	Friends Seminary Legitimates Anti-Semitism	Gatestone Institute/ The Jerusalem Post	January 13, 2012	85
17	A Victory Over Bigotry at Friends University	The Algemeiner	February 2, 2012	87
18	Friends Seminary Plays Bait and Switch on Anti-Semitism	Gatestone Institute / Huffington Post	February 26, 2012	89
19	Should Harvard Sponsor a One-Sided Conference Seeking the End of Israel	Huffington Post/ Gatestone Institute	February 27, 2012	91
20	Brooklyn College Political Science Department's Israel Problem	Huffington Post/ Gatestone	January 1, 2013	94
21	Does Brooklyn College Pass the "Shoe on the Other Foot" Test?	Huffington Post/ The Jerusalem Post/ Gatestone Institute	February 3, 2013	97

22	The Brooklyn College BDS Debate and Me: The Critics' Real Agenda	The Guardian	February 8, 2013	99
23	Did Brooklyn College's Political Science Department Violate the First Amendment?	Huffington Post/ The Jerusalem Post/ Gatestone Institute	February 12, 2013	102
24	Boycotting Israeli Universities: A Victory for Bigotry	Haaretz	December 17, 2013	109
25	Israel and the Myopic BDS Campaign	The Boston Globe	December 27, 2013	112
26	An American Academic Supports the Targeting of Innocent Israeli Civilians	Gatestone Institute	April 11, 2014	66
27	Harvard's President Stops an Anti-Israel Boycott	Gatestone Institute/ The Jerusalem Post	December 19, 2014	123
28	A Brandeis Student Refuses to Show Sympathy for Assassinated Policemen – and Her Critic Is Attacked	Gatestone Institute/ The Jerusalem Post	December 28, 2014	127
29	Brandeis University: Both Pro-Israel and Pro-Free Speech	The Jerusalem Post	January 12, 2015	131
30	Universities Should be Unsafe for Political Correctness	Gatestone Institute/ The Jerusalem Post	May 28, 2015	144
31	Debating Against BDS– and Winning	Gatestone Institute/ The Jerusalem Post	November 3, 2015	156
32	Selective Outrage on Campus	Gatestone Institute/ The Jerusalem Post	November 12, 2015	161

33	Safe Spaces for Hypocrisy: The Dangerous Sensitivity Double Standards at Play on America's College Campuses	New York Daily News	November 22, 2015	164
34	Both the Left and the Right Must Guard Against Campus Extremism	The Boston Globe	August 31, 2017	263
35	Berkeley Must Defend Ben Shapiro's Right to Speak	FOX	September 14, 2017	268
36	Listen or Censor? Columbia's Free-Speech Test	NY Daily News	September 26, 2017	272
37	An Anti-Semitic Caricature of Me Generates No Criticism from Berkeley Hard Left	The Daily Californian	October 26, 2017	286
38	*Forward* Defends Anti-Semitic Cartoon	The Forward	October 31, 2017	289
39	Taylor Crosses His Own Line into Bigotry	The Daily Californian	November 7, 2017	291

Domestic Efforts to De-legitimize Israel

40	Hampshire Administration Does the Right Thing	Gatestone Institute	March 9, 2009	27
41	Bernie Sanders Must Clarify Where He Stands on Israel	Gatestone Institute/ The Jerusalem Post	April 13, 2016	169
42	New York is Right to Counter-Boycott Anti-Israel Boycotters	The Daily Beast	June 6, 2016	180
43	How to Assess the Bannon Appointment	Gatestone Institute	November 17, 2016	203

44	Ellison Wrong Man at Wrong Time for DNC	The Hill/ Gatestone Institute/ Newsmax	December 1, 2016	206
45	Keith Ellison Defeated by His Own Actions, Not Any Smear	Washington Examiner/ Gatestone Institute	February 27, 2017	291
46	I Will Leave Dems if Ellison Elected Chair	The Hill	February 24, 2017	226
47	The President Has a Special Obligation to Condemn Nazis and KKK	Gatestone Institute/ Washington Examiner	August 23, 2017	260
International Efforts to De-legitimize Israel				
48	Confronting Evil at Durban II	Huffington Post	April 28, 2009	30
49	Sweden's Refusal to Condemn Organ Libel is Bogus	Gatestone Institute	August 25, 2009	32
50	Singling Out Israel for "International Investigation"	Gatestone Institute	June 3, 2010	53
51	Bishop Tutu Is No Saint When it Comes To Jews	Gatestone Institute	December 20, 2010	54
52	Norway's "Boycott" of Pro-Israel Speakers	Gatestone Institute / The Jerusalem Post	March 31, 2011	60
53	South African Charge of Israeli Apartheid Rings Hollow	Gatestone Institute / The Jerusalem Post	April 5, 2011	63
54	The United Nations Should Not Recognize an Apartheid, Judenrein, Islamic Palestine	Huffington Post/ Gatestone Institute	September 21, 2011	75
55	Europe's Alarming Push to Isolate Israel	Newsmax	March 11, 2014	114

#	Title	Publication	Date	Page
56	The Case Against the International Criminal Court Investigating Israel	Gatestone Institute / The Jerusalem Post	January 23, 2015	134
57	A Jurisprudential Framework for Defending Israel	The Algemeiner	July 1, 2015	147
58	The Global Community Is to Blame for Palestinian Obstinance	Haaretz	November 10, 2015	158
59	Terrorism Persists Because It Works	FOX/ Gatestone Institute	May 23, 2017	243
Cultural Boycotts of Israel				
60	Filmmakers and Writers Seek to Censor Israeli Film	Gatestone Institute	September 4, 2009	34
61	Alice Walker's Crass Bigotry Exposed	Haaretz/ Gatestone	June 24, 2013	106
62	Metropolitan Opera Stifles Free Exchange of Ideas about a Propaganda Opera	Gatestone Institute / The Jerusalem Post	October 21, 2014	118
63	Oliver Stone's Response to Being Laughed at for Defending Putin: Blame the Jews	Gatestone Institute	June 14, 2017	253
BDS and the Contemporary Hard Left				
64	How the Hard Left, By Focusing Only on Israel, Encouraged Arab Despotism	Huffington Post/ Gatestone Institute	February 2, 2011	57
65	Pink Anti-Semitism Is No Different from Brown Anti-Semitism	Gatestone Institute	February 26, 2013	104

66	How Amnesty International Suppresses Free Speech	Gatestone Institute / The Jerusalem Post	November 10, 2014	120
67	Hard Leftists are as Guilty of Censorship as North Korea's Dictator	Haaretz	December 27, 2014	125
68	Who Do Bigots Blame for Police Shootings in America? Israel, of Course!	Gatestone Institute / The Jerusalem Post	July 13, 2016	186
69	*The New York Times* Makes a Shocking Mistake	FOX	July 28, 2016	189
70	Black Lives Matter Targets Israel	Newsmax/ Washington Times/ The Boston Globe	August 16, 2016	191
71	Are Jews Who Refuse to Renounce Israel Being Excluded from "Progressive" Groups?	Gatestone Institute/ The Jerusalem Post	August 24, 2016	194
72	Why Must Women Choose between Feminism and Zionism, but Not Other "Isms"?	Washington Examiner	March 15, 2017	232
73	A Supporter of Israel Must Have a "Bias" on Trump Travel Ban: The Newest Bigotry!	Gatestone/ The Jerusalem Post/ Newsmax	March 17, 2017	235
74	The Bigotry of "Intersectionality"	Gatestone Institute	March 29, 2017	237
75	How Can LGBTQs Oppose Israel?		August 8, 2017	258
76	The Hard Right and Hard Left Pose Different Dangers	The Wall Street Journal	September 10, 2017	266

From the Obama Administration to President Trump

77	*Tablet* Magazine: A Conversation with Alan Dershowitz	Tablet Magazine	August 24, 2015	150
78	Obama Meddles in Brexit But Shuns Netanyahu When He Speaks Up About Iran	FOX	April 22, 2016	172
79	Obama: Don't Destroy the Peace Process by Turning It Over to the U.N.	Gatestone Institute / The Jerusalem Post	November 1, 2016	199
80	Trump Rightly Tried to Stop Obama from Tying His Hands on Israel	Newsmax	December 23, 2016	209
81	The Consequences of Not Vetoing the Israel Resolution	The Boston Globe	December 27, 2016	211
82	Britain and Australia More Supportive of Israel than Obama and Kerry	Gatestone Institute / The Jerusalem Post	December 31, 2016	215
83	Obama's Mideast Legacy Is One of Tragic Failure	The Hill/ Gatestone Institute	January 15, 2017	217
84	Trump Welcomes Netanyahu	Gatestone Institute / The Jerusalem Post	February 13, 2017	220
85	Trump: Palestinians Must Earn a Two-State Solution	Gatestone Institute / The Jerusalem Post	February 20, 2017	222
86	Trump's 'Calm Before the Storm' is a Message to North Korea and Iran	FOX/Gatestone Institute	October 8, 2017	278
87	President Trump Did the Right Thing by Walking Away from UNESCO— for Now	Gatestone Institute/ The Jerusalem Post	October 15, 2017	280

Anti-Semitism and BDS

88	Confronting European Anti-Semitism	The Jerusalem Post	January 30, 2015	137
89	A Visit to the Old and New Hells of Europe Provides a Reminder of Israel's Importance	Gatestone Institute	March 17, 2016	166
90	Israel Does Not Cause Anti-Semitism	Gatestone Institute / The Jerusalem Post/ Newsmax	February 22, 2017	224
91	A New Tolerance for Anti-Semitism	FOX/ Gatestone Institute	June 6, 2017	245
92	Plame Knew What She Was Tweeting	FOX/ Gatestone Institute	September 22, 2017	270

Other Efforts to De-legitimize Israel

93	Guess Who's Not Speaking at the J Street Conference?	Gatestone Institute / The Jerusalem Post	March 20, 2015	142
94	What North Korea Should Teach Us about Iran	Gatestone Institute / FOX	April 19, 2017	241
95	So Now American Zionists Want to Boycott Israel	Gatestone Institute / FOX	July 14, 2017	255
96	Why Are So Many Claiming that Iran Is Complying with the Deal, When Evidence Shows They Aren't?	Gatestone Institute	October 19, 2017	283

ENDNOTES

1. Brackman, Harold, "BDS Against Israel: An Anti-Semitic, Anti Peace, Poison Pill," Simon Wiesenthal Center, accessed April 28, 2017
2. Dan Diker, Jerusalem Center for Public Affairs, BDS Unmasked, accessed May 2, 2017 http://jcpa.org/pdf/Unmasking_.pdf
3. Ibid., pp23
4. Morris, Benny, "Arafat Didn't Negotiate—He Just Kept Saying No," *The Guardian*, May 22, 2002
5. See Dershowitz, "The Case Against Israel's Enemies," p69.
6. Richard Gizbert, "US, Israel Pull Out of Racism Conference," ABC News, September 3, 2001, http://abcnews.go.com/International/story?id=80564&page=1
7. The Durban Debacle: An Insider's View of the World Racism Conference at Durban, Tom Lantos, 2002, http://www.humanrightsvoices.org/assets/attachments/articles/568_durban_debacle.pdf
8. Unmasking BDS p25
9. "PACBI Guidelines for the International Cultural Boycott of Israel," BDS Movement, accessed April 30, 2017, https://bdsmovement.net/pacbi/cultural-boycott-guidelines
10. Ibid
11. "Call for an Academic and Cultural Boycott of Israel," BDS Movement, accessed April 30, 2017, https://bdsmovement.net/pacbi/pacbi-call
12. Ali Mustafa, "Boycotts Work: An Interview with Omar Barghouti," *The Electronic Intifada*, May 31, 2009 https://electronicintifada.net/content/boycotts-work-interview-omar-barghouti/8263
13. Archbishop Tutu has touted traditional anti-Semitic tropes on numerous occasions saying, for example, that people in the United States are "scared" to criticize Israel because the "Jewish lobby" is "very powerful." https://www.theguardian.com/world/2002/apr/29/comment. I have written extensively about Archbishop Tutu's flirtation with anti-Semitism and anti-Zionism. See my article "Tutu and the Jews," on page 54.
14. In 2006, the boycott movement changed its strategy slightly by offering "an exemption from the boycott to Israelis who," according to David Hirsh

of London's Goldsmith University, "could demonstrate their political cleanliness." In practice, this proposed "institutional boycott" tested an academic's willingness to publicly disavow their own institution and Israel's so-called policy of 'apartheid.' Hirsh aptly notes that this tactic was essentially a "political test" for Jews. Hirsh states: "targeting of the ones who are likely to refuse to disavow their institutional affiliations, is likely to impact disproportionately Jews." (David Hirsh, "The Myth of Institutional Boycotts," *Inside Higher-Ed*, January 7, 2014 https://www.insidehighered.com/views/2014/01/07/essay-real-meaning-institutional-boycotts)

15 Omar Barghouti, "Boycotting Israeli Settlement Products: Tactic vs. Strategy," *The Electronic Intifada*, November 11, 2008 https://electronicintifada.net/content/boycotting-israeli-settlement-products-tactic-vs-strategy/7801

16 Jeffrey Herf, "Haj Amin al-Husseini, the Nazis and the Holocaust: The Origins, Nature and After Effects of Collaboration," *Jerusalem Center for Public Affairs*, January 5, 2016, http://jcpa.org/article/haj-amin-al-husseini-the-nazis-and-the-holocaust-the-origins-nature-and-aftereffects-of-collaboration/

17 NGO Monitor: http://www.ngo-monitor.org/press-releases/new-study-european-union-major-financial-backer-bds-organizations/

18 Raphael Ahren, "EU Declares Israel Boycott Protected As Free Speech," *The Times of Israel*, October 31, 2016 http://www.timesofisrael.com/eu-declares-israel-boycott-protected-as-free-speech/

19 NGO Monitor: http://www.ngo-monitor.org/press-releases/new-study-european-union-major-financial-backer-bds-organizations/

20 NGO Monitor: http://www.ngo-monitor.org/press-releases/new-study-european-union-major-financial-backer-bds-organizations/

21 NGO Monitor: http://www.ngo-monitor.org/press-releases/new-study-european-union-major-financial-backer-bds-organizations/

22 "Global BDS Week of Action Against HP," BDS Movement, accessed April 26, 2017, https://bdsmovement.net/boycott-hp/week-of-action

23 Barak Ravid, "Largest Dutch Pension Fund Boycotts Israeli Banks Over Settlement Ties," *Haaretz*, January 8, 2014 http://www.haaretz.com/israel-news/.premium-1.567548

24 'German BDS Hurts Israeli and Palestinian Workers alike," Benjamin Weinthal, Foundation For Defense of Democracies, November 8, 2016, http://www.defenddemocracy.org/media-hit/benjamin-weinthal-german-bds-hurts-israeli-and-palestinian-workers-alike/

25 Jack Moore, "Orange to End Partnership With Israeli Company as BDS Claims Another Scalp," *Newsweek*, January 2, 2016 http://www.newsweek.com/orange-ends-partnership-israeli-company-bds-claims-another-scalp-412202. (Orange, however, has denied that its decision was based on BDS.)
26 Yaniv Halily, "Ahava Closes London Store Over Threats," *Ynet*, September 22, 2011, http://www.ynetnews.com/articles/0,7340,L-4125530,00.html
27 The ACLU is opposing this legislation. On July 17, 2017, the group sent a letter to both houses of Congress stating that, "the government cannot, consistent with the First Amendment, punish U.S. persons based solely on their expressed political beliefs. " It continued to say that the bill "aims to punish people who support international boycotts that are meant to protest Israeli government policies, while leaving those who agree with Israeli government policies free from the threat of sanctions for engaging in the exact same behavior. Whatever their merits, such boycotts rightly enjoy First Amendment protection." The full letter can be viewed here: https://www.aclu.org/letter/aclu-letter-senate-opposing-israel-anti-boycott-act. Efforts are currently underway to amend the bill to eliminate any possible conflict with the First Amendment.
28 The calls for an academic boycott of Israel began in 2002, when two professors at the Open University of Bradford in the United Kingdom (Steven and Hilary Rose) wrote an open letter to the Guardian where they argued that, "Despite widespread international condemnation for its policy of violent repression against the Palestinian people in the Occupied Territories, the Israeli government appears impervious to moral appeals from world leaders.... Odd though it may appear many national and European cultural and research institutions, including especially those funded from the EU and the European Science Foundation, regard Israel as a European state for the purposes of awarding grants and contracts. Would it not therefore be timely if at both national and European level a moratorium was called upon any further such support unless and until Israel abide by UN resolutions and open serious peace negotiations with the Palestinians."
29 Shortly after this transpired, SlutWalk Chicago—a self-described anti-imperialistic, anti-war feminist group—followed suit, tweeting that they would stand by the Dyke March's "decision to remove the Zionist contingent from their event" and said "we won't allow Zionist displays at ours." However, after facing backlash for this flurry of tweets, SlutWalk Chicago issued an apology and reversed its position, stating that it will

no longer ban "any symbols or any kind of ethnic or heritage flags." In response to this swathe of anti-Israel and anti-Semitic declarations, a group of activists calling themselves "Zionist" and "progressive" launched the Zioness initiative in order to debunk the idea that the values of Zionism and feminism are discordant. The Zionesses said that they planned to participate in the SlutWalk march wearing T-Shirts featuring a woman donning a Star of David necklace. While the Zioness group participated in the march, SlutWalk Chicago vigorously denounced the initiative on Facebook, where it wrote: "We find it disgusting that any group would appropriate a day dedicated to survivors fighting rape culture in order to promote their own nationalist agenda."

30 Thomas Doherty, "The Israel Boycott That Backfired," *LA Times*, November 5, 2014, http://www.latimes.com/nation/la-oe-doherty-american-studies-assn-israel-20141106-story.html

31 The Palestinian Authority itself has explicitly rejected boycotts of Israel. This position is rooted in the fact that boycotts predominantly result in economic hardships for Palestinian workers, who will lose their jobs if economic sanctions are directed against firms that employ them. Additionally, the PA has acknowledged that BDS does nothing to advance the two-state prospect, but rather, undermines it. President Abbas himself reflected this position when he said: "No, we do not support the boycott of Israel…we don't ask anyone to boycott Israel itself. We have relations with Israel, we have mutual recognition of Israel." He did, however, express support for "boycott[ing] the products of the settlements." More recently, the King of Bahrain, Hamad bin Isa al Khalifa, also denounced the Arab boycott of Israel and said his citizens—unlike those of other Arab states—are welcome to visit the state of Israel.

32 Benjamin Weinthal, "Major German University Students Say BDS Continues Nazi Boycott," August 4, 2017 http://www.jpost.com/Diaspora/Major-German-university-students-BDS-a-continuation-of-Nazi-boycotts-501624

33 An Open Letter to Radiohead, Artists for Palestine UK, April 24, 2017, https://artistsforpalestine.org.uk/2017/04/23/an-open-letter-to-radiohead/

34 See *Jerusalem Post*, July 15, 2017, Barry Show, Unmaking BDS, http://www.jpost.com/Jerusalem-Report/The-unmasking-of-BDS-498347

35 Debra Kamin, "Rihanna and Other Artists Who Play Israel Feel the Pressure," *Variety*, October 16, 2013, http://variety.com/2013/biz/global/rihanna-and-other-artists-who-play-israel-feel-the-pressure-1200729050/

36 "NO LGTBI Conference in Israel," Peter Tatchell Human Rights Advocate, accessed May 2, 2017 http://www.petertatchell.net/international/israel/no-lgbti-conference-in-israel.htm

37 Ali Mustafa, "Boycotts Work: An Interview with Omar Barghouti," *The Electronic Intifada*, May 31, 2009 https://electronicintifada.net/content/boycotts-work-interview-omar-barghouti/8263

38 Israeli-born musician and writer, Gilad Atzmon has expressed some of the most rabidly anti-Semitic views published in the twenty-first century. In 2011, Atzmon—who has called himself a "proud-self hating Jew"—published the book "The Wandering Who?—A Study of Jewish Identity Politics." Borrowing themes from Nazi publications, Atzmon said that we "must begin to take the accusation that the Jewish people are trying to control the world very seriously." He has also vehemently denied the Holocaust and wrote that "the history of Jewish persecution is a myth, and if there was any persecution the Jews brought it on themselves." In this book, Atzmon also perpetuated traditional blood libels against Jews, asking how one "could know that these accusations of Jews making Matza out of young Goyim's blood were indeed empty or groundless." Needles to say, Atzmon is a strong supporter of BDS. See my article on page 67.

39 Steven Plaut, "The Nazi Roots of the Boycott-Israel Movement," *Frontpage Mag*, February 18, 2013, http://www.frontpagemag.com/fpm/178122/nazi-roots-boycott-israel-movement-steven-plaut

40 "The Boycott of Jewish Businesses," United States Holocaust Memorial Museum, accessed May 1, 2017, https://www.ushmm.org/outreach/en/article.php?ModuleId=10007693

41 "Book Burning," United States Holocaust Memorial Museum, accessed May 1, 2017, https://www.ushmm.org/wlc/en/article.php?ModuleId=10005852

42 Heinrich Heine wrote this admonition in his play, *Almansor*, in 1820-1821.

43 "Joseph Goebbels Urges Germans to Boycott Jewish-owned Businesses," United States Holocaust Memorial Museum, accessed May 1, 2017, https://www.ushmm.org/propaganda/archive/goebbels-boycott-jews/

44 Steven Plaut, "The Nazi Roots of the Boycott-Israel Movement," *Frontpage Mag*, February 18, 2013, http://www.frontpagemag.com/fpm/178122/nazi-roots-boycott-israel-movement-steven-plaut

45 Martin A. Weiss, Congress Research Service Report, *Arab League Boycott of Israel*, p1

46 Ibid., pp2

47 Jewish Telegraphic Agency Staff, "Coca-Cola Issue Settled; Franchise For Israel Given to Feinberg," *Jewish Telegraphic Agency*, April 18, 1966, http://www.jta.org/1966/04/18/archive/coca-cola-issue-settled-franchise-for-israel-given-to-feinberg

48 Abbas Al Lawati, "Alstom Loses $10B Saudi Railway Contract," *Gulf News*, October 28, 2011, http://gulfnews.com/news/gulf/saudi-arabia/alstom-loses-10b-saudi-railway-contract-1.920032

49 "Palestinian Civil Society Calls for BDS," BDS Movement, accessed April 30, 2017, https://bdsmovement.net/call

50 Article 11 states that, "The refugees wishing to return to their homes and live at peace with their neighbors should be permitted to do so at the earliest practicable date, and that compensation should be paid for the property of those choosing not to return and for loss of or damage to property which, under principles of international law or in equity, should be made good by the Governments or authorities responsible…"

51 Israeli officials estimate that Hezbollah now has at least 150,000 rockets, including long-range missiles, capable of hitting Israeli cities.

52 53 The latest singling out and targeting of gay Jews—who proudly identify as both pro-gay and pro-Israel—occurred as recently as June 2017. Jewish participants at the Chicago 'Dyke March'—a parade geared towards that city's lesbian community—were told to leave the parade because their flag—which had a Star of David printed on the LGBTQ rainbow flag—"made people feel unsafe." They were also told that the march was "anti-Zionist" and "pro-Palestinian."

54 The shuttle diplomacy efforts led by U.S. Secretary of State Kerry ultimately fell apart during the summer of 2014. The Israeli and Palestinian sides both blamed the other for the collapse of peace talks.

55 Due to mounting pressure and intimidation, the SodaStream factory has since been moved to a town in Israel's south where fewer Palestinians were able to obtain work permits and hence keep their jobs.

56 In January 2015, the ICC opened a preliminary examination in order to determine whether the criteria had been met to warrant pursuing a formal investigation into the 2014 war in Gaza. This was undertaken despite the fact that Israel always independently conducts its own fact-finding missions pertaining to conflicts it is engaged in, and releases its finding and reports accordingly.

57 This statement was apparently removed from the website, following the publication of my criticism.

58   At the time of this book's publishing, J Street has still not acquiesced to my request to speak at one of their conventions.
59   The entire debate can be viewed on YouTube: https://www.youtube.com/watch?v=5jqXEzplxeo
60   The Jobbik party is currently the main opposition party in Hungary.
61   The Golden Dawn party won 18 seats in Greece's most recent parliamentary election held in September 2015.
62   In the most recent parliamentary election held in the UK in June 2017, the British Labor party—headed by the anti-Semite, Jeremy Corbyn—surpassed expectations, gaining 29 seats in parliament and triggering a "hung parliament." It is worth noting that the Labor leader—who is a supporter of BDS—has a sordid history of engaging in anti-Semitism. Corbyn has associated and shared political platforms with vociferous anti-Semites and Holocaust deniers, and has referred to the genocidal terrorist organizations Hamas and Hezbollah as "my friends."
63   This article is an amalgamation of two articles published on June 6 and, 2016, in the *Daily Beast* and *Newsmax*.
64   It is worth noting that recently, in June 2017, several Western-allied Arab states initiated a "boycott" of Qatar due to its alleged role in funding terrorism, and cozying up to Iran and the Muslim Brotherhood. This has placed the United Stated in a difficult diplomatic position, as one its largest CENTCOM military bases is located in Qatar.
65   And more recently, in July 2017, the UNESCO Heritage Committee (the UN Cultural Organization) rewrote history by denying the Jewish connection to the city of Hebron—which houses the holy Cave of Patriarchs—declaring it an "endangered" Palestinian heritage site.
66   This term is short for Anti Fascist Action

Made in the USA
Lexington, KY
04 July 2019